Magic Lantern Guides®

PENTAX™ K10D

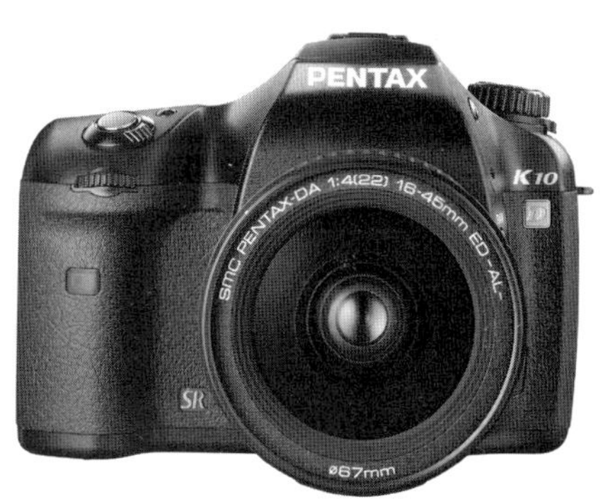

Peter K. Burian

LARK BOOKS
A Division of Sterling Publishing Co., Inc.
New York / London

Book Design and Layout: Michael Robertson
Cover Design: Thom Gaines
Associate Art Director: Lance Wille

Library of Congress Cataloging-in-Publication Data

Burian, Peter K.
Pentax K10D / Peter K. Burian. -- 1st ed.
p. cm. -- (Magic Lantern Guides®)
ISBN-13: 978-1-60059-185-3 (trade pbk. : alk. paper)
ISBN-10: 1-60059-185-X (trade pbk. : alk. paper)
1. Pentax camera--Handbooks, manuals, etc. 2. Digital cameras--Handbooks, manuals, etc. I. Title.
TR263.P4B87 2007
771.3'1--dc22
2007001962

10 9 8 7 6 5 4 3 2
First Edition

Published by Lark Books, A Division of
Sterling Publishing Co., Inc.
387 Park Avenue South, New York, N.Y. 10016

Distributed in Canada by Sterling Publishing,
c/o Canadian Manda Group, 165 Dufferin Street
Toronto, Ontario, Canada M6K 3H6

Distributed in the United Kingdom by GMC Distribution Services,
Castle Place, 166 High Street, Lewes, East Sussex, England BN7 1XU

Distributed in Australia by Capricorn Link (Australia) Pty Ltd.,
P.O. Box 704, Windsor, NSW 2756 Australia

If you have questions or comments about this book, please contact:
Lark Books
67 Broadway
Asheville, NC 28801
(828) 253-0467

Manufactured in USA

ISBN 13: 978-1-60059-185-3

ISBN 10: 1-60059-185-X

For information about custom editions, special sales, premium and corporate purchases, please contact Sterling Special Sales Department at 800-805-5489 or specialsales@sterlingpub.com.

Contents

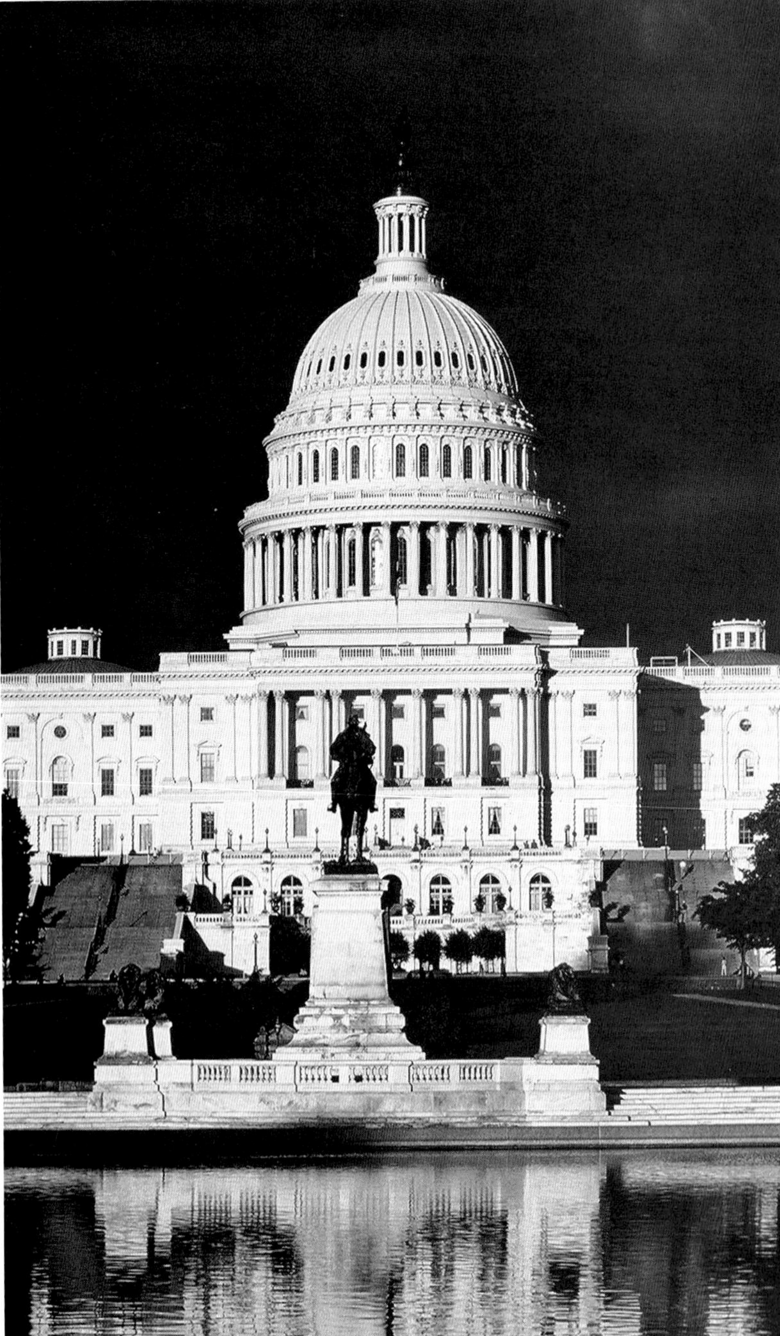

Digital Photography

The Pentax K10D was officially announced in September 2006 as a more advanced digital SLR (D-SLR) than the company's previous models in the *istD and K-series. With its 10.2-megapixel sensor, you can make 13 x 19 inch (33 x 48 cm) prints that look as good, or better, than an enlargement from a 35mm negative. When made from your technically best images, even larger prints can be suitable for framing.

The K10D incorporates an entirely new sensor-dust removal system along with the Shake Reduction (SR) system first introduced with the Pentax K100D. It provides compatibility with manual focus K-mount lenses, as well as autofocus lenses, of course. In fact, this model is the most advanced, sophisticated, and versatile of any Pentax camera to date. It's also remarkably competitive with comparably priced D-SLRs. For example, the K10D is the only non-professional D-SLR that is splash-proof, achieved through a body construction that includes 72 seals, a feature that also helps eliminate dust accumulation. This benefit is usually available only with cameras costing much more than the K10D.

Note about conventions used in this book: Unless otherwise stated, when the terms left and right are used to describe the location of a camera control, it is assumed that the K10D is being held in a horizontal shooting position.

With features not found even on higher-priced models, the Pentax K10D is an innovative contender in the digital SLR marketplace.

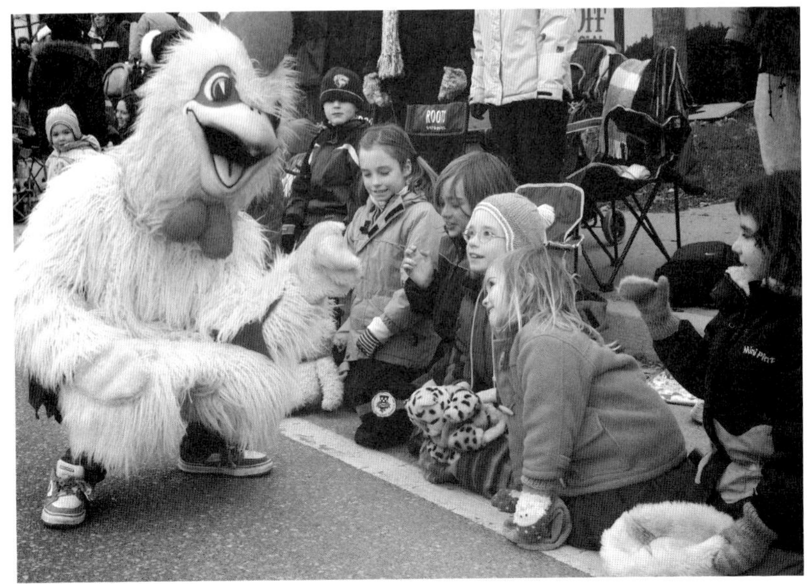

Though equipped with a number of professional-level features, your K10D can easily be used for quick snap shots. For ease of use, set the camera's exposure mode for Green or P (Hyper-program).

Differences Between Digital and Film Photography

Whether shooting with a digital or film-based camera, you regulate the amount of light that will strike the light-sensitive medium (film or sensor) by adjusting the f/stop or the shutter speed. However, in traditional photography the image is recorded on film and later developed with chemicals, while in digital photography the camera converts the light to an electronic image. A digital camera is a mini computer that immediately processes this image internally and stores it temporarily on a memory card for downloading, while a film camera stores the exposed film for processing at a later time. Digital technology allows you several creative possibilities not available with film, such as the ability to change sensitivity (ISO) and/or white balance from shot to shot.

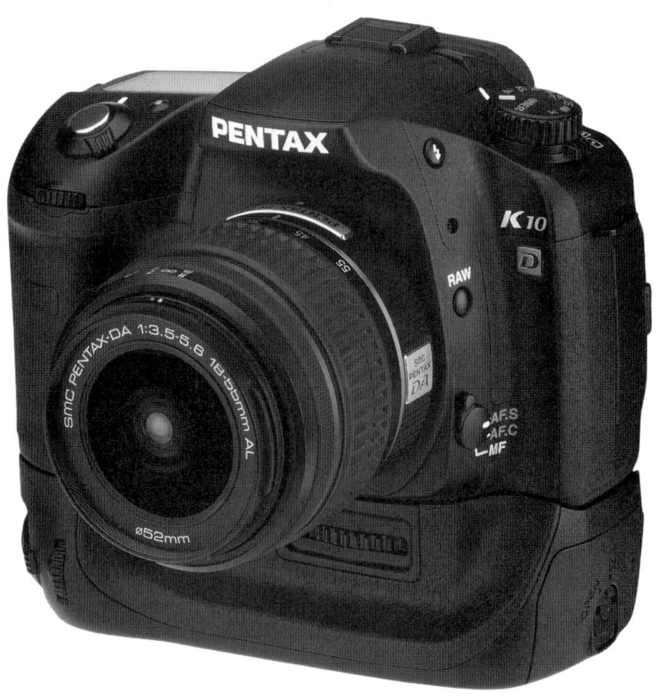

The Pentax K10D has an outstanding line-up of features, including a 10.2MP CCD sensor, shake reduction, and dust removal. Unlike most other D-SLRs in its class, it is also dust proof and weather resistant. Photo courtesy of Pentax Imaging Co.

The Digital Sensor vs. Film

Both film and digital cameras expose pictures in nearly identical fashion. The light measuring (metering) methods are the same, both work with ISO-based systems, and the shutter and aperture mechanisms controlling the amount of light admitted into the camera are the same. These similarities exist because both film and digital cameras share the same goal: to deliver the appropriate amount of light required by the film or sensor to create a good picture.

Not surprisingly, however, digital sensors respond differently to light than film does. From dark areas (such as navy blue blazers, asphalt, and shadows) to mid-tones (blue sky and green grass) to bright areas (such as white houses and sand beaches), a digital sensor responds to the full range of light equally, or linearly. Film, however, responds linearly only to mid-tones (those blue skies and green fairways). It responds in a non-linear fashion to bright and dark areas of the image. Negative film distinguishes tones very well in highlight areas and slide film separates tones well in shadow areas, whereas digital sensors often cut out the bright tones. Digital responds to highlights as slide film does and to shadows as negative film responds.

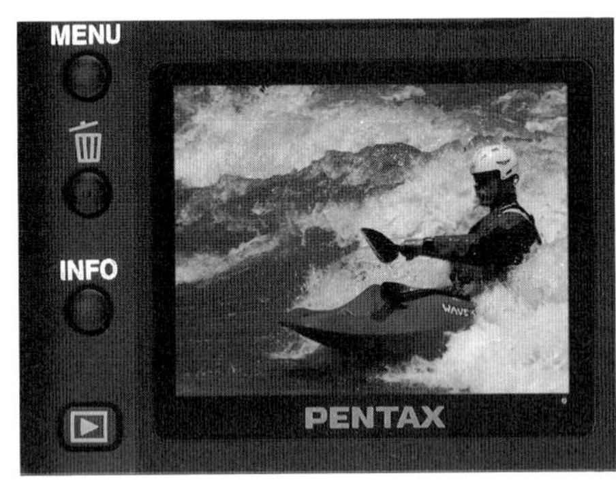

The LCD monitor lets you analyze and edit your photos during playback. With the K10D, you can even apply filter effects and other enhancements in-camera.

The LCD Monitor

In conventional photography, you are never really sure your picture is a success until the film is developed. You must wait to find out if the exposure was correct or if something happened to spoil the results, such as the blurring of a moving subject or unwanted stray reflections from an on-camera flash.

When using a digital SLR, however, you can see an image on the LCD monitor almost immediately after taking a picture. Admittedly, you cannot see all the details that you would see in a print, but this ability means that you can evaluate the picture you have just shot. If the exposure, lighting, or composition is not quite right, simply re-shoot on the spot. This feature is especially useful in flash photography. In addition to confirming correct exposure, the LCD

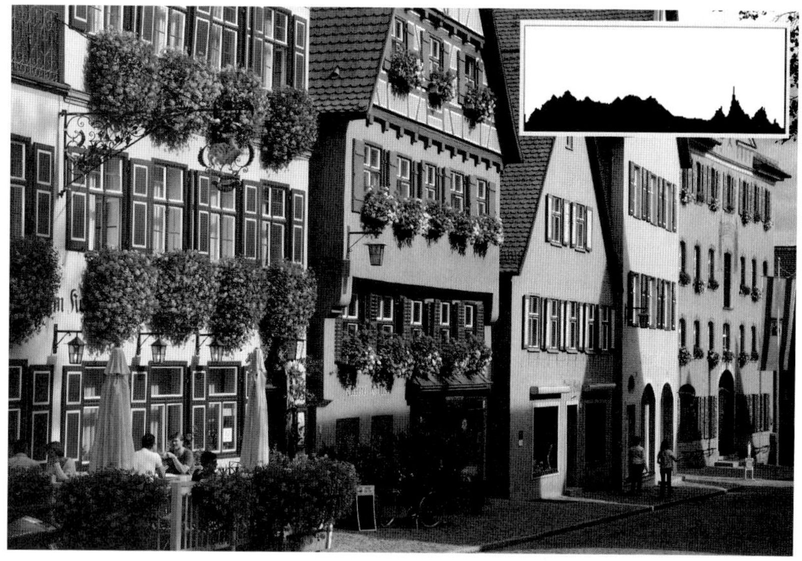

This histogram shows an even distribution of tones from dark (left side of graph) to light (right side of graph). It demonstrates a photo that is well exposed.

monitor allows you to check for any excessively bright highlight areas or dark backgrounds, as well as allowing you to evaluate other factors, such as the effect produced by multiple flash units and/or reflectors.

Exposure and the Histogram

Digital cameras do not offer magic tricks that let you beat the laws of physics, so incorrect exposure will still cause problems. Too little light makes dark images; too much light makes overly bright images. Granted, you can correct digital images to a certain extent afterwards by using software in a computer, but programs can't add details to overexposed images. Also, getting the correct exposure in-camera can save you a great deal of post-processing work.

After you shoot a digital image, a quick glance at the LCD monitor will indicate whether the exposure (image brightness) is close to accurate. Better yet, you can also access two features found in digital photography that give a more scientific evaluation of brightness values: a histogram scale and Bright/Dark area warning (see pages 163–171 for details on both features). Because you are able to check exposure using these tools, there is less need to bracket (shoot a series of images at different exposure levels) when using the K10D than with a traditional film camera.

ISO (Sensitivity)

Digital sensors don't have a true ISO. However, their sensitivity is adjusted electronically to mimic film ISOs. This means you can set the ISO on a D-SLR to 100 for average daylight shooting, 800 for faster shutter speeds or smaller apertures in less bright situations, or 1600 for low-light photography. With a digital camera, you can change ISO from picture to picture. It's like changing film at the touch of a button! This provides certain benefits, such as the ability to first shoot indoors without flash at ISO 800, then follow your subject outside into bright sun and optimize image quality by switching to ISO 100 (or allowing the camera to do so, with the Auto ISO feature).

Noise/Grain

Grain in film appears as an irregular, sand-like texture that, if large, can be unsightly and, if small, is essentially invisible. (A textured look is sometimes desirable for certain creative effects.) It occurs due to the chemical structure of the light sensitive materials and is most prominent in fast films, such as ISO 1600.

The equivalent in digital photography is known as noise, which often occurs as colored specks most visible in dark or evenly colored mid-tone areas. Digital noise occurs for several reasons: sensor noise (caused by heat from the electronics and optics), digital artifacts (when digital technology cannot deal with fine tonalities such as sky gradations), and JPEG artifacts (caused by image compression). Sensor noise is the most common.

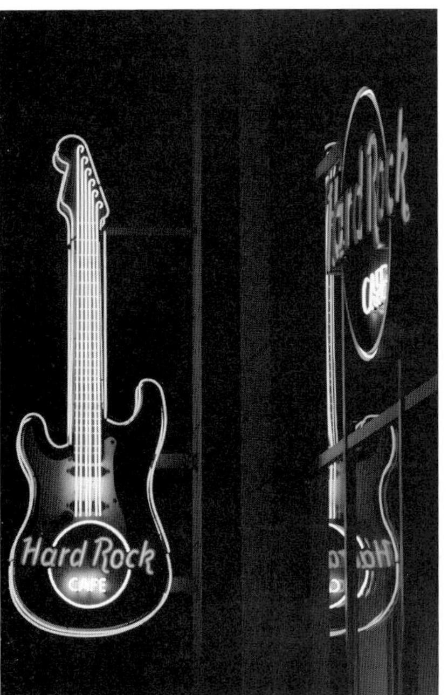

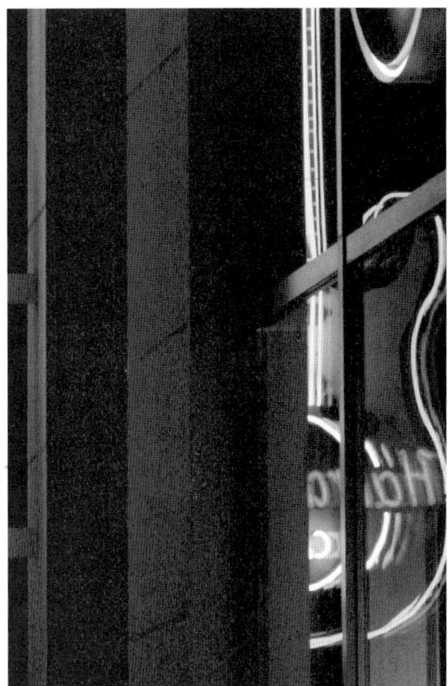

Noise can be a problem, especially when you set long shutter speeds or high sensitivity (ISO) to shoot in low light situations, as demonstrated in the crop on the right. However, noise can be reduced using in-camera processing or special software in the computer.

Although the K10D includes automatically applied noise reduction processing, digital noise is most prominent in images made at high ISO settings (especially at ISO 800 or higher), and will increase as the ISO increases.

The mottled colored specks are even more obvious in images that are underexposed and lightened afterward in image processing software. You can buy aftermarket software for noise reduction, but it's best to use ISO 400 or lower whenever practical for the absolutely "cleanest" images.

Sensor noise may also be increased with long exposures under low-light conditions, as in night photography. However, when you activate the camera's noise-reduction feature, exposures of one second or longer will receive extra processing to minimize the digital noise pattern. In most situations, the K10D produces images with very little digital noise at ISO settings up to 800 and acceptable digital noise at ISO 1600.

File Formats

A digital camera converts analog image information to digital data and records to a digital file. The K10D offers two distinct file formats. The first is JPEG, a universal imaging format. The second is RAW. The K10D also offers another option: RAW+, which will record each photo in JPEG and RAW formats simultaneously.

JPEG: Joint Photographic Experts Group, the most common format in digital photography, is actually a standard for compression of images rather than a true file format. Digital cameras use JPEG because its compression reduces file size, allowing more pictures to fit on a memory card.

RAW: A generic term for a file format consisting of raw data captured by a camera's sensor; a RAW file has little or no internal processing applied by the camera. Most camera manufacturers have developed proprietary versions of RAW. The K10D can record raw data in the Pentax format denoted with the file suffix .PEF. However, this camera also provides another RAW option: recording in the DNG (for digital negative) format. Developed by Adobe, DNG is publicly available for use by any camera manufacturer, although only a few have decided to use it so far. (In this book, I will often use the generic term RAW, but will provide additional specifics about PEF and DNG as appropriate.)

Resolution

Resolution refers to the quantity of pixels being utilized, quantified in terms of megapixels (abbreviated as MP), denoting a million pixels. (Pentax refers to resolution, or image size, as Recorded Pixels). Virtually all of today's digital cameras give you choices about how many of the sensor's pixels to use when shooting pictures. You do not always

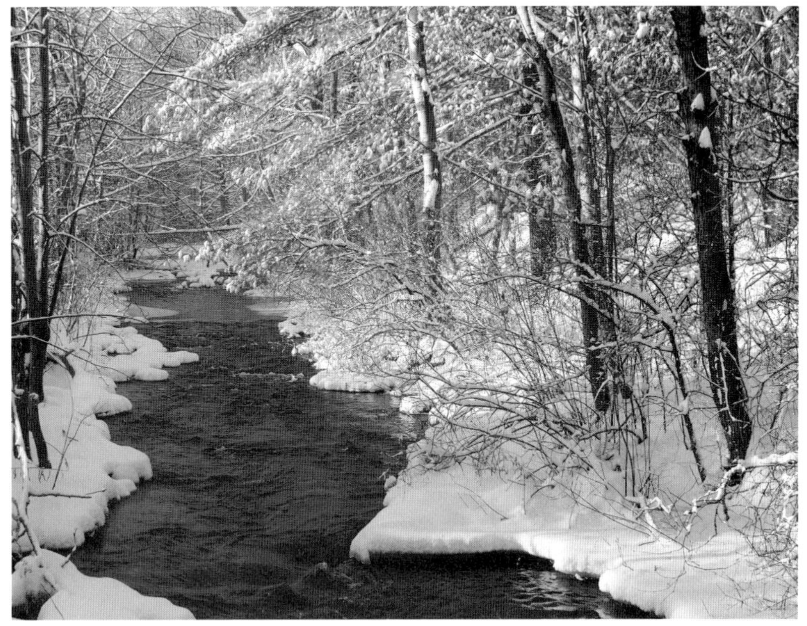

One of the great advantages of digital photography is the ability to experiment while shooting because you can simply delete those photos that "don't work." Try different white balance presets when recording a scene and review the results for creative effects. You can make a daylight snowscape look cooler by setting white balance for Tungsten Light.

need to employ the camera's maximum resolution (10.2 MP with the K10D). When you set the camera to record at a lower resolution, your memory card will hold more images, but it will not capture as much data. That can be a disadvantage however because the more digital information (higher resolution), the bigger print it is possible to make from an image file.

White Balance

Most pros who have shot film over the years can tell you about the challenges of balancing their light source with the film's response to the color of light. For example, daylight-balanced (outdoor) film used indoors under tungsten household lamps will produce pictures with an orange cast. Accurate color reproduction in this instance would require the use of a blue color-correction filter.

The color of light also varies in other circumstances, though our eyes and brain make natural adjustments so we do not notice this variation. Light is quite blue on an overcast day, even bluer in a shady area, green under fluorescent lighting, orange under tungsten lamps, and so on. In film photography, filters attached to the front of a lens can correct for the color cast. But with digital cameras, color correction is managed by the built-in white balance functions. The camera can automatically check the light, calculate the proper setting for its color temperature, and make the necessary modifications using an automated system, called Auto white balance (AWB). It's programmed to produce pictures without color casts or inaccurate tones in many different types of lighting. However, this system is not foolproof, so user-selectable white balance controls are also provided.

Cost of Shooting

While film cameras generally cost less than digital cameras, the cost of shooting digital is lower. A couple of reusable memory cards are much less expensive than a large supply of film, and there's no need to pay for processing or for printing every image on a roll of film. You pay to print only for those photos you select.

More importantly perhaps, you may become a better photographer when using a digital camera. Since you don't need to worry about the cost of film and processing, you'll be more likely to really "work" a subject, exploring it from various angles and trying a variety of creative photographic approaches. This can be liberating because it encourages greater creativity. Any shots that don't work out can simply be deleted.

"Step out of the box"—with no worries about the cost of film and processing, digital photography gives you the freedom to shoot away and experiment with unique photos such as this. ➪

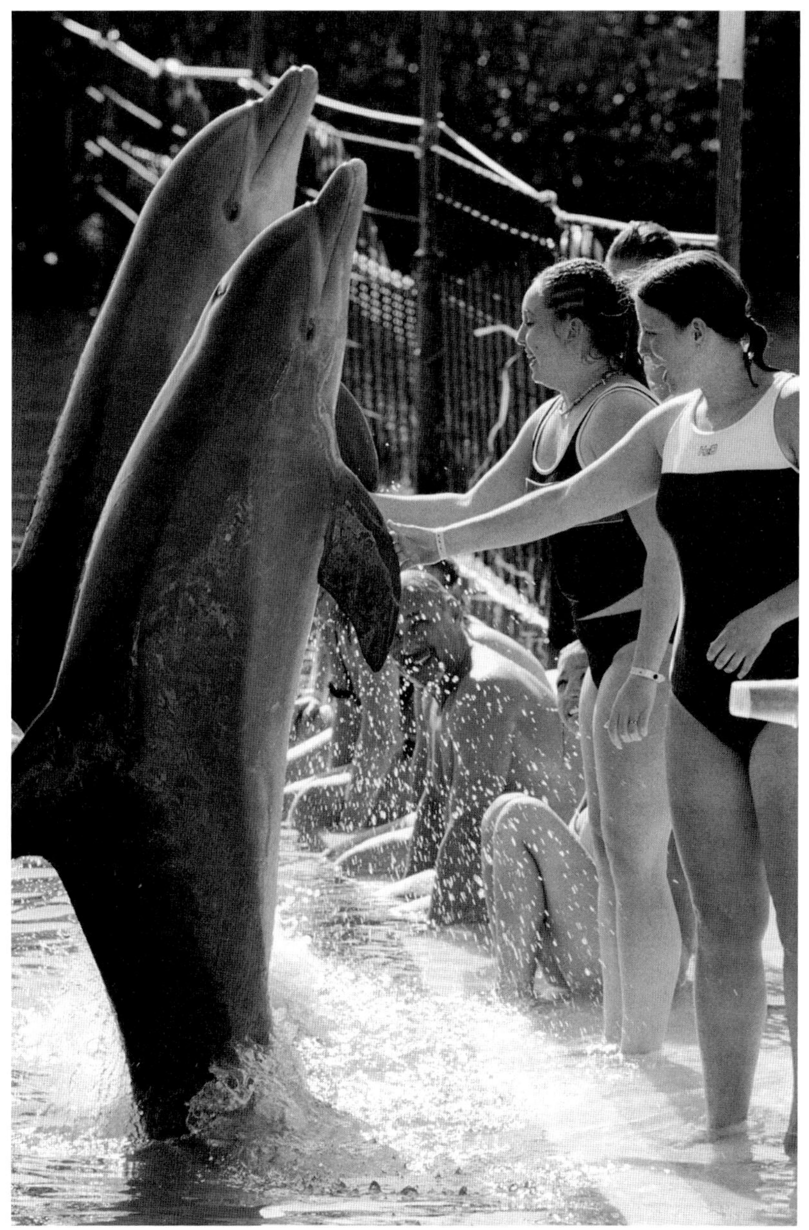

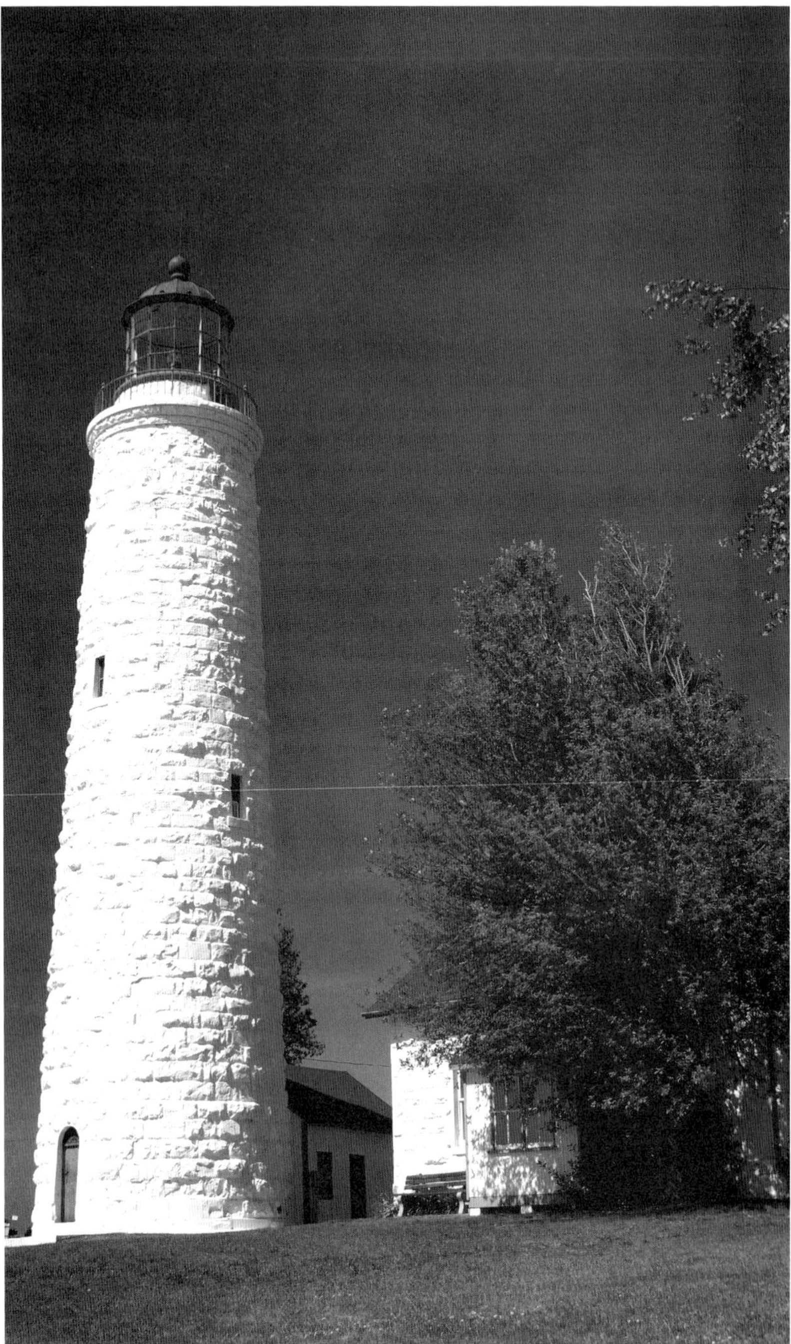

Features and Functions

The Pentax K10D is a sophisticated D-SLR designed to be used by photographers of different abilities. While it's comfortable for those new to digital SLRs, the K10D will also satisfy experienced photographers thanks to its many advanced capabilities. It is remarkably versatile and possesses some high-end technology not available in other cameras in the same class.

This is a moderately large camera with a robust build including a stainless steel chassis and splash-proof, scratch resistant exterior. It has a rubberized handgrip and a large, bright viewfinder. The high-resolution, 2.5-inch (6.2 cm) color LCD monitor provides a relatively wide (140 degree) viewing angle. This screen displays images with certain types of data after they have been taken, plus it displays features for evaluating exposure. There's also a separate LCD data panel on the camera's right shoulder that displays camera settings in use.

Because the K10D is the most advanced Pentax D-SLR to date, it has more external controls than other Pentax D-SLRs. But don't be intimidated; this design actually streamlines operation by reducing the need to hunt through numerous menu pages. Pentax engineers actually minimized the number of buttons and switches by providing an Fn button (back of the camera near lower right corner of LCD monitor) that allows quick access in Capture mode for setting such frequently used functions as the camera's drive, flash, white balance, and sensitivity (ISO). A wide range of additional functions can be accessed electronically by using the various menus.

The Pentax K10D is designed to meet the needs of beginning and advanced photographers. It will grow with you, as you become more familiar with digital photography and progress from simple vacation snapshots to pictures suitable for a gallery.

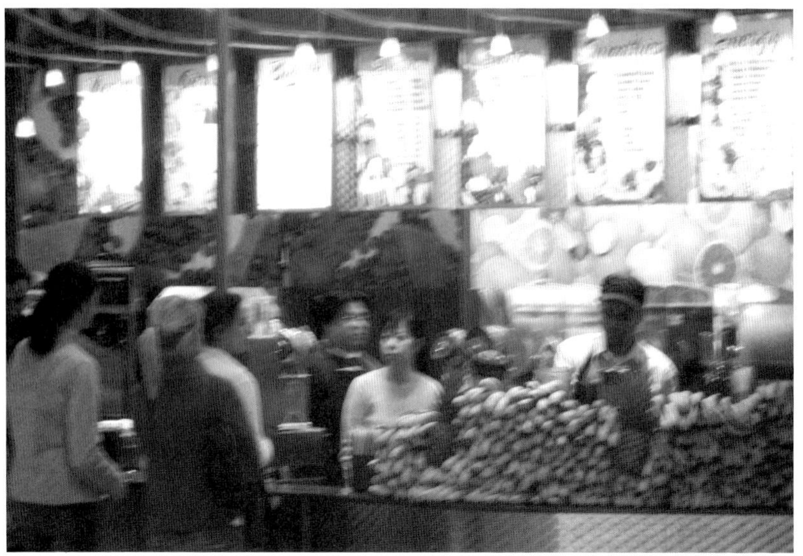

It is difficult to get sharp photos when handholding your camera at shutter speeds longer than 1/30 second.

Shake Reduction

The K10D includes a built-in Shake Reduction (SR) system (as does the entry-level Pentax K100D) that works with any Pentax-compatible autofocus or manual focus lens. In order to correct for camera movement, the system can shift the entire CCD sensor module in any direction. While a few other camera brands also include a built-in device that compensates for camera shake, the Pentax SR system employs a different design, using magnets, ball bearings and coils to shift the sensor module.

Dust Removal

The camera can also vibrate the CCD sensor module at a high speed to shake off accumulated dust particles; the dust is then collected on an adhesive strip below the sensor. Of course, prevention is more important than the cure; in addition to the

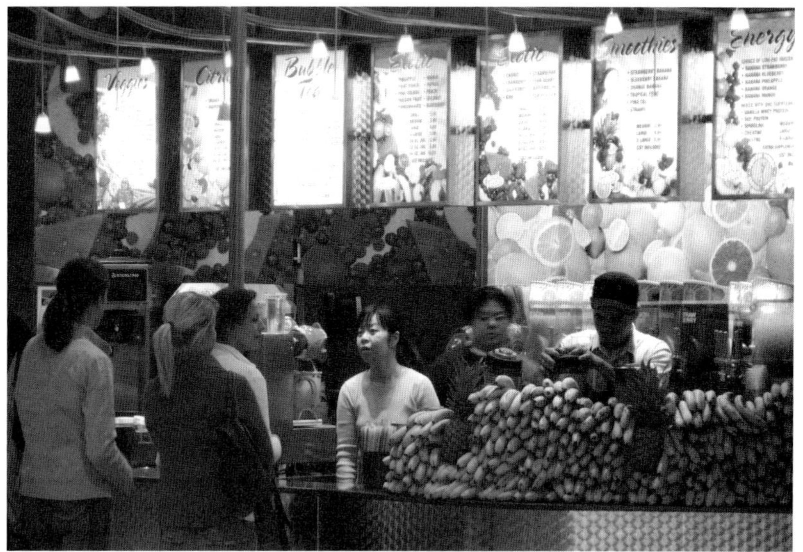

The Pentax Shake Reduction system offers a two to four stop advantage when shooting in low light, allowing you to handhold your camera even at relatively long shutter speeds.

well-sealed (dust proof) body, the low-pass filter over the sensor is anti-static, coated with special fluorocarbon materials to repel dust particles.

Focusing

This is an autofocus camera when used with AF lenses, but allows for manual focusing if desired. The camera features the KAF2 bayonet lens mount, which accepts autofocus KAF2 or KAF lenses as well as the manual focus K and KA mount lenses originally designed for 35mm SLR cameras. With an optional adapter, it will even accept older screw mount Pentax lenses and lenses from the medium format Pentax 67 and 645 systems. Some of the high tech functions will not operate when a manual focus lens is mounted (as discussed on pages 219-220), but the level of compatibility is still notable. Unlike most D-SLRs of other brands, the K10D is compatible with the aperture ring on many older lenses.

Note: Pentax (and some independent lens manufacturers) makes two types of autofocus lenses for Pentax D-SLR cameras. Some are full-size and multi-format, which makes them equally suitable for 35mm film and digital SLRs. The second type is smaller, designed exclusively for D-SLRs that have imaging sensors smaller than a 35mm film frame. The "digital only" Pentax lenses are designated with the suffix DA. Pentax has also announced a new series to be denoted DA*, with plans for them to be weather resistant and to employ a Supersonic (ultrasonic) focus motor.

The SAFOX VIII autofocus system has been developed for the K10D and is unusually sophisticated, with 11 focus-detection points. Nine of these points are cross-hatched, meaning they are sensitive to both horizontal and vertical detail for maximum reliability. The camera's processor, called PRIME (Pentax Real Imaging Engine), is entirely new. It's intended to produce maximum detail, accurate colors, and minimal digital noise. This processor is very fast and the camera has a large buffer, or temporary data storage bank. When using a high speed SD memory card, this processor/buffer combination allows you to shoot JPEGS at 10MP/Best (the largest/least compressed setting) at 3 frames per second until the card is full. Even after taking a long burst of photos, the camera is usually ready for more shots. For maximum speed performance, use a high-speed card, such as the Kingston 100x, Panasonic Gold, Lexar 133x Pro, or the SanDisk Ultra or Extreme series.

Spend time getting to know your K10D well. Become familiar with the purpose of each of the numerous controls. The important data about settings and functions, depending on the camera's current mode, are displayed in the viewfinder, the LCD panel on the top right of the camera, and the LCD monitor on the back of the camera. Many of the abbreviations and icons used to signify the various features are common to other digital cameras, so they may already be familiar to you. Some are intuitive; for example, a trash can icon stands for delete, AF/MF denotes autofocus/manual focus, AE-L stands for auto exposure lock, and so on.

Pentax K10D — Front View

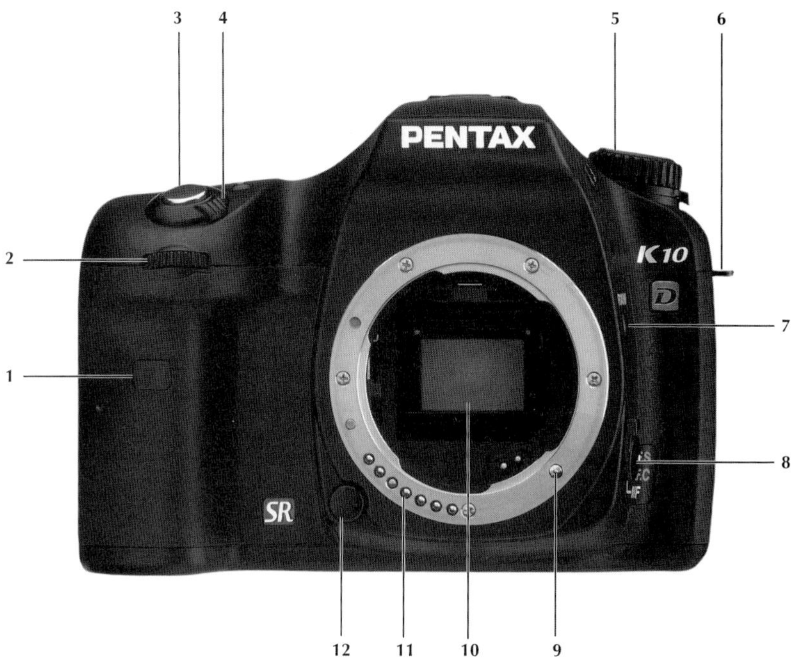

1. *Self-timer lamp/ Remote control receiver*
2. *Front e-dial*
3. *Shutter release button*
4. *Main (power) switch*
5. *Mode dial*
6. *Strap lug*
7. *RAW button*
8. *Focus mode lever*
9. *AF coupler*
10. *Mirror*
11. *Lens information contacts*
12. *Lens unlock button*

Pentax K10D — Rear View

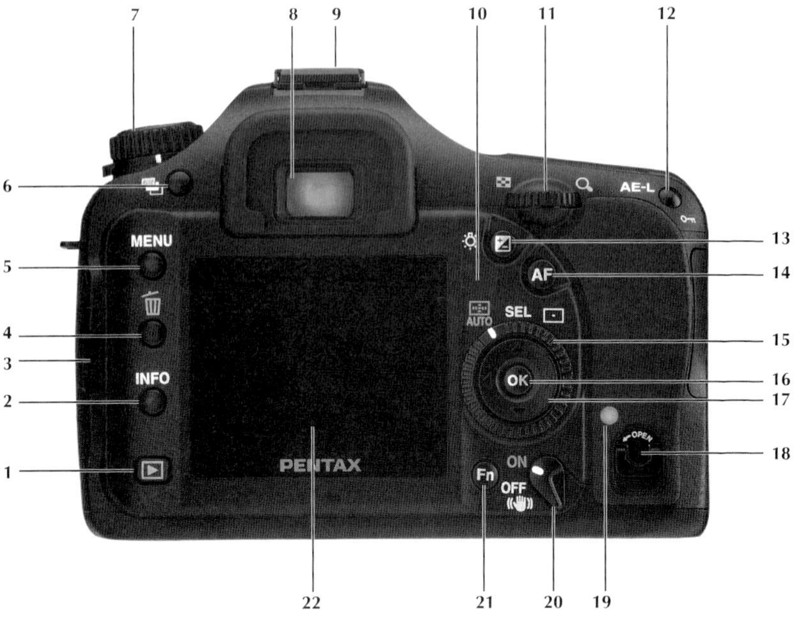

1. Playback button
2. INFO button
3. Terminal cover
4. Delete button
5. MENU button
6. Exposure bracket button
7. Mode dial
8. Viewfinder
9. Hot shoe
10. Self-timer lamp/ Remote control receiver
11. Rear e-dial
12. AE-L (autoexposure lock) button
13. EV compensation button
14. AF (autofocus) button
15. AF point switching dial
16. OK button
17. Four-way controller
18. Card cover unlock lever
19. Card access lamp
20. Shake Reduction switch
21. Fn button
22. LCD monitor

Pentax K10D — Top View

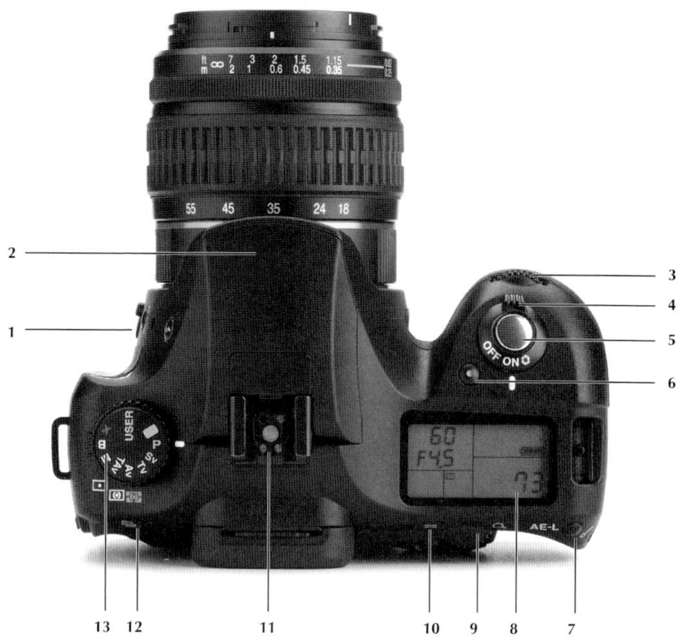

1. ϟ Flash Up button
2. Built-in flash
3. Green button
4. Front e-dial
5. Main (power) switch
6. Shutter release button
7. AE-L (Autoexposure Lock) button
8. LCD panel
9. Rear e-dial
10. EV compensation button
11. Hot shoe
12. Exposure bracket button
13. Mode dial

Pentax K10D — LCD Panel

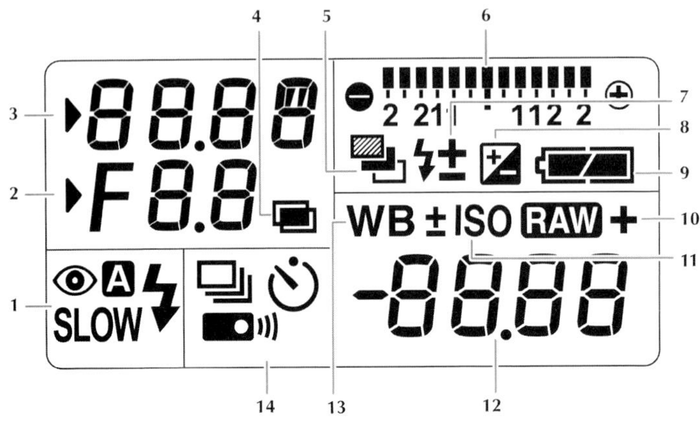

1. *Flash mode*
2. *Aperture*
3. *Shutter speed*
4. *Multi-exposure mode*
5. *Auto bracketing*
6. *EV bar*
7. *Flash exposure compensation*
8. *EV (exposure) compensation*
9. *Battery level*
10. *RAW or RAW+*
11. *ISO (Sensitivity) warning*
12. *Number images/Exposure value (EV)*
13. *White balance/ WB correction*
14. *Drive mode*

Pentax K10D — Viewfinder

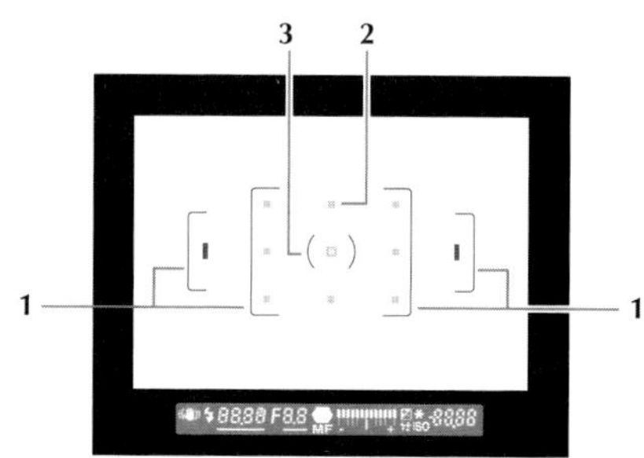

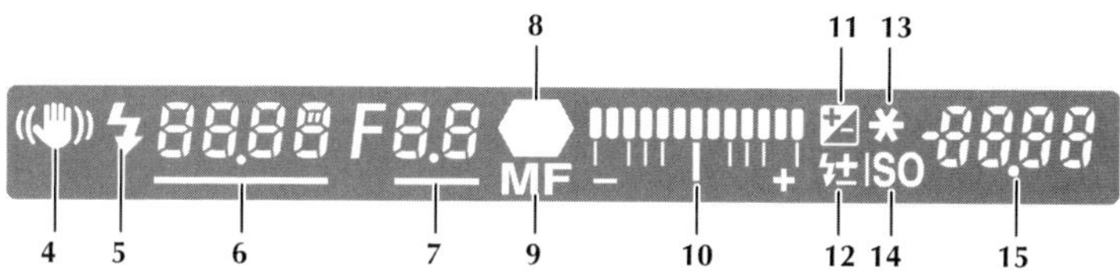

1. *AF frame*
2. *AF point*
3. *Spot meter frame*
4. *Shake Reduction in use*
5. *Flash status*
6. *Shutter speed*
7. *Aperture (f/stop)*
8. *Focus indicator (scene is in focus)*
9. *Manual focus in use*
10. *EV bar*
11. *EV (exposure) compensation*
12. *Flash exposure compensation in use*
13. *AE lock in use*
14. *ISO (Sensitivity) warning*
15. *Number of images/ EV compensation value*

Overview of Features

With its metal chassis and weather-sealed body, the Pentax K10D is an extremely durable camera that has been shutter tested for 100,000 cycles. Its many features include a number of professional-caliber options, making the K10D highly competitive with several more expensive models from other manufacturers. It is easy to use in point-and-shoot modes, but is highly suitable for serious photography due to its outstanding versatility.

- A 10.2MP (effective) CCD sensor.

- A 2.5-inch (6.35 cm) LCD monitor provides a comparatively high resolution (210,000 pixels). It also possesses a wide viewing angle of 140°. The LCD can be adjusted to make it brighter or darker as desired in certain lighting conditions.

- The sophisticated PRIME processing engine maximizes detail and color integrity and minimizes digital noise.

- A Shake Reduction (SR) system compensates for camera shake. This in-camera CCD-shift system minimizes blurring caused by camera shake and is compatible with any Pentax lens.

- A Dust Removal system shakes dust particles from the sensor whenever the camera is turned OFF. The K10D is also equipped with special anti-static coating on the low-pass filter to minimize static electricity and dust attraction.

- A new Lithium-Ion battery (instead of AA's used by other Pentax D-SLRs) is rated to provide 500 shots on a single charge when not using the built-in flash (CIPA standard). The optional D-BG2 Battery Grip (also water-resistant) holds a second high power battery, doubling the number of shots you can take before re-charging.

Specifications

Image Sensor: 23.6 x 15.8 mm CCD with RGB filter array and primary color low-pass and infrared-cut filter; 10.2 million recording pixels (3,872 x 2,592 pixel resolution); 1.5x field-of-view crop.

Processing: PRIME engine with fast DDR2 memory chip; 22-bit analog to digital converter.

Viewfinder and LCD: All glass pentaprism, 95% field of view; 0.95x magnification; Natural Bright Matte II focusing screen; diopter correction, -2.5 to +1.5; rubber eyepiece cup; 2.5″ LCD (6.35 cm) with brightness adjustment and illumination.

Recorded Pixels (Image Size): 10MP, 6MP, and 2MP selectable in JPEG; 10MP capture in RAW.

Quality Level: JPEG Best, Better, and Good; RAW (PEF or DNG) format; RAW+ for simultaneous RAW and JPEG recording.

Sensitivity: Auto ISO (using user-defined ISO range) or manual (ISO 100 to 1600).

Shutter Speeds: 30 to 1/4000 second plus Bulb; maximum flash sync speed 1/180 second.

Exposure Modes: Green (fully automatic), Hyper-program (shiftable), Aperture Priority, Shutter Priority, and Sensitivity Priority, Shutter & Aperture Priority, Hyper-manual; also programs for high shutter speed, small aperture, and MTF Priority (prioritizes best aperture setting for lens in use).

Autofocus: SAFOX VIII system, with 11-point sensor including (nine cross-hatched focus-detection points); automatic or user-set focus point selection. Single mode AF (AF.S), Continuous mode AF (AF.C) with predictive tracking function, and Manual focus (MF); focus-assist beam provided with pre-flash.

Drive: Single frame and Continuous at up to 3 fps advance for an "unlimited" number of JPEGs or nine RAW frames; 12 sec. and 2 sec. self-timer.

Exposure Metering: Center-weighted, Spot (2.5% of center), Multi-segment (16-segment evaluative); exposure and flash exposure compensation; AE lock and Auto bracketing (Exposure bracket and Extended bracket) for ambient light and/or flash.

White Balance: Auto (AWB), Daylight ☼ , Shade ⌂ , Cloudy ☁ , Fluorescent Light ☲ (3 options), Tungsten Light ☀ , Flash ϟ , Manual ▭ , and Color Temperature selectable (K) with Kelvin or Mired scale; WB Shift toward blue/amber or magenta/green; WB Bracketing.

Image Adjustments: Two image tones, Natural or Bright, selectable; also separate adjustments and bracketing available for Contrast, Sharpness, and Color Saturation; sRGB and Adobe RGB color space selectable.

Playback Options: Instant Review time selectable; magnification to 20x; Brightness or RGB (color) histogram on/off; Bright/Dark area warning on/off; Image Rotation on/off; multiple display of 4, 9, 16 images in LCD.

Digital Filter Image Processing: In-camera options include RAW to JPEG conversion, B&W with three selectable filters, Sepia, Color with 18 variations, Soft, Slimming effect, and Brightness adjustment.

Flash: Built-in with manual pop-up control; selectable for Auto discharge, Auto flash+Red-eye reduction, Flash On, Flash On+Red-eye, Slow speed sync, Slow-speed sync+Red-eye, Trailing (second) curtain/slow speed flash; P-TTL metering using pre-flash, distance data and 16-zone meter; field of view coverage for 18mm and longer lenses; flash exposure compensation control; wired or wireless off-camera TTL flash available with accessories; hot-shoe accepts Pentax FGZ-series flashes and off-camera flash cables; high-speed sync available with certain flash units.

Photo courtesy of Pentax Imaging Co.

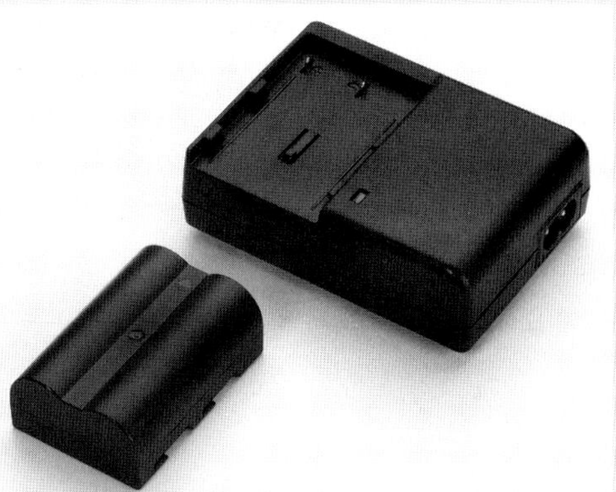

Power: One (1620 mAh, 7.4V) D-LI50 Lithium-Ion rechargeable battery; optional AC adapter and Battery Grip D-BG2 available.

Other Features: Optical depth of field preview or Digital Preview selectable; Multi-exposure mode with automatic exposure correction to create a single picture from multiple exposures; 32 Custom Functions; reflex mirror pre-lock with 2-second self timer; image orientation sensor; User mode for instant recall of favorite settings; SD and SDHC memory cards; PictBridge and DPOF compliant.

Compatible Lenses: KAF2 (including DA and DA* series) and KAF with support for Power Zoom function; manual focus K and KA mount lenses can be used with some limitations according to camera features; screw mount (S) lenses and Pentax 67/645 system lenses can be used with an adapter, also with some limitations.

Connectivity: USB 2.0 Hi-speed; Video out (NTSC or PAL); accepts optional remote control accessories.

Dimensions/Weight: 5.6 x 4 x 2.8 inches (141.5x101x70mm); 25 oz. (710g) without battery.

Software Supplied: S-SW55 on CD, including Photo Browser 3 and Photo Laboratory 3 for RAW enhancement and conversion.

Camera Activation

Power Sources

The single proprietary Lithium-Ion (Li-Ion) D-LI50 battery (included with the camera) will power about 500 frames per charge, though you'll get fewer shots if you use the built-in flash or frequently playback images. The number of shots per charge is also dependent on the external temperature; if bitter cold outside, the battery will be depleted more quickly. Maximum recharging time is about 180 minutes; the process is finished when the light on the charger goes off.

The camera does not accept universally available batteries, such as AAs, so it is wise to carry a spare D-LI50. The camera can also be plugged into household power using the optional AC adapter (be sure to use the correct power cord for your geographic region). This is useful if you download images directly from the camera to a computer, show images on a TV, or if printing directly from the camera while it's connected to a PictBridge compliant printer with a USB cable.

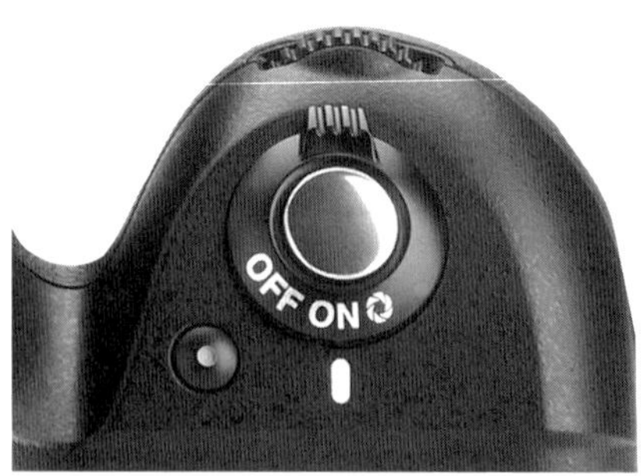

The main switch, located on the top of the handgrip, is used to turn the camera on and off. In the depth-of-field position, it provides a digital or optical preview of the scene.

Main Switch

The main power switch surrounds the shutter release button on the right top of the camera. It can be set to ON, OFF, or Preview (either Digital or Optical Preview, which allow you to check exposure/composition/focus or depth of field, respectively). Preview is an advanced feature discussed on page 146.

Auto Power Off

The K10D will shut down if has not been operated for a given length of time (the default is one minute). This minimizes electrical consumption to save battery power. To reactivate the camera, simply touch the shutter release button, the Playback button ▶ (left back of camera), or INFO button (left back of camera) and it will be ready to shoot almost instantly.

You can use the Set-up menu 🔧 to vary the Auto Power Off time; this allows you to increase the amount of time before the camera will automatically switch to "sleep" mode. See page 106 for details.

External Ports

A hinged cover on the left side of the camera hides and protects several terminals for attaching accessories. Open and you'll find ports for the USB and video cables that are provided with your K10D. The USB cable is used to connect the camera to a computer's USB port for downloading image files. It is also used to connect to some recent PictBridge compatible printers for printing directly from the camera (see page 245 for more information). The video cable is used for connecting the camera to a television monitor's video-in port for showing images. You will also find a terminal for an optional AC Adapter and for an optional CS-205 Cable Switch. The latter can be useful for triggering a tripod-mounted camera without creating external vibration.

A high-speed SD card, in this case 133x, records image data quickly and is more efficient than lower-speed cards when shooting DNGs, PEFs, and high-quality JPEGs. While you probably won't notice the difference with normal shooting, it is helpful when shooting continuous action.

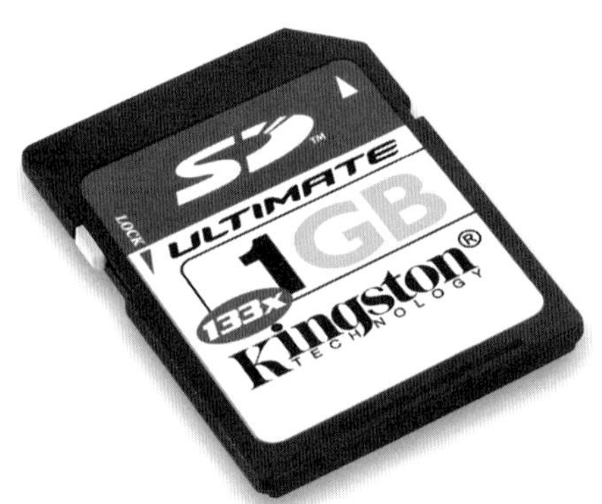

Inserting and Removing the Memory Card

To install an SD or SDHC memory card, first turn the camera OFF. On the right side of the camera body you will find a door covering the memory card slot. Use the card cover unlock lever (bottom right back of camera) to pop card cover open. With the camera turned OFF, insert a card (with the label on the card facing you) and press it down until the card clicks into place. You can then close the card cover.

To remove the memory card, make sure the camera is OFF. Unlock the card cover lever, which again causes the card cover to pop open. Press down on the memory card and it will pop up; you can then pull it out easily.

Caution: Be certain the orange card access lamp on back of the camera (above the card cover unlock lever) is not illuminated. When it is lit, the camera is writing data to the card. Removing a card while data is being transferred can damage the card and cause a permanent loss of image data. To avoid such risks, always turn the camera OFF first; wait until the light is extinguished before inserting or removing a memory card.

Camera Controls

There are several important dials and switches on the K10D that are used to navigate and manage camera functions. Below are basic descriptions; details about these controls will follow throughout this book, explaining exactly when and why you will use each dial, switch, button, or controller.

The mode dial on the K10D contains the unique TAv exposure mode, in which the camera adjusts sensitivity to give correct exposure with the shutter speed and aperture set on the camera.

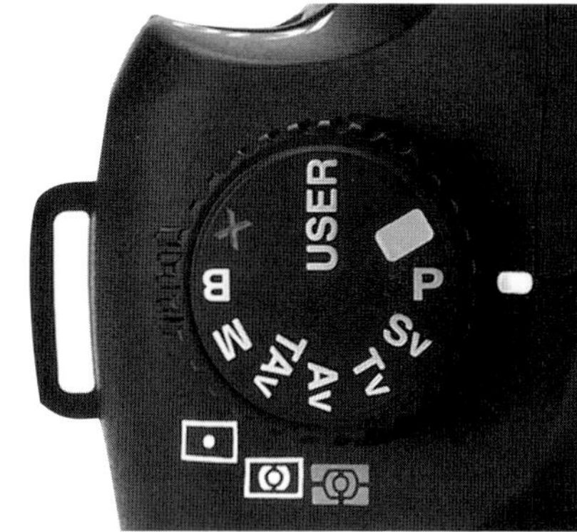

The Mode Dial

Located on the left top of the camera, this dial is used for selecting the exposure mode (see pages 138-156 for discussion of these modes). You'll first need to become familiar with the abbreviations used by Pentax for Green mode (a green rectangle, this is commonly referred to as fully automatic, or Auto, exposure mode), "shiftable" Hyper-program mode (P), Sensitivity Priority mode (Sv), Shutter Priority mode (TV for time value), Aperture Priority (Av), Shutter & Aperture Priority (TAv) mode, the Hyper-manual (M) mode, and Bulb (B). The final option on the mode dial is an X, referring to Flash X-sync speed. It is used with non-dedicated flash units that do not automatically set the camera's shutter sync speed. Select X, and the camera's shutter sync speed will be set at 1/180 second, the fastest shutter (or sync) speed that can be used with flash.

Fn Button

This button on the back of the camera allows quick access to a Fn menu of four frequently used features: white balance, flash modes, ISO, and drive modes. Navigate through the options using the four-way controller on the back of the camera. When you reach a desired option press the OK button in the center of the four-way controller to enter and confirm your selection.

Front and Rear e-dial

Each of these electronic input dials has several functions, depending on the camera mode. However, the front e-dial (right front of camera, below main switch) is most often used to set a shutter speed and exposure compensation value (after pressing the ± button.) And the rear e-dial (right back of camera, below LCD panel) is often used for setting apertures (f/stops) and ISO levels.

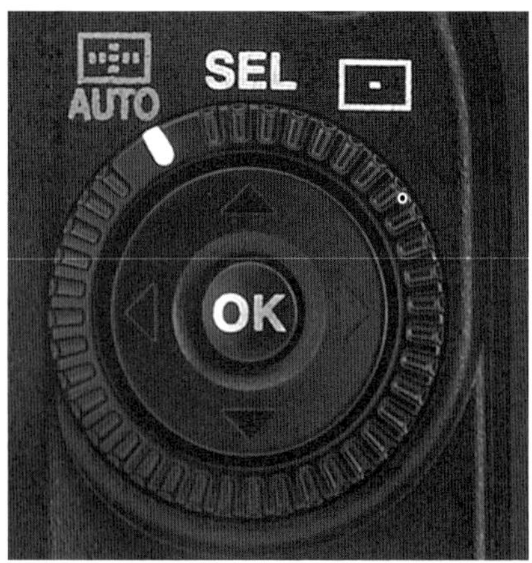

The four-way controller is used to navigate the K10D's menu system.

Four-Way Controller

This circular pad with arrows is on the camera back and is primarily used for up/down and left/right navigation within the various menus. Simply press the up, down, left, or right arrow on the controller to move in a certain direction. The OK button in the center of the controller is used to confirm a selection that you have made within any menu.

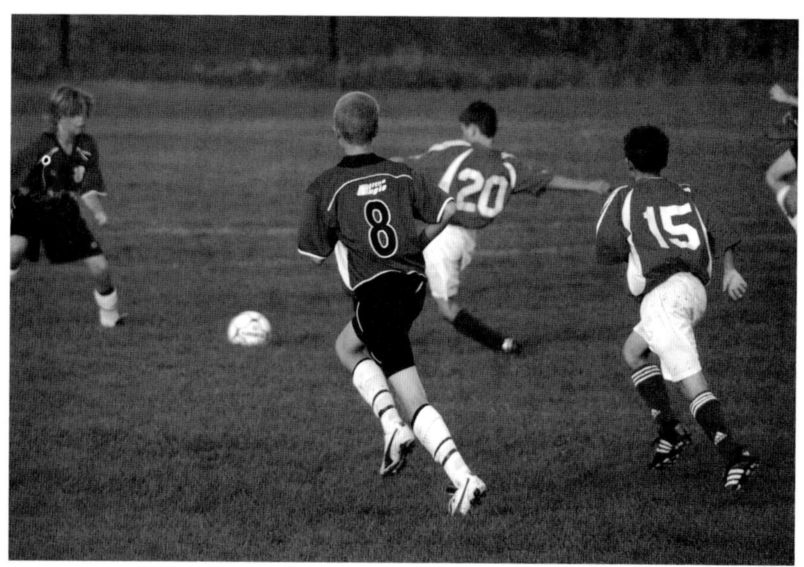

Use the rear e-dial to quickly increase the camera's ISO setting, which will allow a faster shutter speed to capture quick action.

In the camera's Playback mode, the four-way controller can be used for scrolling through images recorded on the memory card. (The front electronic dial can also be used for the same purpose.) Also, it can be used for up/down navigation through data that is available in Playback mode after you press the INFO button (on left back of camera). And finally, the controller can be used for navigating through the options available for image modification in Playback mode (such as converting images to black & white or altering image color.)

INFO Button

This button is pressed one, two, or three times in Playback mode to display various screens in the LCD monitor. Each display shows different shooting data from basic to detailed. View the two types of histograms by pressing the up/down controller arrows in conjunction with this button

In Capture mode, you can press the INFO button at any time to see a summary of more than 30 current camera settings, including exposure mode, ISO setting, shutter speed, aperture, drive mode, file format, metering mode, and lens focal length.

MENU Button

The K10D provides several distinct electronic menu screens accessed with the MENU button. The available screens include Rec. Mode , Playback , Set-up , and Custom Setting C, each with its own tab. You can use the rear e-dial or the four-way controller to move from tab to tab; then use the controller to scroll up/down within the items in any menu screen. When you reach one that you want to set, use the controller to scroll to the right; then scroll up/down and right/left as required within the item to select the desired option. (Green arrows on the screen will indicate directions for scrolling.) Press the OK button to enter and confirm your selection.

Flash Up Button

Because the K10D does not automatically activate the built-in flash, this button (on the left side of the pentaprism) must be pressed to do so.

Metering Mode Lever

Rotate this lever located under the mode dial to select Multi-segment, Spot, or Center-weighted metering. I recommend using Multi-segment initially if you are not familiar with these different metering systems.

Autofocus Control

A ring that surrounds the four-way controller, called the AF point switching dial, can be rotated to select any of three focus-detection options. First, mount an autofocus lens and make sure the camera is set for autofocus (AF.S or AF.C) using the focus mode lever on the left front of the body near the lens mount. Activate the camera and rotate the AF point switching dial to select *Auto* (AUTO automatic focus point detection), *Select* (SEL manual selection of any of the 11 focus-detection points), or *Center* (for quick activation of only the central focus point.)

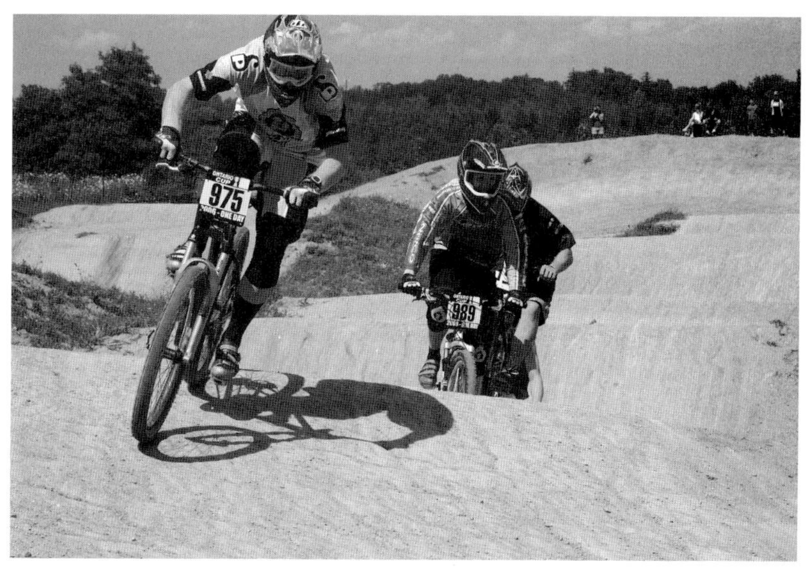

For great reliability in action photography, select the AF.C mode for Continuous autofocus (tracking) and choose automatic focus point detection (Auto).

Shake Reduction

When you are hand-holding the camera, flip this switch located on back of camera) to On in order to activate the SR system; it will then minimize blur from camera shake. Pentax recommends turning SR off when the camera is mounted on a tripod.

Resetting Controls

While experimenting with various controls and menu items during the familiarization process, you're likely to change settings often. Sometimes you may want to quickly return to the original default settings. To do so, use the *Reset* option in the Set-up menu (see page 107). However, this control will not reset any Custom Functions that you might have changed; if you need to do that, access the Custom Settings menu (see pages 107-117) and use the last item, *Reset Custom Function*.

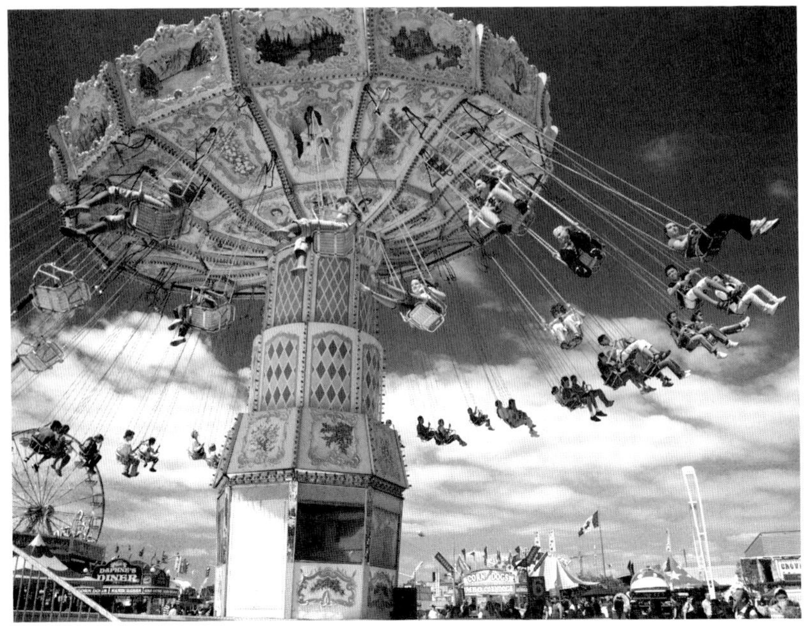

Instant Review is fine for a quick look at an image. However, for a more thorough evaluation, take advantage of the features available in Playback mode, including detailed information on camera settings and histogram analysis of brightness.

Playback Options

Instant Review

Instant Review occurs automatically after you shoot a photo, displaying what you have just recorded. The default time period for viewing is one second, which can be changed to a longer time by selecting the *Display Time* option under the *Instant Review* item in the Playback menu (see page 102). That item also allows you to select *Histogram* in Instant Review, though I don't recommend doing so because the image portion of the display will be very small. However, it would be wise select the *Bright/Dark area* option in Instant Review because it will provide a blinking overlay. This highlights areas in your photo that are too dark or bright to exhibit detail.

Playback Mode

Although Instant Review is useful for a quick look, the full Playback mode offers you the ability to thoroughly review all of the images stored on your memory card. Access this mode by pressing the Playback button ▶ . Use the controller to scroll through the images and press the INFO button one or more times depending on the amount and type of data you want to consider in the full Playback mode.

To view a photo's brightness histogram, press the INFO button once. If you wish to see individual histograms for the image's Red, Green, and Blue channels, press the top or the bottom of the four-way controller. (Frankly, that is more information than most photographers need unless they are digital imaging experts.) To view a great deal of data about settings used to make an image, press the INFO button again.

Note: I recommend activating the *Bright/Dark area* (highlight and shadow detail warning) for full Playback mode. You can do so by selecting the *Playback display* item in the Playback menu. When you do so, the warning about lost highlight and/or shadow detail will blink even if you do not press the INFO button. That will allow you to identify any serious exposure problem and decide whether to re-shoot after setting plus or minus EV (exposure) compensation for a brighter or darker image, as discussed in detail on pages 156-157.

There are two additional options in Playback mode that are quite useful. The first is a magnification feature 🔍 . Use it to check sharpness in specific areas of an image, look for red-eye, gauge facial expressions in people pictures, and so on. In order to magnify an image in Playback mode, rotate the rear e-dial to the right; to decrease the level of magnification, press the ± button one or more times. During magnified view, you can scroll around the image area using the four-way controller.

To display multiple images, rotate the rear e-dial to the left, toward the ⊞ icon. This index display allows for reviewing thumbnails of nine images at one time. This feature is useful to search for a shot stored on your memory card because you can look at more than one picture at a time (but the images are small). The number of thumbnails displayed can be changed from *9* (default) to *4* or to *16* by selecting the desired option in the Function menu, accessed with the Fn button. Select an image from the index display by using the controller arrows to scroll. To view the selected image as a full size display, press the OK button. Rotate the rear e-dial to the left once again and you enter folder browse mode; this will display the folder–or several folders–of images on your memory card; you can then select a desired folder.

You can also review images as a slide show on the LCD monitor. Select the *Slideshow* item in the Playback menu; that also allows you to set the time period that each image will be displayed. Use the Fn menu while in Playback mode to start the slide show. Each picture stored on your memory card will display for the number of seconds that you had selected as the desired option in the menu; the next image will then automatically appear.

Deleting Images

You can delete pictures one at a time in either Instant Review or in Playback mode. Simply press the delete button on the camera back while an image is displayed, then scroll up to *Delete* and press the OK button to confirm your selection.

Deleting in index display mode is more versatile. While viewing the index of several images, press the button. Small boxes now appear on each thumbnail image. Scroll using the four-way controller to select an image and press the OK button if you want to tag a photo for deletion; that step will place a checkmark in the box on that photo. Repeat that step if you want to identify other photos for deletion. After identifying all photos that should be deleted, press the button again; scroll up to select *Delete*. Press the OK button and all selected images will be deleted.

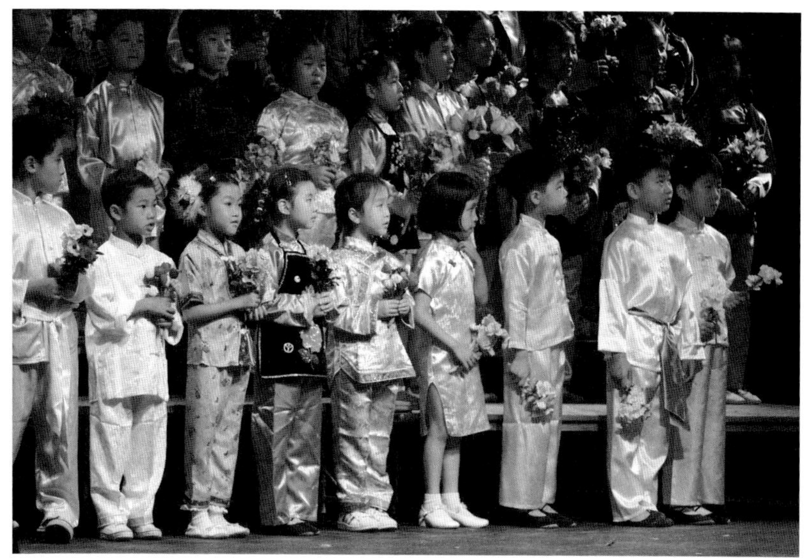

Take care not to inadvertently delete favorite photos; use the Protect function to safeguard image files on your memory card.

In addition to this feature, the K10D allows you to delete all images on the memory card. After pressing the 🗑 button while viewing one image in Playback mode, press it again. An enquiry will appear on the LCD screen: *Delete all images on memory card?* If you are certain that you wish to do so, scroll up to *Delete All* and press the OK button.

Note: Although there is no in-camera method for recovering deleted images, several companies market software that's designed for this purpose. These programs do not provide a 100% success rate, but some are quite good at recovering deleted JPEGs and, sometimes, RAW files. Some memory cards even come with such software. Look for reviews on the Internet through a web search using keywords such as, "image recovery software programs."

Protect Images from Deletion O‑π

To protect important images from unintentional erasure, use the lock feature. While viewing any image (full size or as a thumbnail) press the Protect button (O‑π, but also marked AE-L). Use the four-way controller to scroll to *Protect* and press the OK button. The image will then be locked; a subsequent delete command will not delete it from your memory card.

You can also quickly protect all images on the memory card; use the same procedure but press the O‑π button twice, and select *Protect*. You can always remove the lock from any image–or all images on the card–later. Simply use the O‑π button but then select *Unprotect*.

Caution: All images, including those that are "protected" will be deleted if you decide to format the memory card.

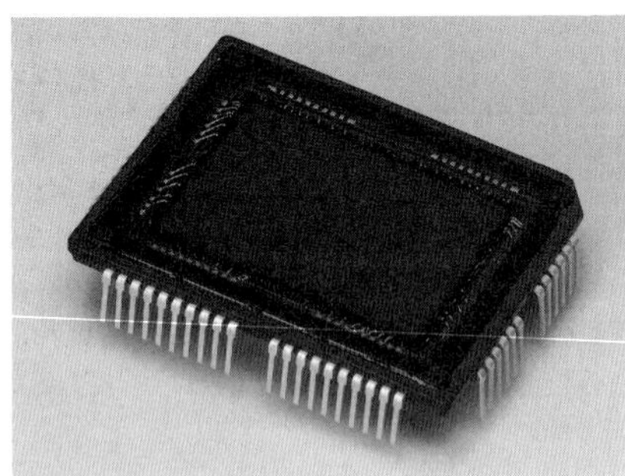

The 10.2MP CCD imaging sensor used in the K10D has a special coating that helps prevent dust accumulation. Photo courtesy of Pentax Imaging.

The CCD Imaging Sensor

Each of the 10.2 million pixels in the K10D captures a portion of the total light falling on the sensor. While the camera provides images in full color, its CCD sensor records only the intensity of light, not wavelengths (color). Therefore, filters are placed in front of the pixels so each will only record one of the three primary colors (red, green, and blue) of light. These filters are arranged in a specific order, most commonly using the Bayer pattern where there are twice as many green pixels as there are red and blue.

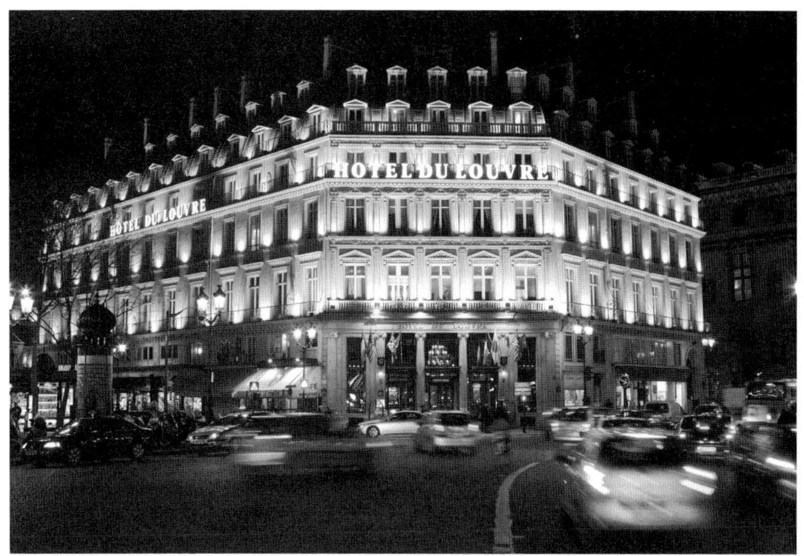

When traveling with your camera, take a camera-care kit with you for quick clean-ups. A soft brush and microfiber cloth are safe, handy tools for removing dust and grim from a day of shooting.

When the light projected by the lens comes into contact with the imaging sensor during exposure, the light-sensitive pixels accumulate an electrical charge. More light striking a particular pixel translates into a stronger electrical charge. The electrical charge for each pixel is converted into a specific value based on the strength of the charge so that the camera can actually process the data.

Because each pixel on the sensor only records the value of one of the primary colors, full color must be interpolated based on information from adjacent pixels. The final image data is then written to the camera's memory card as an image file. An exception to this would be RAW capture, which records raw data (actual pixel values) from the sensor and stores it in a special file format (PEF or DNG) that needs to be processed using special software.

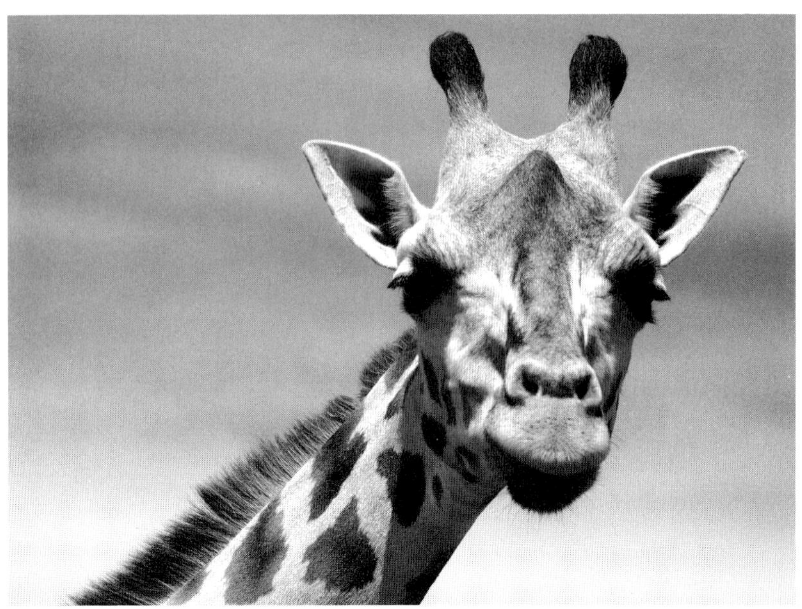

With your K10D, a lens focal length of 200mm is more than a moderate telephoto lens.

The camera also has a low pass anti-aliasing filter located in front of the sensor that reduces the wavy colors and rippled surface patterns (moiré) that sometimes occur when small, patterned areas are photographed with a camera that uses a high-resolution sensor.

The Sensor and Effective Focal Lengths

As with the vast majority of digital cameras, the K10D's sensor is smaller than a 35mm film frame, which measures 36 x 24 mm. Because of the sensor's smaller size (23.5 x 15.7 mm), the view through a lens is different than it would be if the same lens were mounted on a 35mm camera. A number of photographers like to think in 35mm SLR terms, so they often describe lenses on digital SLRs by their effective focal lengths (EFL). The EFL is what the angle of view would look like with that lens mounted on a camera using 35mm film.

To calculate this effective focal length for the K10D, multiply a lens' focal length by 1.5. For example, a 28–75mm zoom becomes equivalent to a 42–112.5mm zoom in the 35mm format. As you can note, the smaller sensor in the K10D reduces the wide-angle capability of the lens, but increases its capacity for telephoto.

This 1.5x factor for effective focal length, or "focal length magnification," is actually a field-of-view crop. In other words, the focal length is not actually increased. The apparent magnification occurs because the sensor records a smaller portion of the scene than a larger 35mm film frame would. Consequently, the image appears as if it had been taken with a longer lens, one with a narrower field of view that encompasses less of any scene.

This factor is certainly useful in wildlife and sports photography as it reduces the need to use super telephoto lenses (i.e., 500mm or greater) for tight shots of a distant subject–the long end of a 75-300mm zoom lens will often now do the job. But in wide-angle photography, the effective focal length magnification is a drawback because we need extremely short focal lengths to create images with a true ultra-wide effect. That's why Pentax is offering shorter, or wider, lenses, such as the 12-24mm f/4 AL zoom.

Camera Care and Cleaning

Keep your K10D and all lenses clean and well protected when not shooting. Do not expose the camera or especially the lenses and their caps–to water, dust, sand–or salt. A camera bag and a clean, dry storage environment should prevent dust and dirt buildup. Always keep the body cap on the K10D when a lens is not mounted; this will prevent dust and contaminants from getting inside the body and settling on the sensor. Keep the front and rear caps on your lenses as well; be sure to clean them occasionally. And keep your camera bag immaculately clean; use a vacuum cleaner on a regular basis to remove dust and other contaminants from the bag.

Always switch the camera OFF before mounting or removing a lens. This will minimize static electricity, reducing the amount of dust that will be attracted to the CCD sensor. When shooting in a location with a great deal of sand or dust, do your best to change lenses quickly in a protected spot. Hold the camera pointing downward when changing lenses.

In addition, do not leave the camera in hot locations, such as the interior of an automobile parked in the sun. Try to minimize exposure to extreme humidity. In such conditions, keep the camera/lens in a camera bag when not in use. (When you set the camera down, be sure that the lens is not pointing toward the sun, to prevent damage to the CCD sensor.)

When storing the camera for more than a week, remove the battery and the memory card. In order to minimize the risk of lost data, do not place the card near a magnet (as in audio speakers) or near any appliance that produces high static electricity discharge.

Put together a basic camera care kit, including two microfiber cloths and photographic lens cleaning solution, plus a large blower bulb for blowing dust out of the camera interior. All such accessories are available from photo retail stores. Also carry a soft, absorbent cotton cloth (an old T-shirt perhaps) to dry off the exterior of the camera and lens when working in damp conditions. Do not shoot in rain or snow unless the lens is well protected. While the K10D is splash-proof, only the DA* series lenses will be water resistant and they may not be impervious to heavy rain.

Dedicate a microfiber cloth for the purpose of cleaning your lenses; do not use it for other purposes, such as cleaning a smudged LCD monitor; use a cloth of a different color for that. To remove stubborn smears or fingerprints from your lens, use a photographic lens cleaner solution. Do not use solutions designed for other purposes such as cleaning eyeglass lenses. Apply a drop of solution to a small part of the microfiber cloth; do not pour it onto the front or rear element of the lens because liquid may seep into the optics. Then wipe using a dry part of the cloth.

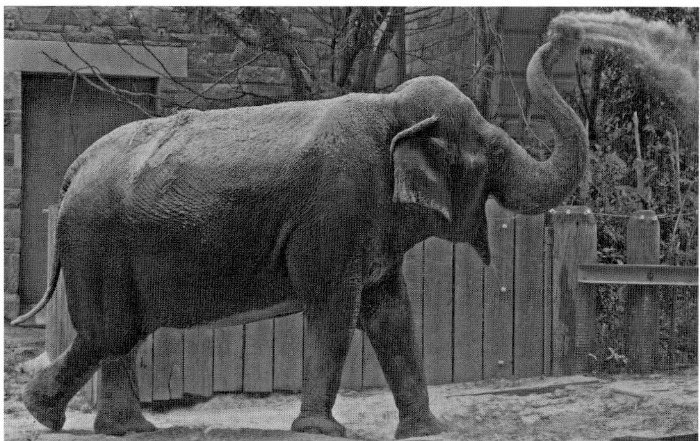

Even though the Pentax Dust Removal system greatly reduces the accumulation of dirt on the sensor, it is still a good idea to use care, especially in dusty environments. Change lenses quickly with the camera powered off and the mirror box pointed down. Always use lens and body caps and store your gear in a clean camera bag.
© Kevin Kopp

Cleaning the CCD Sensor

Because dust specks on the camera's sensor can be visible in your images, it's wise to activate the camera's Dust Removal function. In the Set-up menu, scroll to the *Dust Removal* item and select the *Start-up action* option. Press the OK button to confirm your selection.

Afterwards, whenever you turn the K10D ON, the Dust Removal system will shake loose particles off the CCD sensor. (You'll be able to hear the CCD module shaking for about one second at startup.) However, sticky particles or dust in dry climates may remain on the sensor. Prevention of dust accumulation is definitely preferable to cleaning. You'll know if the sensor becomes dusty because spots will appear in your images. If several Dust Removal cycles do not solve the problem, you may need to clean the sensor. (The exact method for doing so is discussed on page 107).

Getting Started in Ten Basic Steps

Although we have not yet covered all of the operations and features of the K10D in detail, the following steps will allow you to quickly set up your camera and begin taking photos without the need to make a series of complex photographic decisions.

1. With the camera OFF, load the (fully charged) battery and a memory card; mount an autofocus lens.

2. Turn the camera ON and set the time and date; the pertinent screen appears automatically. Navigate using the four-way controller and use the OK button to confirm you selection. The time and date will then be recorded for each image you make and will be available as part of the "EXIF" data for the file. You will be able to access that information with the INFO button in Playback mode or with image editing software in your computer.

3. Make sure the K10D is set for its default modes by selecting the *Reset* item in the Set-up menu. This ensures that all overrides are set to a suitable starting point.

4. Using the mode dial, select the P (Hyper-program) mode for automatic camera operation, and choose the Multi-segment metering option (green item) using the metering mode lever. If you want to shoot a series of frames in a burst, select Continuous shooting ⧉ in the Fn menu, using the four-way controller to navigate and the OK button to confirm your selection.

5. You can simply use the default settings in Rec. Mode 📷 for Recorded Pixels (resolution: 10 megapixel 10M) and quality level (Best ***). Or, you can use the Rec. Mode menu to choose a lower Recorded Pixels setting, such as 6M, and a lower quality setting, such as (Better **). The default file format (in the same menu) is JPEG, which is suitable for most picture taking.

6. Set the camera to Single mode (AF.S) with the focus mode lever. Choose the green Auto option [AUTO] to make the camera select the AF point. (Neither of these AF settings are provided by default, so cannot be reset to default in the menu.)

7. By default, white balance is set to AWB. To confirm that, press the Fn button and scroll through the various white balance options as part of the familiarization process using the four-way controller, but select AWB by pressing the OK button two times.

8. By default the sensitivity (ISO) is set for Auto, which you can confirm in the Fn menu. The camera will now select a suitable ISO depending on the brightness of the environment.

9. Adjust the viewfinder diopter for your eyesight. Make sure the camera is activated by pressing the shutter release button part way, then fine-tune the diopter adjustment lever (on back of camera at bottom of viewfinder eyepiece) while looking into the viewfinder; stop when the data display (at the bottom of the viewfinder screen) appears sharpest to your eye.

10. Point the lens at a desired subject and press the shutter release button part way to activate the autofocus and light metering systems. Depress the button to take a photo. After you do so, the image will appear for one second (Instant Review) on the LCD monitor. Extend the duration of Instant Review to a more useful period, such as 3 seconds, using the Playback menu.

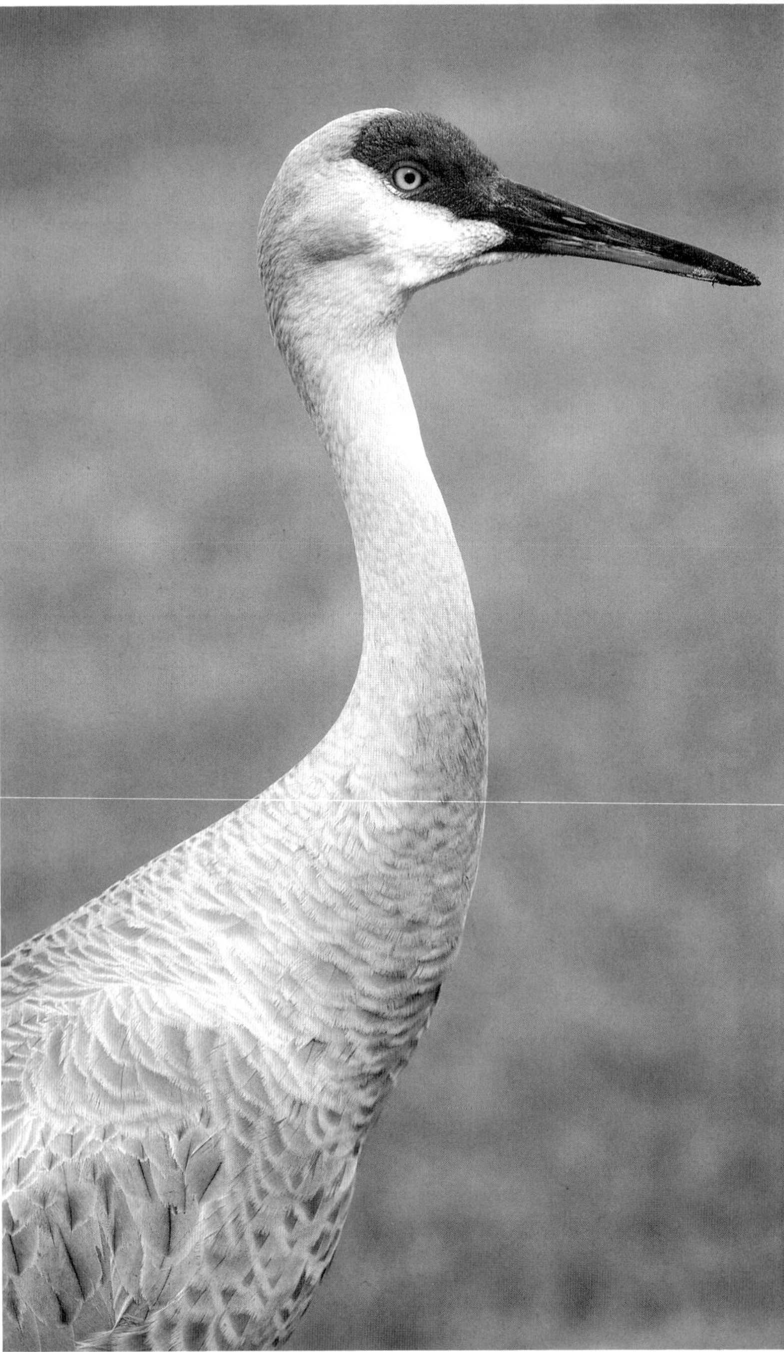

Digital Recording and In-Camera Processing

Formats for Digital Recording

A digital camera processes analog image information from its sensor and converts it to digital data. While the camera can capture 22-bit data, this is converted to 8-bits for JPEG images or as 12-bits in a RAW file. This color data is stated in bits for each of three different color channels: red, green, and blue. A bit is the smallest piece of information that a computer uses–an acronym for binary digit (0 or 1, off or on).

One great feature of the K10D is its ability to record a RAW data file in either Pentax' proprietary PEF format or in Adobe's DNG format. RAW files are different than other image files because they have undergone very little, if any, internal processing by the camera.

The other recording option for the K10D is JPEG, an abbreviation for Joint Photographic Experts Group. This is an international standard for the compression of images and is the most common file-type created by digital cameras. When a photo is recorded as a JPEG, extensive in-camera processing is applied to the image data. The camera's processor evaluates the 22-bit image, makes adjustments to it, and compresses the image to a color depth of 8-bits, thereby reducing the size of the file substantially, allowing more pictures to fit on a memory card. Because this process discards what it deems "redundant" data, JPEG compression is referred to as "lossy." When the file is opened in a computer using image-processing software, the program will rebuild

⇦ ***The K10D records both JPEG and RAW files. JPEGs are convenient and useful for photo-transfers, while RAW files offer a greater potential for image adjustments without creating artifacts.***

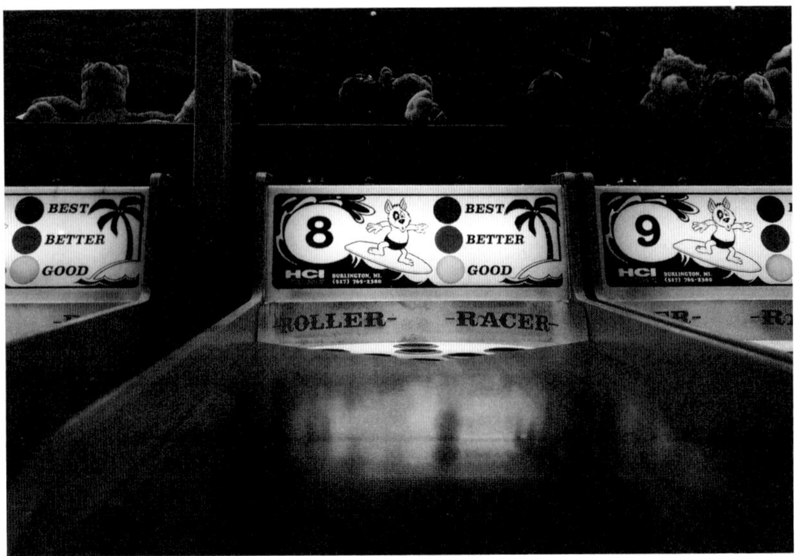

This photo, shot in mixed lighting, showed a slight color cast when reviewed with the in-camera settings. However, because it was recorded as a RAW file, it could be adjusted in the computer.
© Kevin Kopp

the JPEG file based on existing data. However, the better the JPEG quality option, the less original data is discarded; hence, the overall image quality is superior when using the Best quality versus the Better or Good quality options available with the K10D (see page 62).

After the JPEG file is downloaded and enhanced using image-processing software in the computer, it should be saved as a TIFF or in the software's native format (such as Photoshop's .psd). That will prevent further loss of quality due to additional compression that can occur when re-saving a file as JPEG.

Both RAW and JPEG files can give excellent results. The unprocessed data of a RAW file can be helpful when faced with tough exposure situations, but the small size of the JPEG file is faster and easier to deal with.

The RAW Difference

When recording in RAW, the camera's processor documents the in-camera settings used for such aspects as color saturation, color mode, contrast, white balance, and sharpness. However, those aspects are not actually applied to the RAW file by the camera as they are with JPEGs. Because they are not locked-in, you can retain the in-camera settings, or change them as desired.

Let's say you are shooting inside a stadium under sodium-vapor lighting and you forget to change from Auto white balance. At the end of the day you notice all your images exhibit a strong color cast. Or, perhaps your exposure was a bit off for some of the shots of one end of the field. You'll usually have better results correcting these types of problems if you were recording in RAW format.

RAW files contain 12-bit color information, which is considerably more data than an 8-bit JPEG. This large amount of information allows greater latitude for making corrections during image processing. You can alter the RAW file's attributes to a greater degree with less file degradation than you can when adjusting JPEGs. Generally you can also expect more pleasing prints at larger sizes from files originally shot in RAW.

However, to process RAW images you must use software (such as Pentax PHOTO Laboratory bundled with the K10D) that is compatible with your camera's particular RAW file format. Examples of additional programs include Adobe Photoshop Lightroom, as well as Adobe Photoshop CS (version 2 and later) and Adobe Photoshop Elements (version 3.0 and later), as long as Adobe's Camera Raw plug-in version 3.7 or later is being utilized.

While no software can work miracles with a grossly over or underexposed image, you should be able to correct moderate exposure errors (plus or minus one stop) without giving the RAW image an artificial look. As well, major changes can be made to other aspects of an image, such as color, contrast, and white balance, without negative effects on the pixels.

Yet working with RAW does have certain drawbacks. As mentioned, PEF and especially DNG files consume more space on a memory card than JPEGs. In addition, converting and adjusting RAW files adds extra post-processing time. That can be a problem after you return from a long trip with hundreds of images.

The choice between RAW and JPEG is up to you. Determine the advantages and limitations of each and use what works best for your situation. One important factor is your personal working style. If you want to shoot quickly and spend less time in front of the computer, JPEG might be the best choice. If you loved working in the darkroom and processing film, then RAW is a great continuation of that process. If you are dealing with problematic lighting, shoot in RAW for the superior correction possibilities available with the PEF or DNG format files. If you have tons of images to deal with, JPEG may be the most efficient because you will not need to first convert every photo. Of course you can always use the option to shoot RAW and JPEG simultaneously (see page 64).

Recorded Pixels (Image Size/Resolution)

For digital cameras, resolution indicates the number of individual pixels contained on the imaging sensor. Sometimes this is referred to as image size, while Pentax calls it "recorded pixels." Resolution, or recorded pixel size, is usually expressed in megapixels (MP), an abbreviation for millions of pixels. Thus, a 10-megapixel camera has 10 million pixels covering the sensor.

You don't always have to utilize the camera's maximum resolution. The K10D offers the choice of three different JPEG recorded pixel settings. Generally it is best to use the highest resolution to take the most finely detailed pictures. This also gives you more flexibility to crop or to make large prints. You can always reduce resolution with image-processing software in a computer.

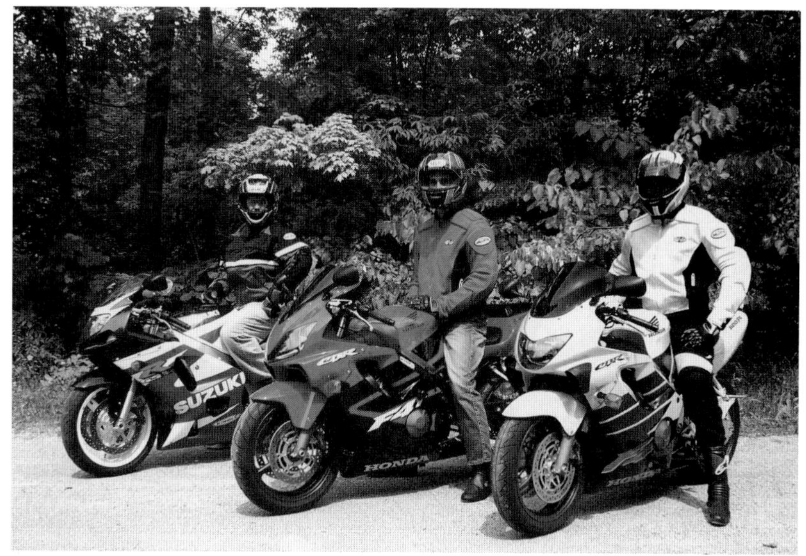

In difficult high-contrast lighting, RAW is the best choice because of the greater latitude for making modifications.

Below are the three options available for creating JPEG files. To choose your desired resolution, press the MENU button and navigate to the Rec. Mode menu , then scroll using the up/down controller arrows to select the *JPEG Rec. Pixels* item. Continue scrolling right to select a resolution setting, then press the OK button:

- 10M: 3872 x 2592 pixels
- 6M: 3008 x 2000 pixels
- 2M: 1824 x 1216 pixels (actually, 2.2 megapixels)

It is usually best to record using the highest resolution, though there may be situations where it is preferable to shoot at less than the maximum. Lower resolution (smaller) image files require less storage space and processing time. You can fit more of them on your memory card than those captured using higher resolution settings. Also, servers and browsers can handle smaller files used in emails or on web pages more easily and quickly than large files. Do note however, that even the 2M recorded pixel level produces files that are larger than you'll usually want for uploading to a Web site or for sending as an attachment with an e-mail message. In that case, you would still want to down-size the JPEGs in your image-editing software.

JPEG Quality Level (Compression)

Quality level refers to the amount of compression applied to your JPEG files by the in-camera processing engine. The K10D allows you to select the quality level in the Rec. Mode menu. The *Best* option produces the least compression, so the file will be larger and the quality will be higher. *Better* applies a medium amount of compression. Selecting *Good* quality will provide the smallest JPEG files because of greater compression; that can be useful when you don't have much storage capacity left on your memory card. However, be aware that increased compression creates an image that is less fine. When a highly compressed file is opened in a computer, discarded data is restored but the process is not perfect; some artifacts, such as jagged subject edges, may appear.

As the labels in the menu imply, applying the least amount of compression to an image file will give you the best quality.

Recording Formats

The default recording mode is JPEG (10M, Best), but the Rec. Mode menu also allows you to select RAW format using the *File Format* item. You can choose several format options for recording:

JPEG: change recorded pixels and quality level using the *JPEG Rec. Pixels* option as discussed on page 61.

RAW: only a raw data file will be recorded, and PEF is the default.

RAW+: a raw data file plus a JPEG will be recorded.61

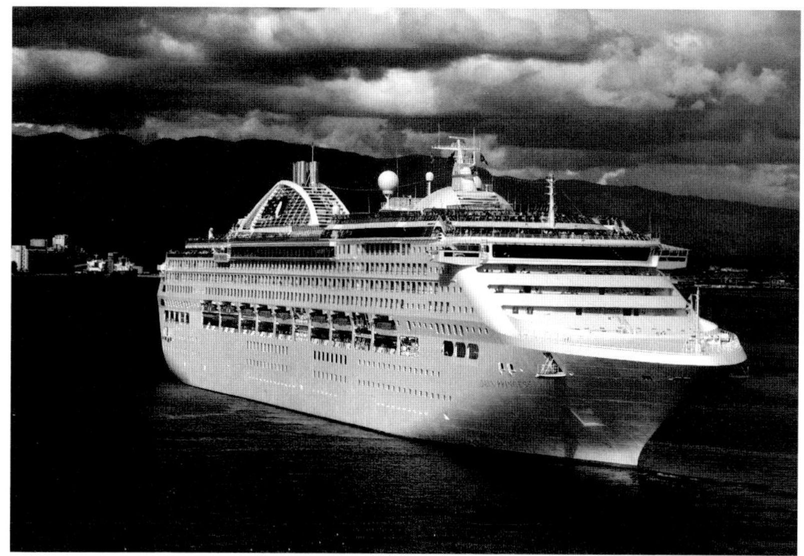

For superior JPEG images with a lower risk of artifacts, be sure to select the largest image size (JPEG Rec. Pixels) along with the Best quality (lowest compression).

There is an added selection option for *RAW file format* in the Rec. Mode menu that allows you to choose either PEF (the Pentax RAW format) or DNG (developed by Adobe). Some photographers prefer to use the DNG format because it is supported by a broader range of image-processing software.

Do note that there is one technical benefit to using PEF files rather than DNG files: they are smaller thanks to greater lossless compression (as noted in the File Size Chart on page 65). Consequently, any memory card will hold more PEF files than DNG files. In spite of the file size difference however, there is not a great difference in terms of "burst depth:" the number of consecutive shots you can record. In DNG format using a fast memory card, I was able to take 12 shots in a single burst. Switching to PEF reduced that to 9 shots in a sequence, perhaps because the extra compression applied to PEF format files requires additional processing.

When you record in either of the two RAW formats, the files are always created at the full 10MP resolution. Since RAW files are significantly larger than JPEGs and consume more memory in both your card and your computer, I recommend a high capacity memory card, at least 2 gigabytes (GB), if you plan to frequently shoot in RAW format.

RAW+JPEG Recording

The K10D gives you the option to shoot a RAW file plus a JPEG image simultaneously. If the camera is set to default, RAW+ will produce a 10MP RAW file and a 10MP Best JPEG, recording both to the memory card. However, you can choose to generate a lower resolution and/or lower quality JPEG in RAW+ capture mode. (Neither aspect can be changed for RAW files, however.) Simply select different JPEG Recorded Pixels and/or Quality level while the camera is set for RAW+ recording.

The RAW+ recording mode can be useful if you want JPEGs for making prints quickly–or for viewing images in some browser software program–as well as RAW files for later modification and processing in your RAW converter software. The combination of RAW and JPEG means that more data must be recorded to the memory card. (The higher the JPEG size/quality that you select in RAW+ mode, the more space the image will consume on the memory card.) Hence, this option will fill your card more quickly and you will be able to shoot fewer images in a sequence, depending on the speed of your card and the JPEG size/quality selected in RAW+ capture. That's understandable, because the camera will need to save two files for every image to its buffer and then record two files to the memory card.

Approximate File Sizes

The chart below shows memory card file sizes in megabytes (MB) with the various options for format, quality level, and recorded pixel size (resolution) offered by the K10D. These are merely rough estimates, because file size can vary significantly depending on the amount of fine detail in an image.

This data was produced by taking a photo of exactly the same scene. Later, when I opened each of those JPEG images in my computer, the JPEG decompressed. My image-processing program rebuilt the data (by adding pixels) that were discarded during in-camera processing. Hence, the JPEG 10MP files were actually 28.7MB in size when opened in the computer.

A RAW file will also be larger after it is decompressed (even RAW files may undergo a certain degree of lossless compression) and processed by the special software and converted to a format such as TIFF. Both my PEF and DNG files were 28.7MB in size after conversion.

Memory Card File Size Chart

Quality Level	10MP Recorded Pixels	6MP Recorded Pixels	2MP Recorded Pixels
JPEG Best	2.56MB	1.63MB	0.82MB
JPEG Better	2.03MB	1.24MB	0.53MB
JPEG Good	0.98MB	0.66MB	0.32MB
PEF	13MB	N/A	N/A
DNG	16.2MB	N/A	N/A

Note: To estimate the total size of a RAW+JPEG image on a memory card, add the size of the RAW file plus the size of the pertinent JPEG file.

Memory Card Capacity

The number of images that any memory card will hold varies, depending on the number of recorded pixels and level of compression of the images. The values in the chart below are only approximate and relate to the use of a 1GB memory card. In fact, actual file size–and hence, the actual card capacity–can vary widely depending on the type of scene and the amount of fine detail.

Comparative Capacity of 1GB Memory Card

Recorded Pixels (Resolution)	Quality Level (Compression)	Approx. Number of Files per Card
10MP	JPEG Best	202
10MP	JPEG Better	244
10MP	JPEG Good	592
6MP	JPEG Best	336
6MP	JPEG Better	574
6MP	JPEG Good	990
2MP	JPEG Best	914
2MP	JPEG Better	1548
2MP	JPEG Good	2626
10MP	RAW - DNG	60
10MP	RAW – PEF	77

Note: Estimates for JPEGs were provided by Pentax while the estimates for DNG and PEF format are based on my actual picture taking experiences using "average" outdoor scenes.

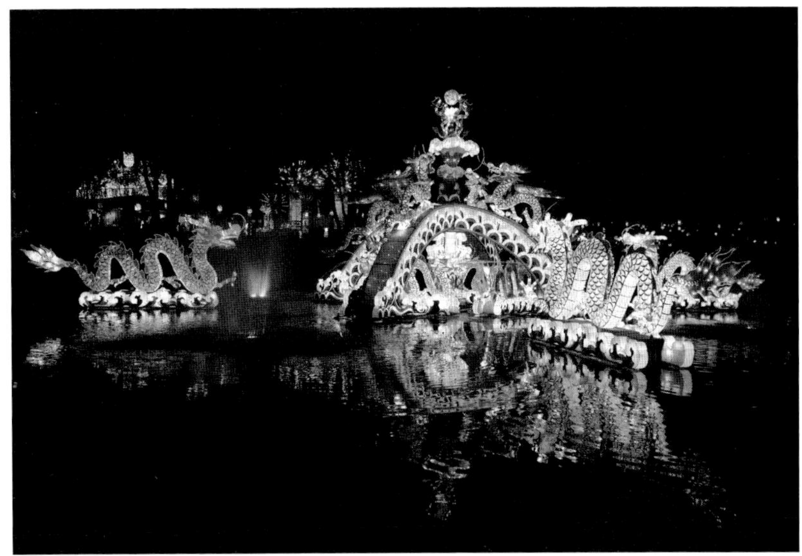

Invest in a large-capacity memory card if you intend to often record PEF or DNG files. These RAW files require much more memory than even the largest size/least compression JPEGs.

In-Camera Processing

A digital SLR is far more versatile than a film camera because it allows the owner to control many more aspects of an image. While the default settings can be useful for quick shooting, your K10D provides a wealth of user-selectable options for managing the "look" of a photo–both before and after you take the shot. It's time to take a closer look at some of the ways you can use your K10D to process and enhance different qualities of your image files.

White Balance

The sensors in digital cameras can be adjusted for different color temperatures of light. In other words, the camera can produce a natural-looking image, rendering whites as pure white, in various types of lighting. When the whites are accurate, generally other tones are accurate as well, without a strong color cast. This is known as adjusting the white balance (WB).

White Balance—How It Works

Every light source emits a different range of wavelengths, varying from primarily short (appearing blue) to primarily long (appearing red.) Even the light from the sun can look different due to time of day and atmospheric condition. It is cooler (bluer) on overcast days than during a sunrise or sunset (warmer, redder). While our brain perceptually adjusts for some of these differences, digital sensors record them more objectively.

The color of light is defined numerically using the Kelvin color temperature scale. Lower Kelvin temperatures denote the warm, reddish light produced by a bonfire, an incandescent lamp, and the sun when it is low in the sky. Higher Kelvin temperatures denote the cool, bluish light at twilight, on heavily overcast days, or in a shady area.

On the Kelvin scale, full sunlight (mid day) is typically between 5100K and 5500K. The light on an overcast day is usually between 5500K and 6500K. In full shade, the light is even bluer: typically between 7000K and 8000K. The range provided for these different types of light is quite broad because it's affected by the time of day, the extent of the clouds that filter the light from the sun, the time of year, and atmospheric factors such as haze, smog, fog, or dust particles in the air.

Artificial light sources also produce light with certain color temperatures. Household tungsten lamps produce light with an orange cast (about 3200K). Some fluorescent tubes produce greenish light, although that's not true with the newer Daylight or White balanced tubes. Unusual lamps, such as sodium vapor and mercury vapor, produce light with a strange color that can be difficult to define.

Since digital cameras can be adjusted somewhat for the color temperatures produced by these various light sources, it is possible to greatly reduce or eliminate color cast from your photos. This is referred to as white balance control.

To select different white balance options, press the Fn button and scroll left to AWB. The screen will now show the white balance options available. Scroll down using the four-way controller to the WB option you want. For example, you may decide to select the preset option for Cloudy ☁ when shooting on an overcast day. Press OK again to confirm your selection. That WB option will be applied and used for all subsequent photos.

Auto White Balance (AWB)

This option is designed to let the camera analyze the color of light and automatically set an appropriate color temperature between 4000 and 8000K. This system works quite well outdoors, especially on sunny or partly cloudy days, and indoors with flash. It's an especially useful choice when the light is changing rapidly (from sunny to cloudy to sunny again), or when shooting subjects that move from one type of lighting to another—sunlight to shadow, for example. But AWB does not always work as well under manufactured lighting such as tungsten or sodium vapor.

Preset White Balance Selections

You can usually get more accurate white balance rendition than AWB in particular lighting situations by selecting a specific WB setting—called a preset—designed specifically for those conditions. That's particularly important when shooting JPEGs, but can be useful for RAW capture too. While a PEF or DNG file can be extensively corrected in the special converter software, it's still wise to get white balance as close to accurate as possible; that can save a great deal of time and effort later.

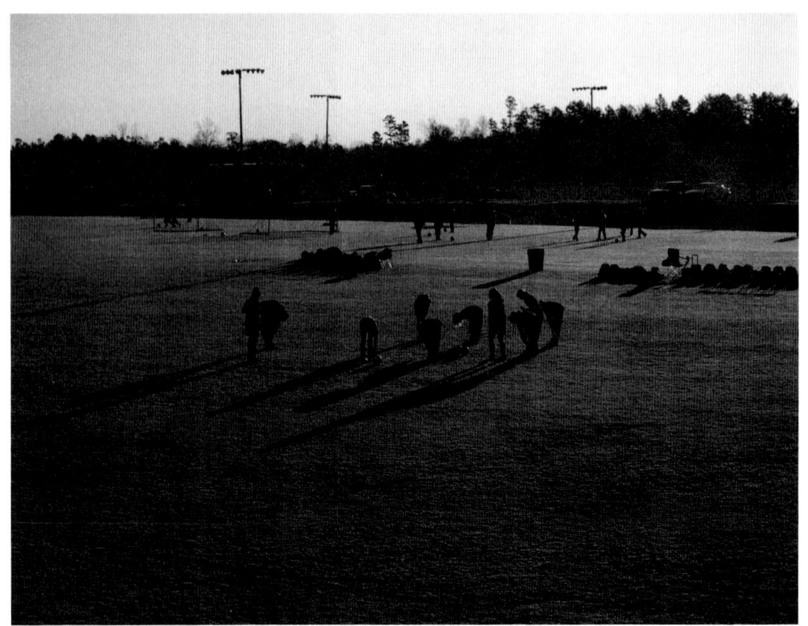

Manual, or custom, white balance is usually the best way to accurately capture the warmth of early morning light. © Kevin Kopp

To select a preset WB, scroll down to the second option in the LCD monitor and then scroll right. Now, several white balance preset options will be visible, each with an icon and a description in words:

Daylight
Shade
Cloudy
Fluorescent (There are three different types of Fluorescent WB from which to choose: D (6500K), N (5000K), and W (4200K)).
Tungsten (household lamps)
Flash

Scroll to the desired option with the controller and press the AF button to confirm your selection. There are also icons available for Manual and Color Temperature. We will discuss these separately (see pages 75 and 76).

Note: When using flash as fill merely to lighten shadows in a scene where sunlight (or another light source) is the primary source of illumination, do not select the Flash white balance preset. Instead, use AWB or make your white balance selection based on the type of illumination that is the main light source for the shot. For best results, if color is critical, filter the flash so it matches the ambient light in the scene. Reserve the Flash preset for low light photography when the subject will be primarily lit by the electronic flash.

Digital Preview for White Balance

The Pentax K10D provides a white balance evaluation feature that is unique to this camera. Digital WB Preview is easy to use. Activate the camera's circuitry by gently touching the shutter release button. Compose and focus for the scene that you plan to photograph. Remove your finger from the shutter release button. Press the Fn button to select the WB screen and any WB option. While viewing the scene again through the viewfinder (but without touching the shutter button), rotate the camera's On/Off switch to the far right, to the Preview position .

You'll hear a click and the scene will be displayed in the camera's LCD monitor but not written to the memory card. While the scene is displayed, scroll through the various WB options to see the effect that each WB setting will have on the image. When you find the one that is most accurate or most pleasing, select that WB option (with WB Fine-tuning if desired) and take a photo using the normal picture-taking procedure.

Fine-Tuning White Balance

After selecting any WB option except AWB, you can fine-tune the white balance level for that option by biasing it toward green or magenta, blue or amber. This feature is most useful when taking advantage of Digital Preview for white balance. From any preset WB item in the screen, scroll right to access the White Balance Fine-tuning rectangle.

Note: Fine-tuning can also be activated for AWB. To do so, scroll to the Custom Setting menu tab. Scroll down to the *Fine tune when AWB* item. Then scroll right, select *Enabled* and press the OK button to confirm your selection. I recommend this, and in the rest of this chapter I will assume this function has been set by all readers on their own cameras.

Scrolling through the rectangle in the appropriate direction–by moving the cursor toward the G, M, B, or A side–allows you to adjust the color balance toward green, magenta, blue, or amber, respectively. The farther you scroll toward the appropriate edge of the rectangle, the stronger the effect will be. Watch the WB preview changing as you move the cursor to different locations within the rectangle. When the color balance of the image appears to be the most accurate or the most visually pleasing, press the OK button to confirm your selection. Take the photo and the adjusted WB setting will be used.

WB Fine-Tuning Feedback: When the WB Fine-tuning option is active, you can scroll through the rectangle, placing the cursor in any desired position to bias WB toward a certain color. As you do so, the K10D provides feedback about the extent of the setting. In addition to the preview image, it provides alphanumeric abbreviations for data that's important to understand; it becomes significant when using the White Balance Bracketing feature (see page 78).

This feedback notation is based on the blue, amber, green, and magenta axes for correction. For example, a level of A4 indicates a +4 adjustment toward amber, for a fairly strong warming effect. A notation of B1 indicates a slight (+1) bias toward blue, giving a moderate cooling effect. G5 would indicate a setting with a strong green bias, as M5 would tell you the same for magenta. If you moved the cursor toward both the magenta and amber portion of the fine-tuning rectangle, you might see data such as M2 (+2 magenta) and A2 (+2 amber).

Note: Once set, white balance fine-tuning will remain active for that particular WB option whenever it is selected. In order to cancel it, reset the cursor in the fine-tuning rectangle to the default position by placing the cursor back in the center of the rectangle using the four-way controller. You can also cancel all WB Fine-tuning that has been set by selecting the *Reset* tab in the Set-up menu and scrolling to select the *Reset* option. Activate by pressing the OK button.

Creative Use of White Balance: Intentionally using the "wrong" white balance setting can yield some interesting creative effects. For example, if you select the Cloudy WB preset on a sunny day, the image will be warm with a slight amber cast. That can resemble the effect produced by a warming filter attached to the front of a lens in film photography. The Flash WB preset produces a milder warming effect, while the Shade WB preset produces a more obvious yellow/orange color cast. The Tungsten setting produces the opposite effect–a strong blue cast that can be useful with some winter scenes to show a cool appearance. Experiment with using the various preset choices–as well as the fine-tuning option–for creative purposes. As already described, you can preview the result that each will produce, a definite benefit not available with most other digital cameras.

Of course you can always decide, for example, to leave the K10D set to a slight amber adjustment in fine-tuning for AWB. That can be useful if you always prefer a slight warming effect for all photos. Or, you may decide to use the Shade WB preset instead of Cloudy WB preset on overcast days for warmer looking images in such conditions. Or set a slight blue fine-tuning adjustment for the Shade WB if you

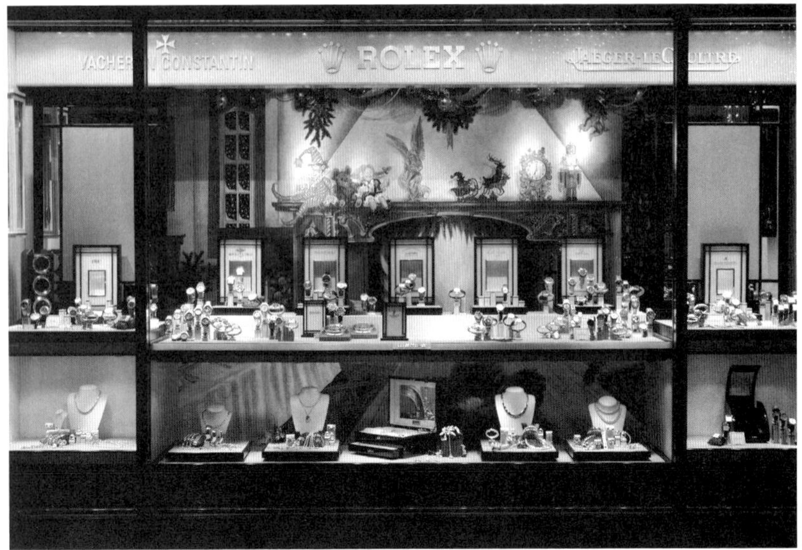

Manual WB is useful when a scene is lit by mixed artificial light. In most cases this option produces more accurate color than the white balance presets.

find the camera routinely produces images that are slightly too amber with that WB preset.

However, remember that the WB strategy that you use may not be ideal in every situation. That's because the exact color of light often varies within a broad range. Also, when shooting in tricky lighting conditions where the camera routinely makes images with inaccurate white balance, I strongly recommend using the Manual (custom) WB feature instead.

Manual White Balance

Often referred to as Custom WB, the Manual WB setting in the K10D allows you to tailor the white balance value to any type of lighting. Though a sophisticated function, it is not overly complicated to set. It is well worth the bit of extra effort to learn the procedure because this setting virtually guarantees good white balance; it's particularly useful for artificial or mixed artificial lighting.

Note: Manual WB is unnecessary when electronic flash will be the primary light source, even when shooting under artificial light. If you routinely use flash indoors, stick with the Flash WB preset option, perhaps using the WB Fine-tuning if you prefer a warmer or cooler result.

For Manual WB, a sheet of white paper or a Gray Card is used as a target in order to calibrate the camera for a specific lighting condition. It is a good idea to photocopy the following steps to keep as reference in your camera bag.

1. Press the Fn button; select the WB screen; scroll down to the Manual icon .

2. Use the controller keys to scroll right from . The words *Manual White Balance* will appear at the top of the screen and the WB Fine-tuning rectangle will be circled to indicate that it is active.

3. Place the white or gray card in the same light that illuminates your subject. (If the lighting is not identical for the entire subject, place the sheet at the most important subject area: near a person's face, for example.) If the light is very bright, you may get a better reading off the gray side of the card.

4. Look through the viewfinder and point the lens so the white target fills at least the central area of the frame (within the rectangle on the viewing screen). Be careful not to cast a shadow over your target. The white card does not need to be in focus; if the AF system has difficulty finding focus, switch the camera to manual focus (MF).

5. Press the shutter button all the way down. The camera will create a preview image of the card. When it does so, it also calibrates the WB system. An image of your target will appear in the LCD monitor.

If the target looks white or neutral in the preview image, the calibration process has been successful. In truth, it may look grey because the camera's light meter may have under exposed the white target. That's not a problem. But if there is a strong color cast, turn the camera off and on, and repeat the Manual WB calibration procedure.

When you're satisfied with the color balance of the preview, press the OK button to confirm this Manual WB selection. Then, you can use the WB Fine-tuning feature to bias Manual WB toward amber, blue, green or magenta if desired. I find that a slight adjustment toward amber is often useful to prevent Manual WB from generating images that appear quite "cool;" however, this is a subjective preference.

Press the OK button twice. The camera will record the Manual white balance setting and it will return to normal operation in all other respects. You can now begin taking photos under the specific lighting condition and the images should exhibit correct white balance.

Note: The K10D saves the Manual WB setting even when the camera is turned off. When you move to entirely different lighting conditions–outdoors after shooting in a sports arena for example–remember to switch to another WB option, such as AWB or the Sunny or Cloudy WB preset. That will prevent serious white balance errors. At a later date, when shooting in the same arena, you can recall the setting (if you haven't changed it in the meantime) simply by selecting Manual white balance. Press the OK button to confirm your selection. However, since the system only retains the last calibration, be sure to recalibrate Manual WB if you decide to shoot in different light. Note too that selecting the *Reset* item (in the Set-up menu) will clear any Manual WB and WB Fine-tuning that has been set.

K Color Temperature

This option allows you to set a specific color temperature (in degrees Kelvin) for white balance purposes. It is intended for photographers who use a color temperature meter or shoot under lighting with a known color temperature, or who follow the manufacturer's recommendations for certain types of lighting. If you aren't using these methods, the camera's other white balance options will be more useful.

Enter the Fn menu and scroll left to *AWB*. From the option screen for white balance, scroll down to the last item, which is the control for Color Temperature (the default listing is 5000K). Then follow this procedure:

Scroll to the right to highlight the first of the three 5000K items: the words White Balance Color Temperature will appear in the LCD monitor, confirming the name of this feature. Next, set the desired degrees Kelvin. (Remember, it is best to use this feature when you already know already know what the Kelvin setting should be.) Use the camera's front e-dial to make smaller changes (in increments of 100 degrees K), or the rear e-dial to make larger changes (in increments of 1000 degrees K). Press the OK button twice and the K10D will be set to your selected degrees Kelvin.

From this point on, the camera will use that WB setting until you select another WB option in the Fn menu. However, even if you change WB settings, that previous setting for degrees K will be saved by the K10D. In fact, you will note that there are three listings when you scroll to the Color Temperature (K) option. Each of these three Kelvin selections can be changed, so you can set three specific and distinct color temperatures. Each will be saved until changed. This means you can quickly select and activate one at any time, which can be useful if you often shoot in the same three types of lighting conditions.

After setting the desired color temperature in degrees Kelvin, you can further modify the white balance by applying White Balance Fine-tuning to bias the image toward blue, amber, green or magenta. However, photographers who are advanced enough to use the Color Temperature WB control are unlikely to want to bias the white balance. Hence, that is not a step that I would recommend.

Note: The K10D includes an option for selecting color temperature in Mired steps (in increments of 20 mired). This is available under by choosing *Color temp. steps* in the Custom Settings menu. When that option is activated however, the color temperature will still be shown in degrees Kelvin in the WB Fn menu. Frankly, the vast majority of photographers have absolutely no experience with the mired steps, so I will not comment further on this option.

White Balance Bracketing

The K10D can be set to generate two extra JPEGs of any single photo that you shoot, varying the white balance for these additional images. This is an option that's available in the camera's Extended Bracket feature selected in the Rec. Mode menu . Scroll to the *Extended Bracket* tab using the controller; then scroll right to *Off*. In order to activate the bracket using white balance, scroll to the right once more. That causes the K10D to list the bracketing options available: *White Balance*, as well as *Saturation*, *Sharpness*, and *Contrast*. (The other three are discussed later in this chapter; see pages 82-85).

Scroll down to the *White Balance* item and press the OK button. Now, scroll down to the *Bracketing amount* item and then scroll right. This produces a screen with all of the available options for WB Bracketing. They're listed as BA and GM abbreviations, indicating Blue/Amber and Green/Magenta, as explained in the WB Fine-Tuning section, on page 72. For example, BA+1 indicates that the white balance will be modified by one increment (a small amount) toward blue for one photo and toward amber for another photo. And GM+3 indicates that the white balance will be modified by three increments (a fairly large amount) toward green for one photo and toward magenta for another photo.

White Balance Bracketing can be selected no matter which WB option was set from the Fn menu. It's available only in JPEG (when shooting RAW+JPEG, only the JPEG will be bracketed–it will not function when RAW is used, which makes sense since you can easily change the white balance when processing your DNG or PEF format files in the computer.)

Only the last of the three JPEG images will be displayed in instant preview on the LCD monitor, but you can view all three in the camera's Playback mode. After you decide that you no longer need to bracket, remember to set the Extended Bracketing menu item to *Off*, or activate *Reset* in the Rec. Mode menu to return the camera to all of its default settings.

In my experience, this feature is most appropriate when using Manual white balance or one of the preset white balance options such as Cloudy or Shade. It increases the odds of getting an image with the most pleasing color. The BA (blue/amber) option is frequently useful since a cooling or warming effect more often desirable. The GM (green/magenta) bracketing is useful when shooting in fluorescent lighting.

WB Bracketing has a disadvantage: the extra two files consume more space on a memory card and the processing time is about a second longer. That delay is not significant but occasionally, it may cause you to miss a fleeting gesture in candid picture-taking if using Single Shot drive mode.

Color Spaces and Modes

Digital cameras render color based on combinations of red, blue, and green and in terms of hue, saturation, and brightness. The various systems that define these colors are called color spaces. Color spaces were invented with different biases based largely on how images will be created or viewed. Two color spaces are common in digital imaging: sRGB and Adobe RGB. With the K10D, sRGB is the default color space and it's ideal for on-screen viewing and Internet use.

Most photofinishers (kiosks, in-store labs, and on-line printing services) also work with sRGB images because that is the standard color space with the vast majority of digital cameras. So, this option is fine for images that you take or send to a printing service. Most (but not all) firms will accept files in Adobe RGB color space, but will usually convert them to sRGB before making prints simply because their equipment is optimized for that color space.

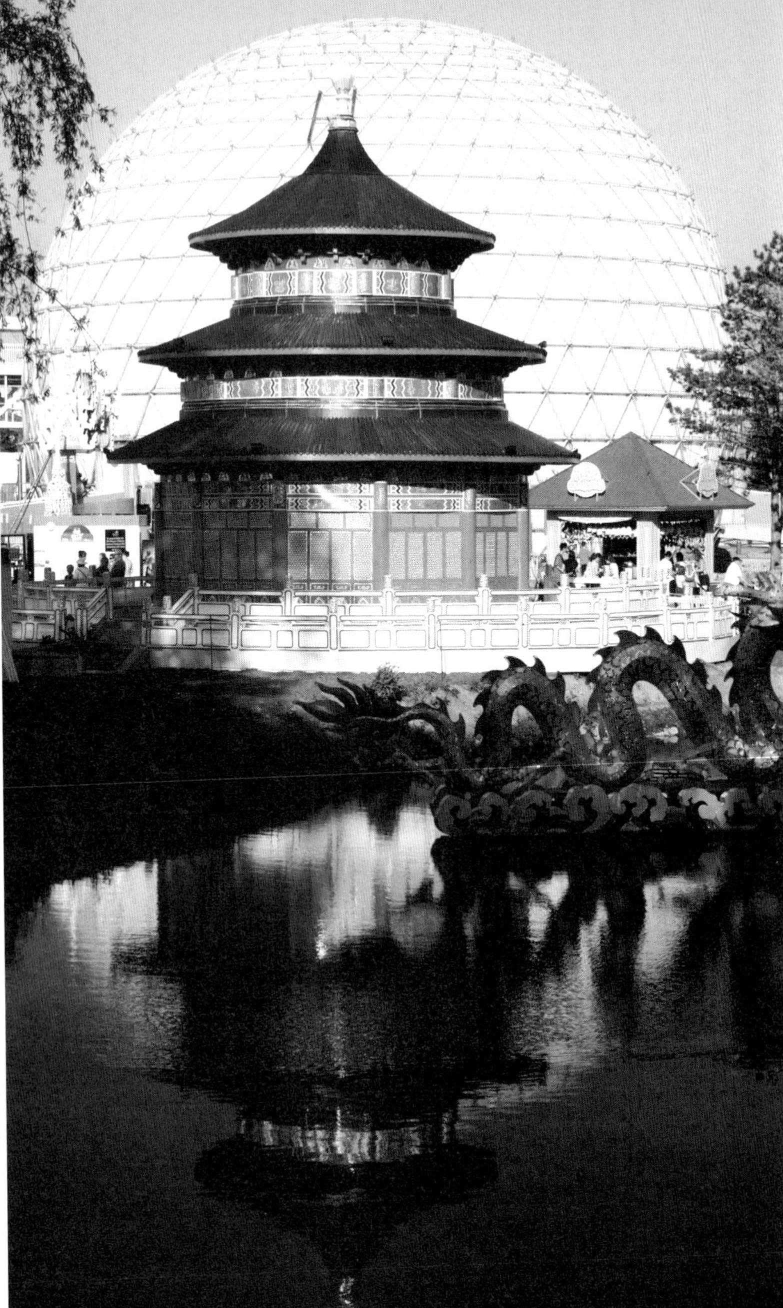

Note: When viewed on a computer monitor, Adobe RGB exhibits less rich colors than sRGB, making sRGB a preferred option for electronic display, as on a Web site, for example. That's one reason why Adobe (and some other brands) of imaging programs allow for converting Adobe RGB files to sRGB color space.

On the other hand, the Adobe RGB color space has a wide color gamut or recording range: it can record far more colors or shades of any single color than sRGB. So, it's a preferable choice if you plan to make inkjet prints using a photo printer. As well, labs offering professional quality custom printing often recommend making images in Adobe RGB color space for the same reason: to take advantage of its wider color gamut. While your imaging software may allow you to convert sRGB files to Adobe RGB color space, doing so offers little value; the key is to capture images in Adobe RGB if your primary plan is inkjet or professional printing.

The default for color space in your K10D is sRGB, you can switch to shooting in Adobe RGB with the *Color Space* item in the Custom Setting menu. Scroll to that tab, and then scroll right. Select the *AdobeRGB* option and press the OK button to confirm your selection. Later, you can select *sRGB* again or use the camera's *Reset Custom Fnction* option in the Custom Setting menu to revert to the default color space.

Note: Some brands of image-processing software are not compatible with Adobe RGB color space, though the Pentax and Adobe brand software programs are certainly compatible. Programs that are incompatible with Adobe RGB might automatically convert the images to the standard sRGB color space, or may produce an "incompatible color space" error message, or they could generate an inaccurate display of the colors on a computer monitor and in inkjet prints. If your favorite imaging software is not compatible with Adobe RGB, simply avoid the problem by using sRGB color Space with your K10D.

Adobe RGB is an ideal choice if you plan to make inkjet prints and have compatible software in your computer.

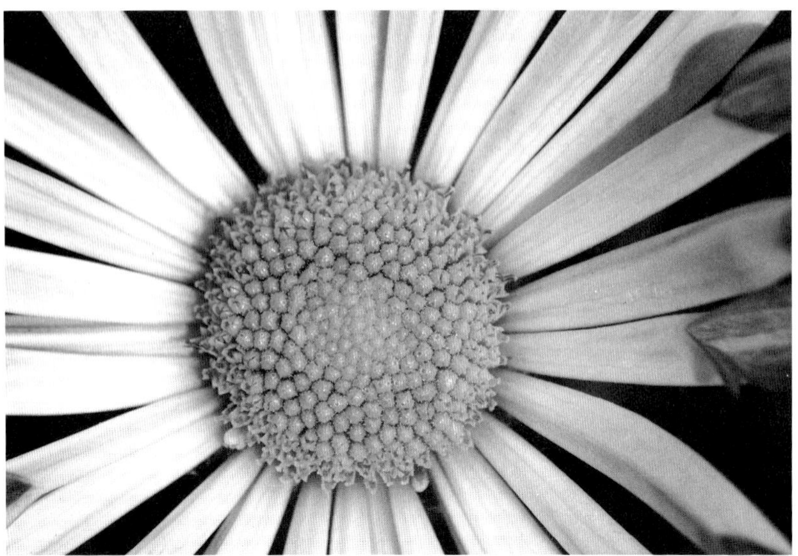

Subjects such as this colorful flower often benefit from a +1 increase in saturation.

Saturation/Sharpness/Contrast Adjustment

While the K10D is programmed to produce sharp, colorful images with snappy contrast, you may prefer a different "look" for some types of subjects. For example, for a graphic mural on a building you might want to make a photo that's even more dramatic by over saturating the colors. On the other hand, for a portrait of your grandmother, you might prefer a softer effect, with lower sharpness, contrast, and color intensity.

The K10D offers several options for modifying images in Capture mode. (It also provides some in-camera effects that can be applied later, in Playback mode, as discussed on pages 88-89.) The most straightforward adjustments in the Capture mode allow you to alter the level from very low to very high for three of these: color saturation, image sharpness, and contrast.

Select one of these three desired attribute in the Rec. Mode menu. Note the scales that appear for each. You can scroll right (to the + side of the scale) to set a higher level, or scroll left (toward the minus side of the scale) to set a lower level. The default for these is 0, and they can be adjusted within a range from –3 to +3 using the controller's left/right keys. After you make any change, press the OK button to confirm your selection.

There's no need for this feature if shooting in RAW format because those image parameters can be adjusted in the converter software before conversion to TIFF or another format. If you're shooting JPEGs, it is best to experiment with your K10D before adjusting any of the three parameters. It's important to get a feel for the level of sharpness, contrast, and color saturation the camera produces at the default level. When you do start experimenting with adjustments, error on the side of caution, making increases in small increments, such as +1, for *Saturation* and *Contrast*. For *Sharpness*, +2 may produce very good results.

Note: Once set, the level for saturation, sharpness, and contrast will be maintained even after you turn the camera off. You can change the levels at anytime, of course. As well, using the *Reset* control in the Set-up menu returns all adjustments to the default level of zero.

Saturation

At its default setting, the K10D produces images with rich color saturation appropriate for most subjects. (When using a polarizing filter over the lens, color saturation can be even more vivid.) However, if you find the colors to be excessively rich, set a minus factor when shooting JPEGs. Decreased saturation may be useful in portrait photography where a muted color rendition often produces more pleasing skin tones.

I find that a -1 saturation level produces color that is preferable for close-up photos of people, but this is a subjective judgment. For some very colorful images in travel photography, I might set a +1 level for saturation. However, it's easy to boost color saturation in image editing software, with full control over the exact amount of the increase. If you plan to manipulate your JPEG photos in a computer, you'll probably want to use the default or -1 in-camera level for saturation. Think twice about selecting a +2 or +3 saturation level. Excessive color richness can lead to loss of detail; that problem can be very difficult to correct later in the computer without creating an artificial-looking effect.

Sharpness

The camera produces moderately sharp images. However, many K10D owners will prefer a higher level for their JPEGs. A +1 setting is fine, but you may want to set +2 if you do not plan to do extra sharpening in image-processing software in the computer.

Some imaging experts prefer to select the lowest in-camera sharpening level available (–3 with the K10D) for recording images. Later, they use special sharpening techniques in computer software to achieve exactly the sharpness level that's ideal for any specific image and print size. Frankly, I don't subscribe to that theory and find that a +1 level for Sharpness is ideal; it produces a slight increase in sharpness that looks quite natural and not excessive. Before making a print, I can still apply additional sharpening if needed using Unsharp Mask or Smart Sharpen in an image-processing program to fine-tune.

Contrast

Without internal adjustment, the K10D produces images with snappy contrast. To reduce contrast in harsh lighting conditions, or to create flattering portraits that benefit from a soft look, you may want to adjust the contrast to -1 or to -2. In flat light, such as an overcast day, you might want to try a +1 level for more separation of light to dark elements; but think twice about selecting a contrast level higher than +2 for any other type of lighting. Low contrast is easy to fix in image-processing software, but excessive contrast can be difficult to moderate. In fact, you may want to permanently set a -1 level if you plan to enhance all of your JPEGs in image-processing software.

Saturation, Sharpness, and Contrast Bracketing

We've already considered the bracketing feature for white balance, one of the four options available when *Extended Bracket* is selected in the Rec. Mode menu. The other three options allow for bracketing the amount of saturation, contrast, or sharpness that the camera's processor will apply to JPEGs. (It's not available for RAW recording.) At any one time, you can set bracketing for only one of these processing parameters.

Note: The K10D will also bracket exposures, varying the exposure level. That is an entirely different function than Extended Bracket, and is selected with a dedicated button . Exposure bracketing is discussed on pages 157-158.

Select *Saturation, Sharpness,* or *Contrast* from the *Extended Bracket* tab. The method for activating any of these is the same as it is for bracketing white balance, though the setting labels differ a bit. The selectable levels are +1, +2, and +3. Just as in WB Bracketing, after an option has been set, the K10D will generate two extra JPEGs after recording a single JPEG photo, each image with a higher or lower level of color saturation, contrast, or sharpness.

In my experience, this feature is occasionally useful, especially for bracketing color saturation or contrast. When you're not sure which level of saturation or contrast might produce the most pleasing image, set the Extended Bracket feature; one of the three JPEGs should be perfect. I suggest using the +2 level; that will usually make the difference obvious but not overly excessive. After you decide that you no longer need to bracket, remember to set the Extended Bracket menu item to *Off*, or activate *Reset* in the Rec. Mode menu to return the camera to all of its default settings.

Image Tone

Image tone has an affect on the way the picture will look. From the Rec. Mode menu, scroll down to *Image Tone*. Scroll right to choose between two options. The default selection is *Natural* , which does not add a great deal of tone processing. The selection for *Bright* , however, offers a quick, automated method for combining increased sharpness, color saturation, and contrast in an image to produce an extremely bold, snappy effect. Frankly, I see no need for this feature since the three characteristics are so easy to set individually, as discussed in the previous sections.

Note too that you can activate bracketing for saturation, contrast, and sharpness when either Bright or Natural image tone is set. You can also adjust the level of each of those attributes individually for full control. For example, you might like the high saturation and sharpness provided by Bright Image Tone, but prefer gentler contrast. In that case, you might set a minus adjustment level for contrast only. Once set, the Bright image tone, as well as any adjustments, will be maintained even after you turn the camera off. You can change them at any time of course; also, the *Reset* item in the Set-up menu returns the K10D to default settings, including Natural image tone and a zero level for all adjustments.

Noise Reduction

Digital images made using long exposures can exhibit noticeable digital noise even when low ISO settings are used. The effect is similar to the grain we see in prints made with high-speed films, but the specks are more colorful. The "noise pattern" is most visible in mid-tone areas or in dark areas that are lightened with image-processing software. Although the K10D automatically applies noise reduction during standard processing, the camera includes a feature designed for additional noise reduction during exposures of one second or longer.

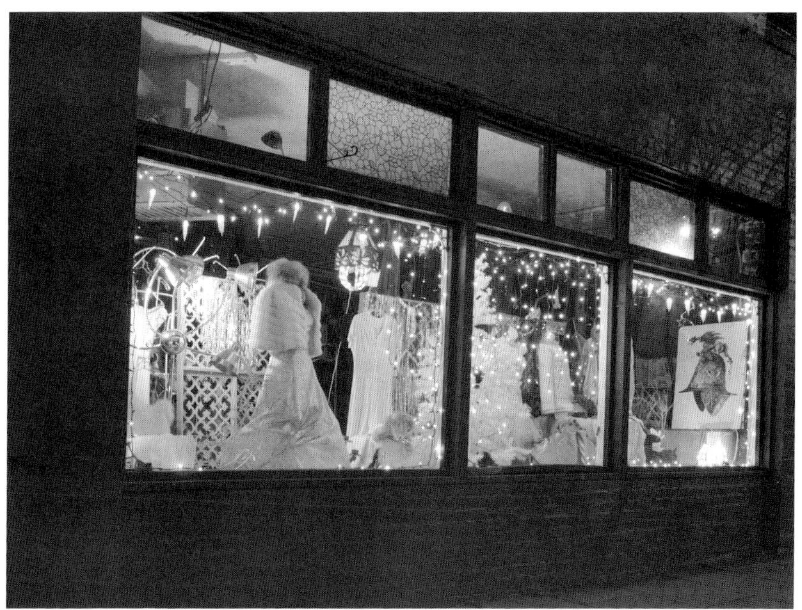

Additional in-camera noise reduction can be effective when shooting at shutter speeds of one second or longer. This may cause the image to be a little less sharp, but often the sacrifice is worth it for decreased noise. ©Kevin Kopp

To activate this feature, scroll to the Custom Settings menu and select *Noise Reduction*. Then scroll right and select *On*. Press the OK button to confirm your selection. When this feature is active, additional in-camera processing, using different algorithms, will be applied only for long exposures. This will minimize the "grainy" effect with special blurring to make the pattern much less noticeable. However, there is one drawback: this process creates a slightly softer image. That can be corrected to a degree with the in-camera control for increasing sharpness or, preferably, in a computer using image-processing software.

Processing With Digital Filters

In addition to features available in Capture mode for altering the look of your images, the K10D includes software that can be applied to JPEGs after they are processed. Press the Fn button while in Playback mode. Then scroll left to select the icon that looks like a circular filter, which will cause a new screen to appear. This is an image in Playback with a display of the available digital filters that you can select by scrolling with the up/down arrows on the four-way controller. However, first scroll left or right through the JPEG to select one on which you can experiment with the filter selection and effects. Then use the front or rear electronic dial to adjust the filter as listed in the following chart.

Using K10D Digital Filters

Filter Name	Effect	Control	Evaluation
B&W	Converts image to black & white. Also allows for application of "contrast filters" said to simulate the effect of colored filters in B&W film photography.	Rear e-dial is used to select red (R), green (G), or blue (B) filter.	A useful feature; Each of the three filters changes the relative brightness of certain tones, and overall contrast.
Sepia	Adds a strong amber (sepia) cast to color photos to produce a "vintage" or nostalgic effect.	Rear e-dial adjusts the density of the sepia color cast from low to high.	In film photography, sepia is a tint usually applied to black & white (not color) images. For best results first convert an image to B&W. Then apply the Sepia filter to that image.

Filter Name	Effect	Control	Evaluation
Color	Adds a color filter to the image for special effects.	Front e-dial selects color: red, green, blue, yellow, magenta, or cyan filter. Rear e-dial adjusts the density (intensity) of the color, from low to high.	May be useful for special effects. More useful for correcting some color casts caused by incorrect white balance.
Soft	Produces a soft image using a simulated diffusion filter.	Rear e-dial adjusts the intensity of softening from low to high.	Especially at highest level, creates a pleasing, artistic effect. Try with land scapes and portraits for a soft, dreamlike effect.
Slim	Changes the horizontal and vertical aspect ratio of an image; simulates the effect of slimming the subject through vertical "stretching" or widening the subject through horizontal "stretching" of the image.	Rear e-dial increases widening effect (rotating to left) or slimming effect (rotating to right.)	May be useful at a low level for a slimming effect, particularly for fun; even at low level, any stretching of an image may produce an unnatural effect.
Brightness	Modifies the brightness level of an image in a range from -8 (darker) to +8 (brighter). Intended for correcting exposure in JPEGs.	Rotating rear e-dial to the left increases the darkening effect; rotating to the right increases the brightening effect.	Surprisingly useful, but avoid setting excessive levels that might cause loss of detail in highlight or shadow areas.

Note: Only a single filter can be applied to an image at one time. When you are satisfied with the effect, press the OK button. Select *Save as* and press OK again. The modified image will be saved as an entirely new JPEG file, with a new name. Afterwards, you can access that file in Playback mode and apply another filter to it for a second effect; for example you might first convert to B&W and later, add a sepia tone. You can also access the original file to apply an entirely different filter; again, after you do so, the modified version will be saved as a new file. The original JPEG will always remain available.

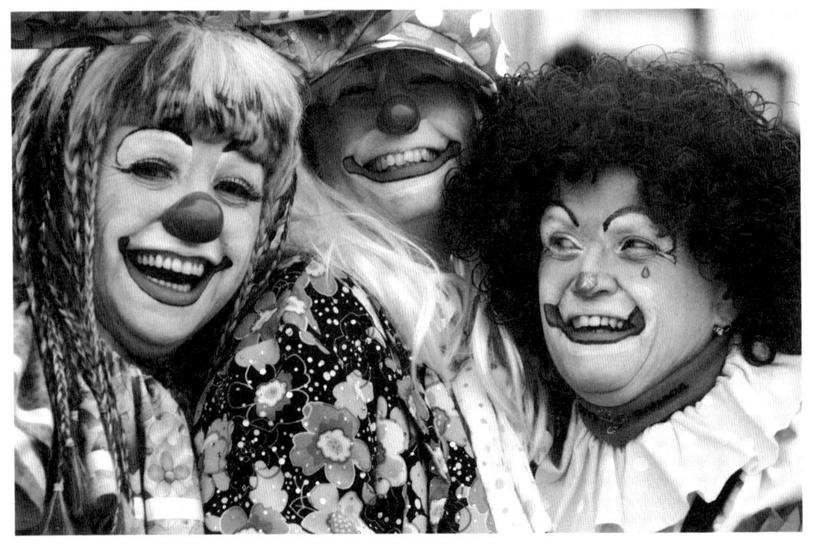

With nearly all digital cameras, RAW files must be modified and converted in the computer, but the K10D allows you to do so in-camera, if desired.

While each of the filter effects can be achieved in certain software programs, the in-camera adjustments are simple and quick by comparison. The process is also intuitive, because the effect of each digital filter–as well as any change in intensity–is visible in the preview image on the camera's LCD screen. The digital filters are most useful when you want to make prints directly from images in the camera; many inkjet photo printers allow you to do so by connecting the K10D with a USB cable or inserting your memory card into a slot on the printer.

The primary disadvantage of digital filters is that it's difficult to fully evaluate a preview image on the 2.5-inch (6.35 cm) LCD monitor. That's a great deal easier to do when viewing a much larger display on a computer monitor. Of course, the original JPEG file remains available for enhancement later with image-processing software, providing another opportunity for further enhancement, or for adding entirely different effects.

Editing and Converting RAW Files

As mentioned several times already, special software is necessary to convert a RAW (DNG or PEF format) file to JPEG, TIFF, or another image format. Normally, that's possible only in a computer, but your Pentax K10D includes built-in RAW software for enhancing and converting RAW files, meaning you can modify many aspects or parameters of an image (originally captured in RAW) before converting it to JPEG, all in-camera. (The modified JPEG image is then saved to the memory card under a new file name.) It's worth becoming familiar with this feature, because at some time in the future, it may well prove to be quite useful.

The process is not complicated, but it does take several steps, as follows.

1. Take a photo in RAW or in RAW+ Capture mode.

2. Display the photo in Playback mode and press the Fn button. Scroll down to select *RAW > JPEG* from the Fn Menu. After you do so, a note on the screen will say *Develop this image*.

3. Press the OK button to proceed. The preview image will remain visible, but the screen will now show a series of items along the right side; the words *Change settings* will also be visible near the bottom of the display.

4. If you want to change some image parameters, press the Fn button. The screen will change slightly, with the addition of a bold indicator to show each item that you will be able to modify.

5. Use the up/down keys on the four-way controller to scroll through the available editing items: Recorded Pixels (for reducing resolution), Quality Level (for selecting JPEG quality from Good, Better, Best), White Balance (for selecting a different WB option), Sensitivity, also shown as ISO but actually an exposure adjustment (for increasing or decreasing image brightness), Image Tone (Natural or Bright), as well as Saturation, Sharpness and Contrast (for setting a higher or lower level for each). Note: The white balance editing item does not allow for WB Fine-tuning, Manual WB or entering a Color Temperature.

6. To make changes to any or all of those image parameters, scroll to the right and left with the controller. You can modify as few or as many as you wish. As you make a modification, the preview image will change to reflect the new effect. If you change from Sunny WB to Shade WB for example, you'll notice that the color balance becomes much warmer (amber) overall.

7. When the preview image looks right, press the OK button to confirm your selections. Scroll to *Save as* and press OK again. The built-in software will then apply the changes you have specified. It will save the modified or "edited" image as an entirely new file, in JPEG format, with a new file name. The original DNG or PEF (RAW) file will not be affected; it will remain available as is.

Note: If you are perfectly satisfied with a RAW image and do not want to make any modifications before conversion to JPEG, simply ignore steps 4, 5 and 6 above. After step 3, simply go to step 7. The built-in software will then save a copy of the RAW file–without any modifications–as a JPEG under a new file name.

The in-camera RAW edit and conversion feature of the Pentax K10D is most useful when you want to modify the technical aspects of a photo without downloading the images to a computer. The processing features allow you to enhance the image and convert it to JPEG quickly. Like applying in-camera filters, you might want use this RAW conversion feature when you plan to make a print directly from the camera or the memory card, using an inkjet printer or a kiosk at a retail store, for example. It also allows you to order prints from a retail lab or an on-line photofinisher. Conversion is necessary for these purposes, because printers and commercial lab machines are not often designed to work with a RAW file. Some custom printing labs offer a service for editing and converting customers' RAW files at an extra charge, which can be quite high. Most photofinishers, however, do accept only JPEG or TIFF files.

While the in-camera RAW processing feature is quite versatile, it does not provide all of the RAW modification tools–or as many different options for some tools–as you can find in many RAW converter programs for your computer. As well, the effects produced by these types of image modifications are easier to evaluate when viewing a much larger display on a computer monitor. There may be certain situations in which the in-camera conversion and processing is useful, such improving the technical aspects of your images for making quick prints, while traveling, or during a Birthday party, for example. But in general, I don't recommend the in-camera feature as a regular alternative to developing RAW files in the computer.

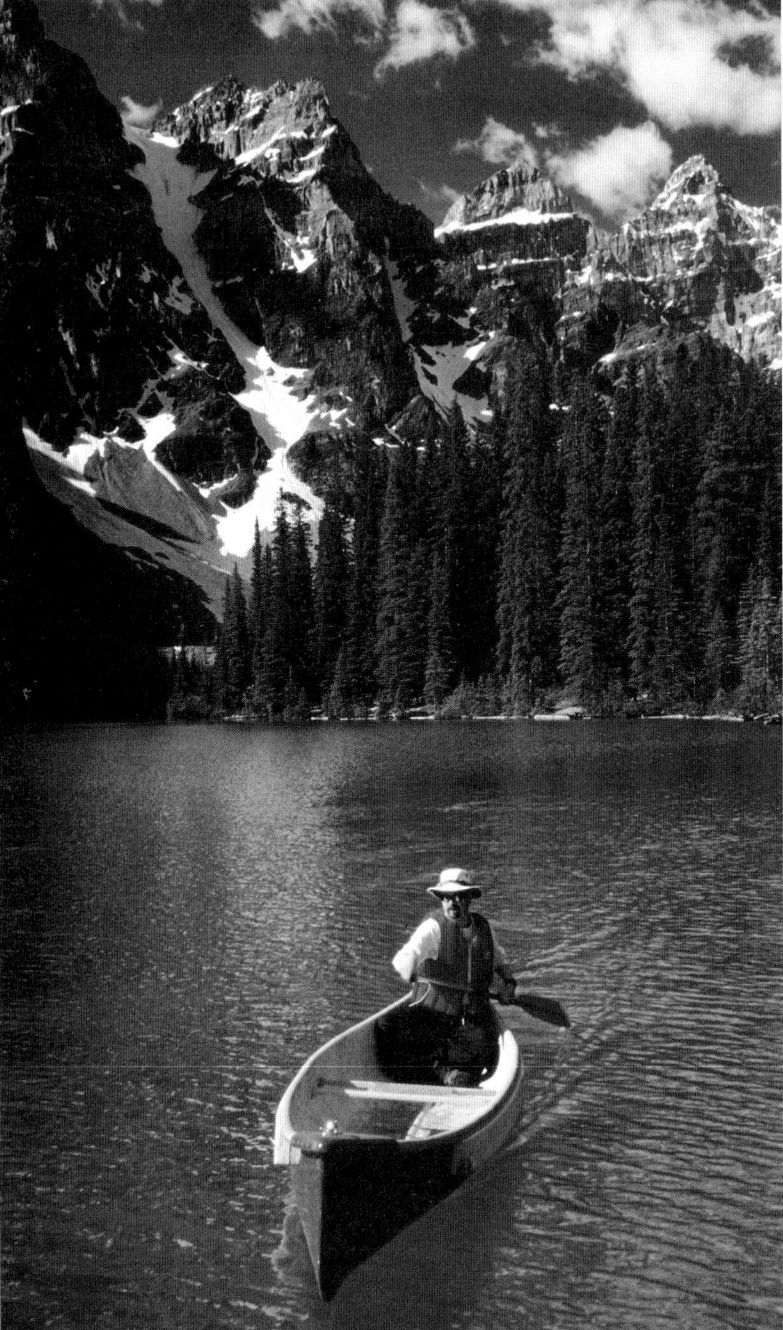

The Menus

Though the K10D offers a thorough set of menu options, many features that require menu access with other cameras are accessible with an analog control or the K10D's Fn menu (available by pressing the Fn button). This design reduces the number of distinct menu screens and the need to dig down into the menu to find commonly used functions.

In addition to the Fn button and its menu options, a different menu can be accessed by pressing the MENU button on the camera back. Scroll to move through the tabs designating the four distinct menu categories (separate tabs) by using the right/left arrows on the four-way controller. Once at your desired tab, scroll down until you reach a desired item. Often you'll need to scroll to the right to access a list of several options within an item. Scroll up/down to select the option you want and confirm your selection by pressing the OK button in the middle of the four-way controller. The four different menu tabs available through the MENU button are the *Rec. Mode* menu , the *Playback* menu , the *Set-up* menu , and the *Custom Setting* menu (C).

Starting with the Function menu, the rest of this chapter details the k10D's menu system and options.

The menu systems in digital cameras provide access to a large number of operations and features. Among the many selections are choices for file format, JPEG image size (Recorded Pixels), quality or compression level, and whether or not to review playback images in landscape or portrait format.

Fn Menu

Pressing the Fn button on the lower right back of the camera opens the Fn menu with its four distinct items, each with its own set of options. Scroll to the desired option using the four-way controller. Continue to scroll as required to select further options within each item, and confirm by pressing the OK button.

Some of the functions can be modified with options available in the other areas of the camera's menu system. Initially however, let's briefly review the basic features available via the Fn button.

☐ Drive Modes

The options include *Single frame shooting* ☐ , *Continuous shooting* (at up to 3 frames per second), and *Self-timer* with options for 12 seconds and 2 seconds (see pages 129-130). When the 2-second self-timer is selected, the K10D provides reflex mirror lock-up: The mirror is raised at the start of the exposure to minimize internal vibrations. As well, two other options are available for use when working with an optional wireless Remote Control F accessory: *Remote Control Unit* (for immediate shutter release), and *3s* to produce a three-second delay for shutter release.

AWB (White Balance)

A wide range of options are available here, discussed in detail on pages 67 to 79, including *Auto* (AWB), presets for use in various common lighting conditions, *Manual* (for setting a custom WB), and *White Balance Color Temperature* (K using the Kelvin scale.) A *White Balance Fine-tuning* feature is also provided (for shifting WB toward green/magenta or blue/amber).

ISO AUTO (Sensitivity)

A feature for modifying camera sensitivity, ISO is discussed in detail on pages 132-133. The K10D allows you to select any ISO from *100* to *1600*, but *AUTO* is the default setting.

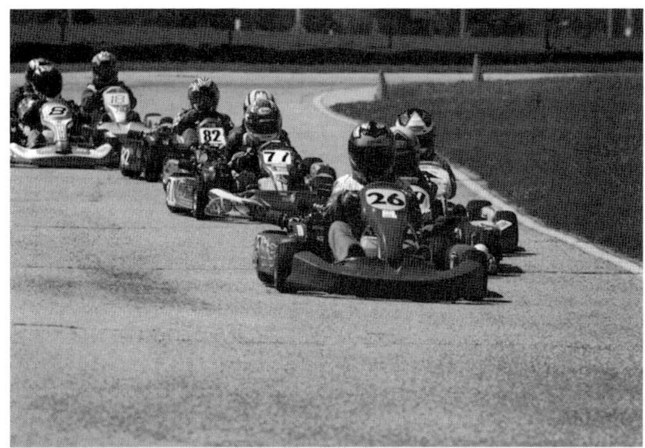

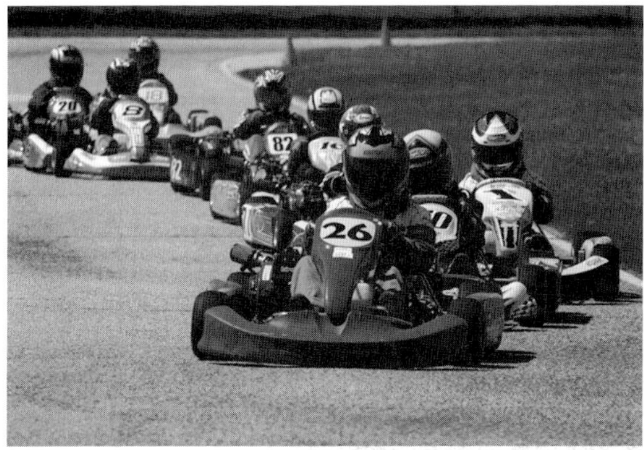

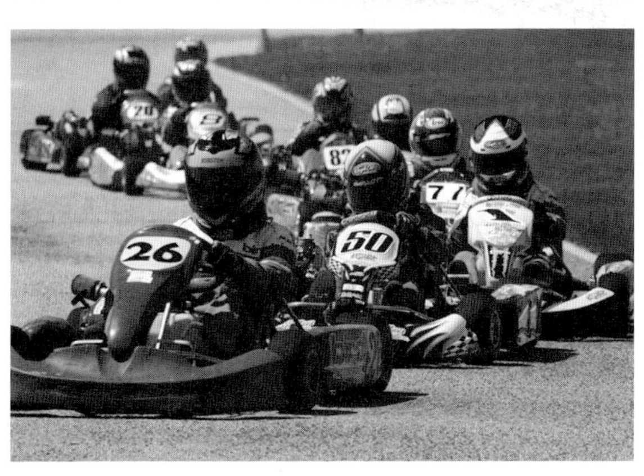

Continuous shooting mode is an advantage at sporting or other events where the action is occurring quickly. At 3 frames per second, this mode helps increase your chances of recording that critical moment–just as your child crosses the finish line, for example. When shooting JPEGs, the K10D will keep shooting until the memory card is full.

AUTO causes the camera to set the ISO automatically; it will usually set a low ISO in bright light and a higher ISO in darker conditions so the camera can provide faster shutter speeds. The automatic system can select from ISO 100 to ISO 400 (unless that range is modified).

Flash Modes

To be discussed in detail in the chapter on Flash, this function provides a wide range of options: *Auto discharge* (flash fires automatically in dark/backlit conditions); *Auto flash + Red-eye reduct* (red-eye reducing flash fires before auto flash); *Flash On* (flash always fires when it is active); *Flash On+Red-eye* (red-eye reducing flash also fires); *Slow-speed sync* (for flash at long shutter speeds); *Slow-speed sync+Red-eye* (adds red-eye reduction); *Trailing curtain sync* (in flash photography at long shutter speeds, the flash fires at the end of the exposure time.)

Note: Not every flash option is available in every camera exposure mode.

Flash Exposure Compensation: This feature allows you to increase flash intensity (to correct for underexposure in backlighting, for example) or to reduce flash intensity (for a gentler flash effect) in 0.5 EV increments. Use the rear e-dial. (See page 157 for discussion of EV).

Rec. Mode Menu (Recording)

A number of items are available for selection when you want to shoot pictures. These are spread over two menu pages, so keep scrolling down in order to view all of the items.

JPEG Rec. Pixels: This option is used to select image size (or resolution). It allows you to set the number of recorded pixels at *10M* (megapixels), *6M* or *2M* (actually 2.2 megapixels), which determines the size of your JPEG image files (see page 65).

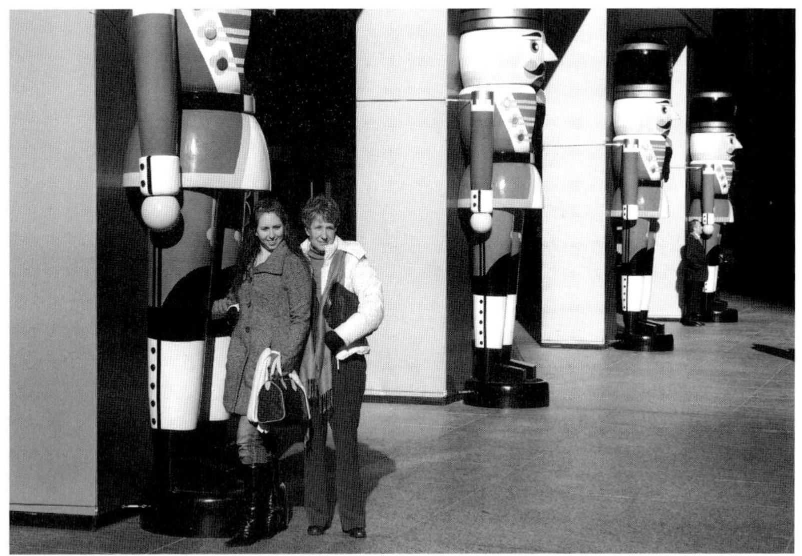

RAW+ is a convenient option for documentary photography. It provides both a RAW file and a JPEG for quick image transfer. File size and quality settings apply only to the JPEG file.

JPEG Quality: This feature allows you to record in *Best* (***) quality with the lowest compression, *Better* (**) quality with slightly higher compression, or *Good* (*) quality with the greatest compression (see page 62).

Note: Also see the *File Format* item in the Rec. Mode menu. All images recorded in RAW format will be 10 megapixels in size and the highest quality. However, if you choose *RAW+*, the number of recorded pixels and quality level you have set in the K10D will apply to the JPEG image that is recorded simultaneously with the RAW file.

Image Tone: Two options are available: *Natural* (default) and *Bright*. If the latter is selected, the K10D will produce images with higher color saturation, contrast, and sharpness (see page 86).

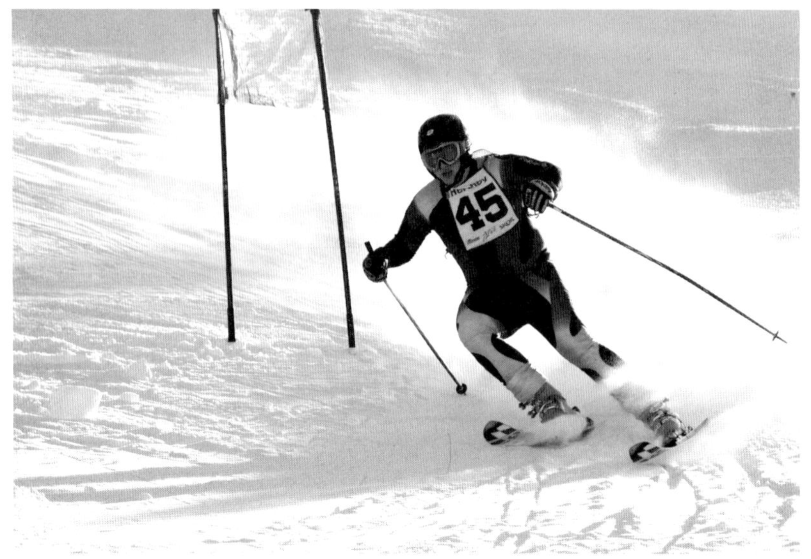

JPEG is an ideal choice for quick, action photography.

Saturation, Sharpness, and Contrast: These are three distinct menu items, but similar in that each can be set for a lower or higher level (-3 to +3) to vary their effect on the image (the default level is zero for each). The full range of adjustments is available whether you had set the K10D for Natural or Bright image tone in the previous item. See pages 82-85 for more details.

File Format: This is the item that allows you to select *JPEG*, *RAW*, or *RAW+* (which allows RAW+JPEG, see page 64). Even if you primarily intend to record RAW files, you might want to shoot a small JPEG file at the same time. That strategy can be useful if your imaging software does not recognize the RAW format generated by the K10D. In that case, you could still view the JPEG file. The JPEG may also be useful for quickly making snapshot size prints directly from the camera or the memory card. (Remember that the JPEG size/quality you set earlier determines the JPEG that will be produced in RAW+ recording mode.)

RAW File Format: Two file format options are available when recording RAW files with the K10D: *DNG* (an Adobe format) or *PEF* (a format proprietary to Pentax.) The reasons for selecting one over the other are discussed on page 63.

Extended Bracket: This feature allows you to bracket not only exposure, but also *White Balance, Saturation, Sharpness*, and *Contrast.* (Default is *Off*. See pages 78 and 85 for details).

Multi-exposure: This item allows you to select the *Number* of shots to be recorded and combined into one image, as well as to set the *Auto EV Adjust* if desired. The latter adds EV (exposure) compensation to automatically correct over-exposure caused by overlapping several photos in a single digital image. This feature is discussed in more detail on pages 159-160.

Memory: The selections in this item are *Flash Mode, Drive Mode, White Balance, Sensitivity* (ISO), *EV Compensation, Auto Bracket, Playback Display*, and *File No.* When an option is checked (default), the camera will record the most recent settings that you have applied in that operation–they will not be cleared when the K10D is turned off, even if the battery is removed. However, this menu item also lets you deselect items. When you do so, those camera settings will be returned to the most automatic option available, or zero for certain overrides. If you deselect *Sensitivity* for example, the camera will always revert to Auto ISO when it is turned off (and not to your most recently set ISO level).

Shake Reduction: This menu item (not to be confused with the Shake Reduction switch) cannot be selected unless you are using an old manual-focus K or Screw mount lens. With a lens of that type, this selection allows you to designate the lens focal length in use, essential data for the Shake Reduction system.

▶ Playback Menu

Playback menu selections let you make settings relating to the display of images after they are taken. In addition, any image displayed in Playback mode can be reviewed using different sets of information about the photo. Press the INFO button to rotate between *Standard* image indicators, *Histogram* (including Brightness or RGB display), *Detailed* information display, and *No* information (only the picture is displayed).

The list of items in the Playback menu is:

Playback Display: This item allows you to activate *Bright/Dark area* (a feature that is sometimes called shadow/highlight detail warning) when you review images in Playback mode. When selected, a colored overlay blinks over the areas of an image that are either too bright or too dark to hold detail or texture.

Instant Review: You select from three options that affect the way images will display in the LCD monitor immediately after shooting. These selections are *Display time* (how long the image will display in the LCD), *Histogram* (whether or not a histogram should also be displayed), and *Bright/Dark area* (whether the Bright/Dark area warning should be visible in Instant Review).

Digital Preview: The options in this item apply only when the camera is set for Digital Preview (you have options to select *Digital Preview* or *Optical Preview* in the Custom Setting menu, by selecting the *Preview Method* item. See page 116.) This menu allows you to specify whether or not to display a histogram and/or Bright/Dark area warning in Digital Preview. All of this is discussed on pages 163-171.

Digital Filter: This item gives you access to a wide range of in-camera processing options (*B&W, Sepia, Color, Soft, Slim,* and *Brightness*) designed to modify JPEG's being viewed on the LCD monitor in Playback mode (see pages 88-89). If you do modify an image, the K10D will save the modified image as a separate file with a new name, but will also retain the original image. These options allow you to make technical improvements or add new effects before using image-processing software in the computer. They can be useful when you want to make prints directly from the camera or a memory card without first downloading them to a computer.

Slideshow: Select this item if you want the camera to play back all the images recorded on your memory card in a series, without the need to scroll through them one by one. Scroll right to select *Interval* so you can choose the length in seconds that each image will be displayed. Select *Repeat Playback* and press the camera's OK button when you're ready for the slideshow display to start.

Set-Up Menu

A variety of items are available for setting up the camera or changing certain aspects to meet your own specifications.

USER: This menu option displays a list of the current camera settings, which will be saved and then used whenever you select the USER item on the camera's Mode dial (see page 39). If you are not fully happy with the combination of settings, close the menu, make the desired camera settings, and open to this option again in the Set-up menu. Confirm that the list of settings in the *USER* selection is acceptable. There is nothing to change in this item; it's simply a display of current camera settings.

Format: This causes the memory card in the camera to be formatted, permanently deleting all data. Scroll up to *Format* and press the OK button to start the process. Press *Cancel* if you decide not to format. Never remove a memory card when formatting is underway; it could damage your card. I recommend reformatting the card frequently to keep it at optimal performing level, but always after you have downloaded images to your computer's hard drive or other backup system so you don't erease wanted images.

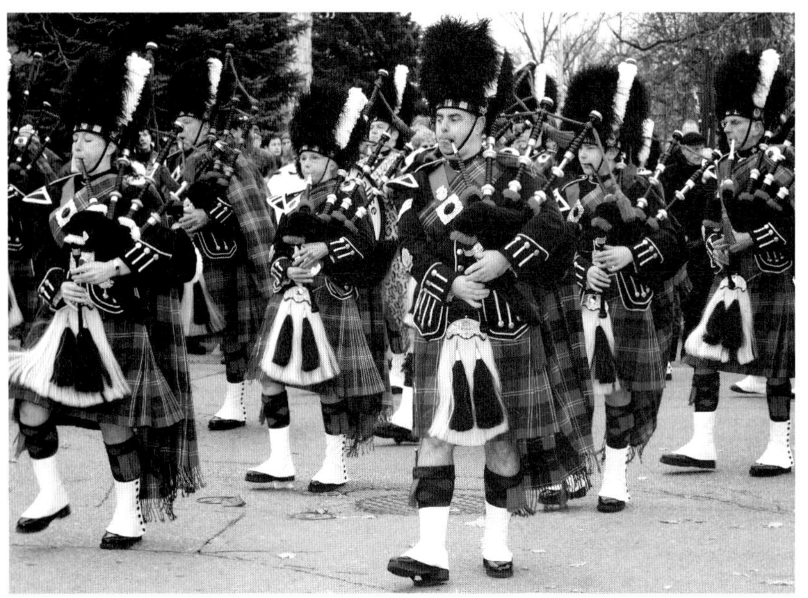

The World Time feature can be set for many travel destinations around the globe.

Beep: This item allows you to decide whether or not the camera should beep to confirm such features as autofocus, self-timer, and remote control operation. From the *Beep* option, scroll to select with a check mark the features that you want to be audible. If you do not want the camera to beep during certain functions, simply de-select those items.

Date Adjust: As you would expect, this item allows you to set the correct time and date as well as the format for date display (from *12h* or *24h* time style, or a sequence variation on the *mm/dd/yy* date style). This data will not be printed on your images. However, it will be recorded by the camera for every image and can later be accessed with the INFO button or with image-processing software in a computer.

World Time: The K10D is set to display the time and date at your own location (assuming you have done so during the initial camera setup.) However, using this item, you can also program the camera to display the time/date at another location, useful when you are traveling. Select the desired location from a long list of worldwide cities by scrolling right and pressing the OK button. Next, scroll to the top of the screen to *World Time*, then scroll right again to place a checkmark in the box, activating this feature.

Language: This item allows you to set the display language (for menu items and camera messages) from a long list of options. Do not press the OK button until you have selected your desired language. Otherwise you may experience problems trying to decipher menu items displayed in a language that is totally unfamiliar to you.

Guide Display: This allows you to set the length of time (*3 sec, 10 sec*, or *30 sec*) that the LCD monitor will display current camera settings. At default, this information is displayed for three seconds to minimize battery consumption.

Brightness Level: This allows you to change the brightness level of the LCD display by using a + slider scale, effective when you need to view images or menu items in bright light–in such conditions set a higher brightness level. Be sure to return to the default level afterwards to prevent an inaccurate view of image brightness in more typical conditions.

Video Out: Select a TV/broadcast standard if you want to playback images on a TV set. Two options are available for video system compatibility: *NTSC* (North American standard also used in Japan) and *PAL* (Europe and many other countries). Find out which standard to use in your geographic area.

Transfer Mode: This item allows you to specify how the camera should be set when connected to a USB cable: *PC mode* (for data transfer to a computer), *PictBridge mode* (for direct printing with a PictBridge compliant printer) or *PC-F* (PC-F is for use with older computers that feature only USB 1.1 connectivity. If your computer is equipped with the more recent USB 2.0 technology, use the PC option instead).

Auto Power Off: Set for 1 minute by default to conserve battery power, this item gives you options to set a longer time before the camera goes into "sleep" mode. (It can then be revived by touching the shutter release button.) I find the *3 min* option to be a useful choice.

Folder Name: The camera assigns names to folders (on the memory card) using letters and numerals such as 100PENTX (*Std*); you can change this by selecting *Date* if you prefer folders to be named by date instead.

Select Battery: Relevant only when an optional battery grip accessory (with a battery) is installed, this item allows you to designate *Auto* for automatic battery selection, or to specify which battery should be used first: *Battery First* (in camera) or *Grip First*.

Dust Removal: You can specify whether or not to activate the automatic dust removal system when the camera is switched on. Checking the option for *Start-up action* will delay camera start up by about one second, but assures that the CCD sensor will be clean.

Sensor Cleaning: Even though the K10D can shake dust particles off the sensor, debris may still accumulate over time. Use this menu item to gain access to the CCD sensor if you notice dust specks in your photos. Two options are available: *Cancel* is the default, and *Mirror Up*, which raises the camera's reflex mirror, reveals the filter over the CCD sensor so it can be cleaned. A fully charged battery or the optional AC adapter is required.

Caution: Improper cleaning may damage the CCD sensor and require expensive repair. Use extreme care when the CCD sensor is exposed. Use a large blower brush (sold by photo retailers) to produce a puff of air to blow away specks (do not touch the sensor cover with the brush). Do not use compressed air because propellant may damage the CCD. Pentax does not recommend the use of sensor cleaning kits (swabs or brushes and liquids) that are marketed by third-party manufacturers. Pentax recommends sending the camera to an authorized service center for cleaning the sensor.

Proceed at your own risk. If you choose clean the sensor yourself, follow these steps:

1. Select the *Mirror Up* option and press the OK button.

2. The camera's reflex mirror now pops up and is locked in the up position so you can gain access to the CCD sensor.

3. Remove the lens or the body cap.

4. Hold the camera facing downward and pump a blast of air from a large blower bulb toward the sensor. (Use a blower bulb without brush attachment.) Repeat this a couple of times to dislodge any dust particles. Use extreme care not to touch anything inside the camera's mirror box.

5. After cleaning is finished, turn the camera off and replace the lens, or body cap. The reflex mirror will return to its normal position.

Reset: When you select the *Reset* option in this menu tab, all menu items (with a few exceptions) will be reset to the factory programmed defaults. Do note that the following are not reset: *Date/Time, Language, Video Out,* and *World Time*. Note too that the custom functions are not reset; the Custom Setting menu includes its own reset control for resetting those items.

Custom Setting Menu (C)

The Custom Setting menu provides a wealth of additional features for customizing the camera. It lists a wide range of options that you may want to explore. The options in this menu are preferences more than necessities, and your K10D will work fine if these functions are left in their default settings. It is a good idea to use your camera for a couple of months and really get to know the basics before plunging into most of these. The really significant or valuable custom functions are discussed in detail in appropriate sections of this book. Nonetheless, here is a brief explanation of all of the items.

Note: To begin, make sure that all options are at their default settings. To do so, scroll down to the first item, *Setting,* then scroll right to remove the check mark from the box. When you do this, the list of custom function items will disappear and all will be automatically reset to default.

To select a specific custom function, scroll down to the desired item using the arrow keys on the four-way controller. Then, scroll right to see a list of options for that item. Scroll down to reach the desired option and press the camera's OK button to select it; that step will make the change and will also return you to the primary Custom Setting menu page.

The list of Custom Setting menu options is:

Setting: This item is checked by default, indicating that the camera will allow you to make changes to any custom function. If the box in this item is not checked, scroll right. The check mark will be inserted and the list of functions will reappear.

Program Line: Instead of the normal program for exposure, you can cause the camera to automatically use one of the other options when Hyper-program (P) is selected on the Mode dial. *Hi Speed* program favors fast shutter speeds; *Depth* favors small apertures for greater depth of field; while *MTF* (Modulation Transfer Function) favors f/stops that will provide optimal image quality, which can vary depending on the lens in use.

EV Steps: The camera allows you to select f/stops, shutter speeds and EV (exposure) compensation in increment selections of *1/2 EV Steps* (default), but you can change to select increments of *1/3 EV Steps*. This is most useful for setting a more precise amount of exposure compensation.

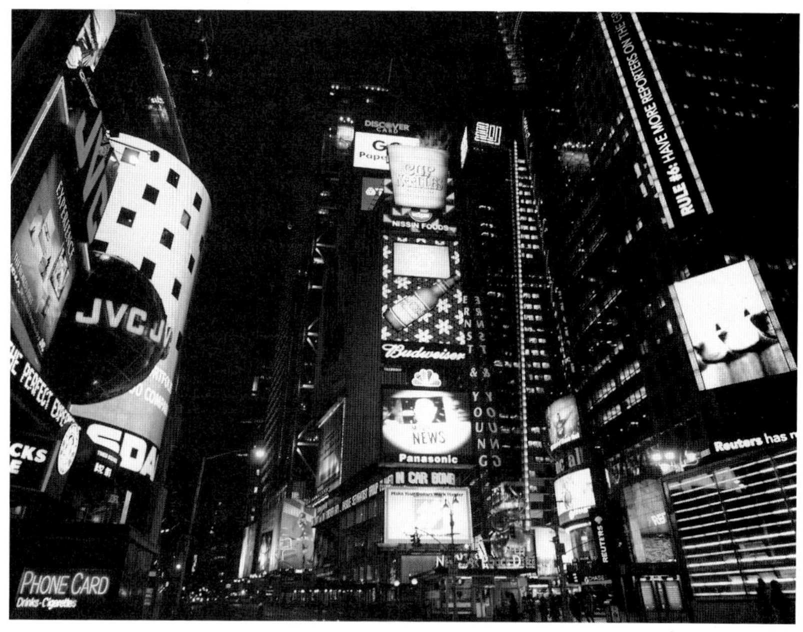

In certain conditions, like urban shooting at night, you may have to raise your ISO setting to 400 or higher. One problem is forgetting to lower the sensitivity for subsequent shooting in brighter conditions. The menu option for ISO warning will tell you when the K10D is still set to a high sensitivity.

Sensitivity Steps: The camera allows you to select ISO in 1 EV increments, but you can change that to smaller increments of 1/2 EV if you want greater versatility.

ISO Warning: This displays ISO in the viewfinder as a warning when an ISO value at or above a certain level is in use. Select options for *ISO 400, ISO 800,* or *ISO 1600*. This is useful as a reminder that image quality may suffer when working with high sensitivity levels. The warning symbol will never appear if you are using the camera's Auto ISO option.

Meter Operating Time: Normally the camera turns off the light-metering circuit after 10 seconds unless you occasionally touch certain camera controls. That conserves battery power but also loses your exposure settings, including any locked with AE-L. You can extend this period by selecting *30 sec,* or shorten the time to a mere *3 sec*. The former is a good choice because it turns the meter off if you haven't used the camera but it doesn't shut it down too frequently, which can be annoying–and cause you to miss a shot. However, the latter might be useful if your battery is almost dead.

AE-L with AF Locked: As discussed in the section on exposure (page 160), the K10D does not lock the exposure value when focus is locked with pressure on the AF button or on the shutter release button. If you do want to lock exposure as well as focus, optimizing both by using a single button, select the *On* option. This precludes the need to use the AE-L button when focus lock is used.

Link AF Point and AE: The camera can be set to weight brightness more heavily than usual for a scene's selected point of focus when the camera is in Multi-segment exposure mode. See page 136 for more details.

Auto Bracketing Order: When you use Exposure Bracket (auto bracketing), the default sequence for three photos is: normal (zero compensation), underexposure (negative compensation), overexposure (positive compensation). However, you can change that order by selecting one of the options in this item, although I cannot provide any reason for doing so.

Auto EV Compensation: The K10D will sometimes be unable to provide a correct exposure in extremely dark or extremely bright conditions at the set exposure parameters. However, the camera will override the settings you have made when necessary to produce a correct exposure when you set this custom function to *On*. This can be useful when shooting quickly, minimizing the risk of exposure error caused by setting an unsuitable f/stop or shutter speed. (When using M, X, or B mode however, *On* will have no effect.)

WB When Using Flash: Normally the K10D applies the white balance you have set, but this selection causes the

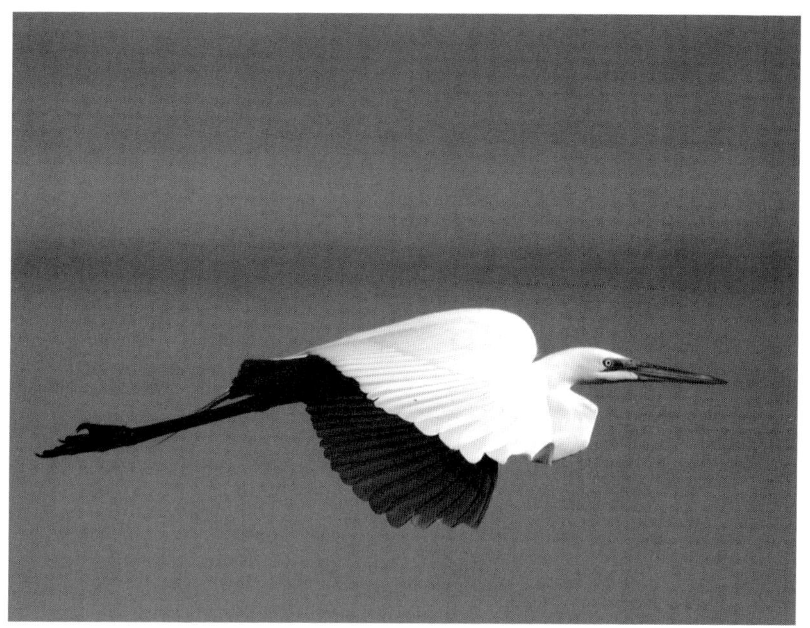

Linking AF point and AE causes the camera's Multi-segment metering system to compute the exposure based on the area in sharpest focus. However, when the subject is not a mid-tone, exposure compensation may be necessary. In this case, +1 EV compensation was used to prevent underexposure.

camera to automatically switch to the Flash preset for white balance ϟ when flash is active. That's useful when taking quick snap shots, especially when flash will be the primary light source.

Fine Tune when AWB: When Auto white balance is in use, the camera will not allow you to fine-tune the white balance (default). Full automation will be used in AWB, and that's fine for preventing inadvertent errors. (Most photographers will select a WB Preset, or Manual WB, before using this fine-tuning process). However, if you insist on the ability to fine-tune AWB, select the *Enabled* option.

AF Button Function: This item changes the operation of the AF button, which by default enables both autofocus and AF lock when pressed, allowing either the AF button or the shutter release button to control these two functions. However, selecting the *Cancel AF* option in this item causes the AF button to disable autofocus when pressed (see page 126 for more details).

AF by Press Halfway: A light touch on the shutter release button normally activates autofocus. Should you select the *Off* option under this item however, autofocus can only be activated by pressing the AF button. (Like the previous item, this one is simply a matter of preference.)

Superimpose AF Area: By default, the active focus-detection point/s (or AF area) will be momentarily illuminated in red on the viewing screen. This indicates the part of the scene that will be in sharpest focus. If you select the *Off* option however, the active AF area will not be illuminated.

AF in Remote Control: This item determines whether or not a remote control accessory will activate autofocus. At default (*Off*) it will not do so, assuming that you have already set focus and merely want to fire the camera. However, when *On* is selected, the remote will activate autofocus before tripping the shutter.

Noise Reduction: Extra noise reduction processing is automatically applied by default during long exposures. That makes sense since digital noise is usually more prominent in long exposures. However, the extra processing does slow camera operation and produces images that are softer than normal. If you prefer quicker camera response and intend to correct for digital noise later in the computer, select the *Off* option. If you do so, the extra processing will not be applied.

Color Space: The default color space for the K10D is *sRGB* (as with virtually every digital camera on the market). However, you can change color space by selecting *Adobe RGB* to generate images with a wider color gamut. That's useful if you usually make inkjet prints or patronize a pro lab that prefers images in Adobe RGB color space instead of the more common sRGB, used by most photofinishing services.

Color Temp. Steps: As discussed in the white balance section (see pages 67-79), the camera allows you to set a specific color temperature in increments of 100 degrees Kelvin (K). However, you can select the *Mired* option in this item. That will cause color temperature to be adjusted in steps of 20 mired, although the camera will use the Kelvin display. Frankly, the default option (*Kelvin*) is the right choice for the vast majority of photographers.

e-dial in Program: In default, the front e-dial is used to select shutter speed and the rear e-dial for aperture selection. With *Option 2*, the front e-dial sets EV compensation while the rear e-dial provides a general program shift. In *Option 3*, the front dial controls program shift while the rear dial sets exposure compensation without the need to press the exposure compensation button. *Option 4* disables both e-dials.

e-dial in Sv Mode: In default, the front e-dial has no effect while the rear dial is used to select an ISO level. *Option 2* allows the front e-dial to control program shift; the function of the rear e-dial does not change. *Option 3* allows for the front e-dial to be used to select an ISO level while the rear dial can be used for program shift.

e-dial in Tv Mode: In default, the front e-dial selects shutter speed while the rear dial provides no function. *Option 2* permits the rear e-dial to set exposure compensation; the role of the front e-dial does not change. *Option 3* causes the front e-dial to set exposure compensation; the e-rear dial will select shutter speeds.

e-dial in Av Mode: In default, the rear e-dial selects apertures; the front has no function. *Option 2* allows the front e-dial to set exposure compensation; the role of the rear e-dial

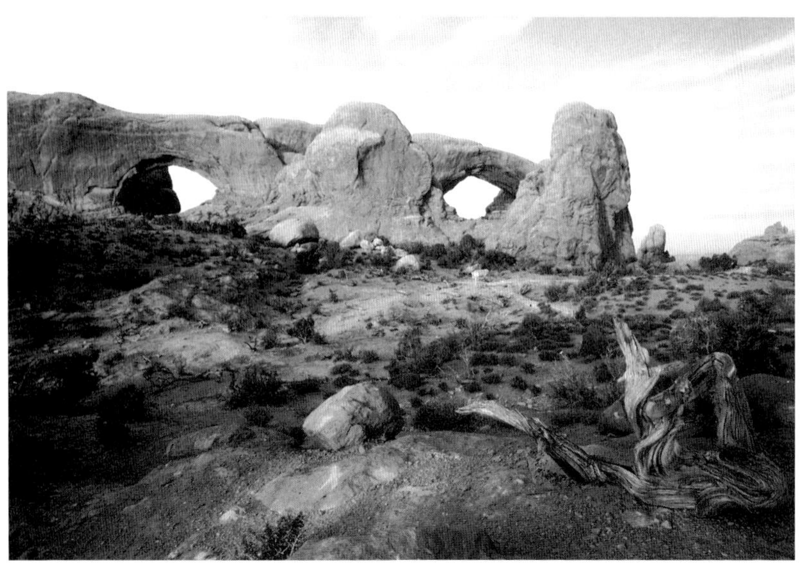

Manual exposure mode provides control of all aspects of an image: exposure, depth of field, as well as shutter speed. Pressing the Green button is a useful way to obtain a reference for "correct" exposure before you begin to make adjustments to achieve a desired effect.

still selects apertures. *Option 3* causes the front e-dial to set aperture while the rear dial will set exposure compensation.

Note: While the default setup is logical and useful, you may want to change the role of the dials after you become fully familiar with the K10D, in order to customize operation to your personal preferences.

Green Btn in Manual: Normally, pressing the Green button in M mode causes the camera to automatically change both the aperture and shutter speed to provide a "correct" exposure, as discussed on page 152. This custom function provides two other options for the function of the Green button while in M mode.

If you select *Tv Shift* (option 2), the camera will automatically change the shutter speed to provide correct exposure at the aperture you have set; however, it will not change your aperture. If you select *Av shift* (option 3), the camera changes the aperture to provide a correct exposure at the set shutter speed; it will not change your shutter speed. One of these options might be useful in a situation where you want to use a specific shutter speed or aperture. Regardless of the option selected for the function of the Green button in M mode, you are free to select a different aperture and/or shutter speed at any time, using the e-dials, if you decide to change the exposure to make a brighter or darker image.

No matter how much resolution a camera provides, image sharpness is the primary pre-requisite for high technical quality. Unless using fast shutter speeds, hold the camera as recommended for great stability and activate the K10D's Shake Reduction (stabilizer) system. Because the latter will operate with any compatible lens, there's no need to buy expensive new lenses with built-in stabilizing mechanisms.

One-touch RAW+JPEG: The items available in the Rec. Mode menu provide the most common method for selecting JPEG, RAW, or RAW+ recording formats. However, the K10D also has a unique control, a button marked RAW under the flash button on the left front of the camera. Here's how it works.

When *RAW* or *JPEG* has been selected in the Rec. Mode menu, pressing the RAW button causes the camera to switch to RAW+ capture for one single photo (default setting). However, if you select the *Continue* option in this item, the camera will keep shooting in RAW+ mode until you again press the RAW button. After you do so, it will revert to RAW only or JPEG only, depending on the setting you had selected in the Rec. Mode menu. This is a quick way to switch to RAW+ capture occasionally, when you only want to take one or a few photos in both file formats.

Illuminate LCD Panel: The button normally has a secondary function when pressed: It illuminates the LCD data panel, which is useful in low light. If for some reason you do not want that button to also turn on the LCD panel illumination, select the *Off* option in this item.

Release When Chrging: When this item is set to *On* (default), the camera will not let you take a photo until the built-in flash has recycled (charged) and is ready to provide full output. That's a prudent precaution since it minimizes the risk of an underexposed flash photo. If you select the *Off* option in this item, you will be able to take a photo at any time, whether the built-in flash has recycled or not. That might be useful on rare occasions, when capturing just the right instant is more important than waiting for the flash to fire.

Preview Method: Allows you to use either *Optical Preview* (default) or *Digital Preview* when switching to the Preview icon found on the main (ON/OFF) switch.

Recordable Image No.: The default option causes the camera to always display a numeral indicating the number of photos that you can take given the current capacity of the memory card in the camera. If you select *option 2* instead, the camera will continue to provide that information, but will provide additional data whenever you maintain slight pressure on the shutter release button, displaying a numeral indicating the number of frames that you can shoot in a single burst, given the recording format and image/size quality options that are in use.

Initial Zoom Display: The camera provides several options for the level of magnification that should be in use when you first activate the zoom feature to review images in Playback mode (by turning the rear e-dial to the right.) You can choose any of several options: *1.2x* (default), *2x, 4x, 8x,* or *16x* magnification. Regardless of the option you select, all magnifications are available when using zoom in Playback mode; simply continue rotating the rear e-dial to select a different magnification level.

Auto Image Rotation: At default (*On*), the camera is set to automatically display vertical images in a vertical orientation on the LCD monitor. That is useful because a vertical image uses the entire LCD area, so it's large; however, you do need to turn the camera to a vertical orientation for convenient viewing of the display. Should you select option 2 (*Off*), the automatic rotation is disabled; a vertical image will be displayed as a vertical without the need to turn the camera on its side. However, the actual image area of the display will be quite small.

Saving Rotation Info: At default (*On*) the camera will save vertical images in a vertical orientation; this time-saving feature will eliminate the need to rotate vertical images after you open them in a computer. If you select option 2 (*Off*) however, the camera will not provide that feature and you will need to rotate all vertical photos in your image-processing software.

Using Aperture Ring: This item is relevant only when using a lens with an aperture ring. The default option, *Prohibited,* prevents the camera from taking photos unless the aperture ring is locked to the A position. If you select *Permitted,* you will be able to take photos at any time, using the lens' aperture ring (instead of the camera's e-dial) to select f/stops, as discussed in a lens compatibility note on pages 219-220.

Reset Custom Fnction: If you select the *Reset* option, all custom functions will revert to their factory-programmed (default) settings. This can be useful after you have done a lot of experimenting with various functions.

IN·FLANDERS·FIELDS
IN·MEMORY·OF
THOSE·WHO·GAVE
THEIR·LIVES·IN
THE·GREAT·WAR
1914 · 1918
WORLD·WAR·II
1939·1945
THE·KOREAN·WAR
1950·1953
·GREAT·BRITAIN·NORWAY·
·YPRES·FESTUBERT·GIVENCHY·
CANADA

Camera and Shooting Operations

Make Sharper Images

Various factors contribute to the sharpness of an image. While focus, depth-of-field, and even the use of flash play a role, proper handholding technique is also essential. If you don't use proper technique, camera movement may degrade image sharpness and your pictures will be disappointing. A good way to evaluate your technique is to review your photos. If the focused subject is not crisp, but another element in the scene is sharp, the problem is usually caused by an improperly focused image. However, if nothing in the photo is tack sharp, the cause is probably camera movement.

Long lenses are more difficult than shorter ones to hold steady. Just as they magnify the subject, longer lenses also magnify movement. Your shutter speed should be fast enough to minimize camera movement at whatever focal length you are using. If you cannot achieve a fast enough shutter speed at your desired aperture setting, you can increase your ISO (but beware of digital noise, especially at ISO 1600). If you want to shoot at long shutter speeds, use a tripod or other camera support.

Proper technique will maximize the odds of a sharp photo when handholding the camera. Hold the camera's grip in your right hand with your index finger on the shutter button. For horizontal (landscape format) pictures, cradle the lens and body in your left hand so that your fingers can comfortably operate the lens if necessary. For vertical (portrait format) shots, turn the camera so your right hand is on top and

No matter how much resolution a camera provides, image sharpness is the primary pre-requisite for outstanding photographs. Always practice proper handholding technique and, at slower shutter speeds, take advantage of the K10D's Shake Reduction system.

the opposite end of the camera is cradled in your left hand. With either format, keep your elbows in, pressed gently against your body for additional support. Spread your legs apart in a firm, but comfortable, stance. When you are ready to take a picture, exhale and roll your finger across the shutter button making sure to hold the camera level.

The Shake Reduction (SR) System

Pentax has incorporated an improved version of the Shake Reduction (SR) system previously used in the entry-level K100D camera as an image-stabilizing device. They indicate that SR should allow you to handhold the K10D at 2.5 to 4 shutter-speed steps longer than the rule of thumb stated on page 149. The system will also allow you to use longer shutter speeds to obtain smaller apertures in order to increase depth of field.

The Pentax SR system consists of gyroscopes that detect motion and magnets that shift the CCD sensor module inside the camera body to compensate for camera shake. It also considers data on lens focal length, the lens aperture in use, and the focused distance. The SR function allows photographers to utilize stabilization with all autofocus and manual focus lenses that are compatible with the K10D (over 20 million Pentax lenses manufactured to date, and most of the aftermarket brand lenses with the appropriate mount).

This feature is intended primarily for hand-held use. Pentax recommends leaving it off when the camera is mounted on a tripod (however, it can be useful when working with a monopod since that accessory cannot eliminate all camera shake). Pentax also warns that the system is not completely effective when using shutter speeds of 1 second or longer (use a tripod instead). The system will usually work well in macro (close-focusing) photography because the focused distance will typically be about six inches (15.24 cm). However, on occasions when the focus distance is only an inch or two (less than 5 cm), the SR system may have difficulty determining distance data, a very important part of the calculations for optimal anti-shake performance.

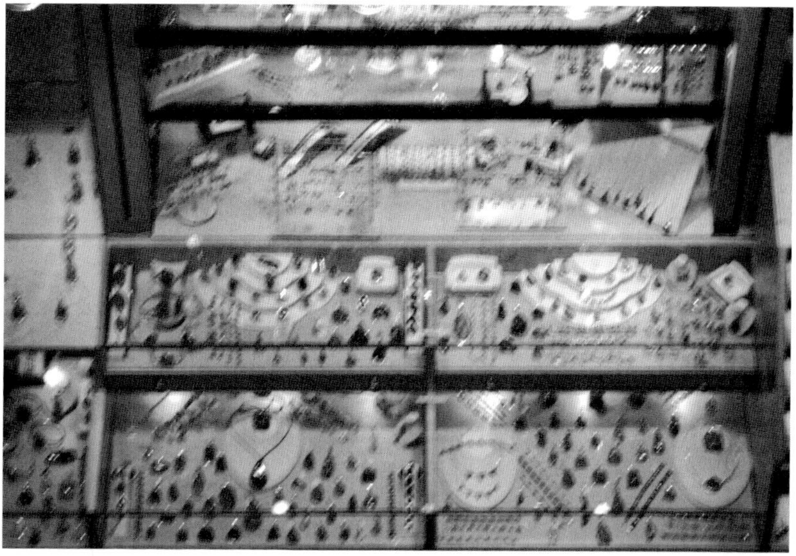

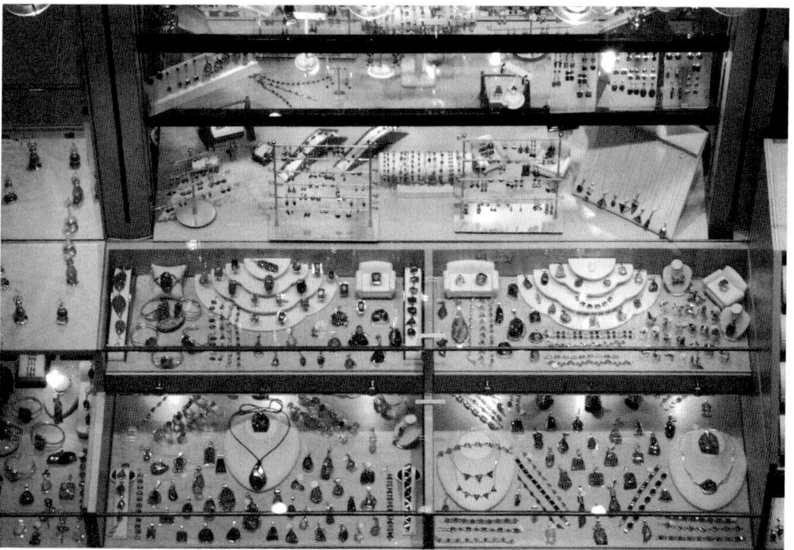

These photos were both made at a shutter speed of 1/15 second using a focal length of 105mm. The camera's Shake Reduction (SR) system was activated for the bottom photo. As a rule of thumb, SR allows the K10D to be handheld at shutter speeds that are about two stops longer than you could use with non-stabilized equipment.

Note: Activate the SR function by turning ON the switch (located on back of camera). The shaking hand icon will appear in the viewfinder data panel. It takes about two seconds for the SR function to become effective when you first turn the K10D on or when the camera is revived from the Auto Power Off mode.

Take a conservative approach to insure photos without blur from camera shake. Stay within two steps of your normal minimum hand-holdable shutter speed. When shooting from an unstable platform (such as a boat) with SR activated, use even faster shutter speeds: at least 1/60 second with a 28mm focal length and at least 1/500 second at the 300mm end of a zoom lens. Finally, be aware that constant SR use will increase power drain, so take an extra battery if you plan on using it a lot during a very long day of shooting.

Lens Compatibility with SR: If you're using the K10D with most types of recent lenses, you'll find that the SR system automatically determines the focal length of the lens in use, an important part of the data required for optimal shake reduction. This applies to DA, DA*, FA, D FA, FA J, FA or F series lenses.

If you use another type of lens, such as an older K-mount series, the SR system cannot determine the lens' focal length. Consequently, you will need to provide that information. When the SR function is switched ON (located on lower right back of camera), the Shake Reduction setting menu will appear on the LCD monitor. Set the focal length information for the lens in use by selecting one of the 34 focal length values provided. Press the OK button.

Note: If the exact focal length value is not one of the options, select the closest numeral, such as 18 for a 17mm lens. When using a zoom lens that does not support automatic focal length data acquisition, do the same: set the focal length that you will use to take a photo, such as 100 for a 70-200mm zoom set to the 100mm focal length.

The Focusing System

The K10D employs the sophisticated SAFOX VIII TTL phase-detection autofocus (AF) system for great accuracy and high speed, using an advanced AF driving mechanism. It's very reliable in most shooting situations, capable of functioning at an ISO 100 equivalent of 0 to 19 EV (from low light to very bright conditions). There is also an AF illuminator (focus-assist feature) available with the built-in flash and with accessory flash units, which helps the camera to focus in much darker locations when flash is active.

Note: Although the K10D can be used with a wide variety of lens types, new or old, full compatibility with all camera features requires a DA, DA*, or FA J series lens or a D FA, FA, KAF2, F, or A series lens with an "A" setting locked on its aperture ring. In that case, all the camera's features, should function as described. However, when used with some older bayonet mount or thread mount lenses from 35mm camera systems, some camera functionality limitations with regard to metering, focusing, and exposure modes should be noted. See section on Lens Compatibility, pages 219-220 for more details.

This book assumes you are using a fully compatible lens, so for the most part does not provide information on non-compatibility issues in discussions of the various camera features and functions.

The system utilizes a wide focus-detection area, with 11 distinct focus-detection (AF) points, so it can usually focus on an off-center subject. All but two of those AF points are cross-hatched, sensitive to both vertical and horizontal patterns.

When *Superimpose AF Area* is selected in the Custom Setting menu, the active focus point/s will light in red on the viewing screen to indicate the area of the scene where the camera is focusing. However, only the central AF point will be active for focus confirmation when using lenses other than DA, DA*, D FA, FA J, or F series. If you do not want the focus-detection points/s to light (when using any lens), you

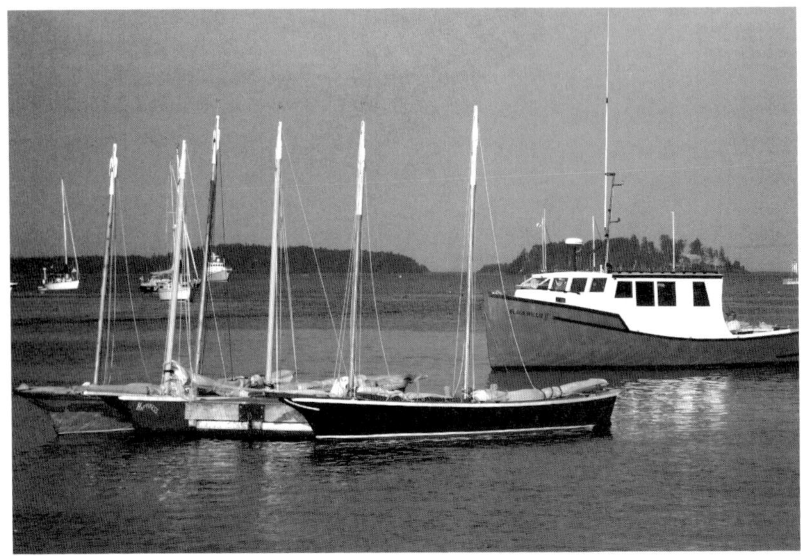

Lock focus in AF.S mode by pressing the shutter release and holding it down half way, then shift your camera to recompose. For instance, you can focus on the bow of the third sailboat in the line and recompose so that it is off center, creating a pleasing composition.

can disable illumination by selecting Off in Superimpose AF Area item.

AF and Manual Focus

Use the focus mode lever (located on lower left front of camera, near lens mount) to select either of two autofocus modes or manual focus. The following are available with an AF lens:

AF.S (autofocus single mode): This option is intended for static subjects. Activate autofocus by holding the shutter button half way down. You can also do so by depressing the AF button on the camera back. When focus is acquired, the camera will beep; also, one or more of the AF points will briefly illuminate in red on the viewing screen. As long as focus is maintained, a green focus confirmation signal (hexagon) will remain lit in the data panel in the viewfinder.

Note: If desired, you can deactivate the confirmation beep for autofocus (as well as for other functions). From the Set-up menu, scroll down to *Beep*, and then to *In-focus*. Next scroll to the left. The check mark in the In-focus box will disappear. You can shut off this feature individually for each of the functions listed, or for all. To deactivate all at once, scroll right from the *Beep* item in the Set-up menu; a message will then appear: *Beep is not activated*. Note that there will always be a beep confirmation when focus has been acquired using Manual focus (MF) mode.

Focus Lock: In AF.S mode, focus is locked as long as you maintain pressure on the shutter button or the AF button. Consequently, after setting focus, you can recompose as you wish, placing the focused subject off center. If your subject moves to another location—or if you want to focus on another subject at a different distance–remove your finger from the button, recompose, and start the focusing process again.

If the camera cannot find focus, the focus signal (hexagon) will blink in the viewfinder data panel. In AF.S mode, you cannot take a picture until focus is confirmed. It may help to use only the single central AF point if the AF system has difficulty finding focus. In low light, raise the built-in flash unit; when you try to focus it will fire several bursts of light, creating a more reliable target for the AF system. You could also mount and activate an accessory Pentax flash unit; that will project a red (near-infrared) beam onto the subject to help the camera focus.

AF.C (Continuous autofocus): AF.C is designed for tracking a moving subject, such as a cyclist approaching your position. Focus is never locked, but shifts continuously as the camera-to-subject distance changes. You can take a photo at anytime, even if the subject is not in focus, although the system is very effective so that most photos will be sharply focused. When AF.C is selected, a flash unit's focus-assist feature will not operate. If you use this mode with a static subject, the AF system will focus on it just as if you were using AF.S mode. The same focus confirmation signals are also provided. However, the focus lock feature is not available in AF.C mode.

Note: An option in the Custom Setting menu, *AF Button Function*, allows you to change the role of the AF button (on upper right back of camera). If you set that item to *Cancel AF*, the AF button will disable autofocus whenever it's depressed. In that case, it will work as a focus lock control, occasionally useful in AF.C mode when you do want to lock focus for some reason.

Manual Focus: Setting the focus mode lever to MF disengages the autofocus system so you can focus manually at any time using the lens' focus ring. The K10D will provide focus confirmation. When focus is acquired, the hexagonal indicator in the viewfinder data panel glows continuously, the camera beeps, and an AF point on the viewing screen is momentarily illuminated in red. Of course, in Manual focus mode you can take a picture anytime, even if focus is not confirmed.

If you are having trouble focusing in a very dark location, or you want to set focus in anticipation of an event, you can estimate the subject distance and set the focus accordingly. (Of course, this is effective only with lenses that include a focus distance scale.)

I recommend switching to MF occasionally, especially in macro, landscape, and architectural photography, when you may want to set the point of focus in the scene to control depth of field. The Manual focus mode is also ideal for critical focus on a small, specific subject element: the eyes in a portrait or the stamen in the heart of a blossom, for examples. Finally, it's a convenient method for focusing on one segment of a scene while setting exposure for an entirely different area.

Selecting a Focus Point

The K10D provides three options that define how the focus-detection points–called AF points by Pentax–are used by the system. You can select any of three modes with the AF point switching dial (the ring around the four-way controller located on the back of the camera).

Auto AUTO **:** This mode provides a wide focus-detection area, with automatic focus point selection; the AF system sets focus on a suitable subject, usually on the closest or largest, particularly favoring an area of high contrast. That often works well, even with an off-center subject so it can be useful for shooting quick snapshots.

Of course, the system cannot read your mind. Hence, it may set focus for something other than the intended area: the nose instead of the eyes in a portrait, for example. In a scene with several objects, the system may or may not select what you intended to be the primary subject.

SEL (Select): This allows you to select any single AF point using the four-way controller to scroll up, down, left, or right. When focus is acquired, the active AF point is illuminated briefly on the viewing screen. The camera also beeps (unless that feature was turned off) and the hexagonal focus indicator symbol in the viewfinder lights steadily. If the system has trouble finding focus, the indicator will blink instead.

Occasionally, you might decide to select one of the off-center focus points. That can be useful when you plan to make several images of a scene that include a primary subject always at a certain position in the frame. The scene may be a landscape, for example, with a large, off-center rock that is the intended to be the focal point of the images.

Center [-] **:** In this AF mode, only the single, central AF point is active. While you can also choose the central point with SEL, it's quicker to do so by switching to this mode.

The ability to manually select any of several focus-detection points is common to many brands of D-SLRs. This feature certainly sounds useful and logical. However, unless I'm shooting an action subject that may drift off-center, I generally use only the central focus area. For static subjects, the central focus point, plus focus lock when recomposing, works very well. Nevertheless, you may find circumstances where you'll want to select one of the other ten AF points.

Drive Modes

This function in digital cameras is similar to that performed by the motor drive in a film camera. While no film has to be transported, these modes control the firing and re-cocking of the camera's shutter mechanism.

Set the drive mode on your K10D by pressing the Fn button (bottom right back of camera) and scroll up to the □ icon. The drive mode options will appear in the LCD monitor. Then, scroll to the right or left to select the option that you want to use. Press the OK button to confirm your selection.

□ Single Frame Shooting

The default drive mode, this causes the camera to fire one frame each time you press the shutter release button until the memory card is full. Select this any time you simply want to shoot one image at a time rather than several in a bracket or a burst.

⧉ Continuous Shooting

In this drive mode, the K10D will keep recording images as long as the shutter button is held down. If you are using a high-speed memory card and shooting JPEGs, the camera will fire until the card is full. (With slower cards, the number of frames per burst may be limited.) This is useful when you want to shoot a series of images, whether friends being silly or action at a sports event. It will shoot up to 3 frames per second (fps) as long as the shutter speed is 1/250 second or faster. If longer shutter speeds are used, the framing rate will be slower.

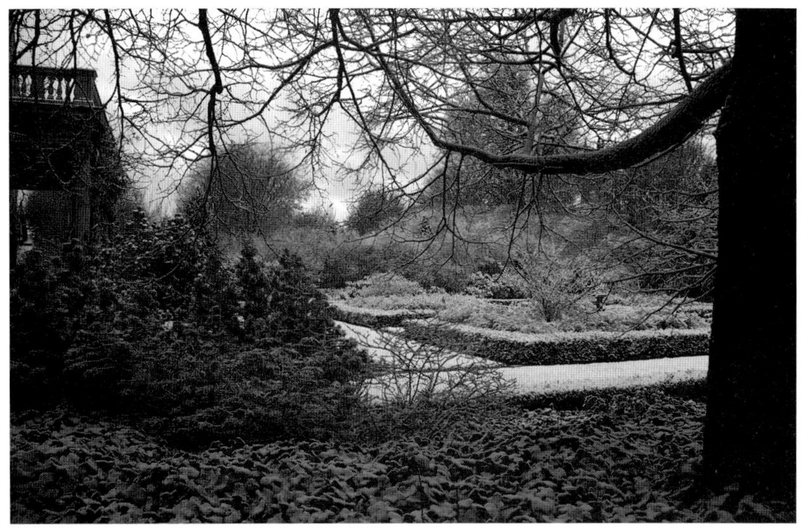

To insure optimal sharpness in a scenic photo, mount your K10D on a tripod and use the self-timer to prevent camera movement or vibration. © Martha Morgan

Note: The framing rate may be slower when flash is used because the flash must recycle after each image in order to fire again. The recycle time depends on the condition of the battery and the amount of flash output used when making an image. There's a long recycle time when high output is required (great flash-to-subject distances), and a quicker recycle time when lower output is required (with nearby subjects, in bright light, or when shooting at a high ISO levels).

Self-Timer (12 seconds)

When this option is selected, the camera waits 12 seconds after the shutter release button is pressed before it fires. This can be useful when the photographer wants to get into the picture and when the camera is mounted on a tripod. Focus and exposure are set when you first press the shutter button. If the lighting changes during the 12-second delay, the exposure may not be correct.

Self-Timer (2 seconds)

Identical in concept to the 12-second Self-timer drive, but this option provides only a 2-second delay after pressing the shutter release. This mode is intended for use while the camera is on a tripod. Because the reflex mirror is raised at the beginning of the countdown, this feature is useful for triggering the camera without creating external or internal vibrations. It is often used for long exposures or when telephoto or macro lenses are used on a tripod. (Such lenses produce high magnification of the subject but also amplify the effect of even the slightest vibration.) Focus and exposure are set when you first press the shutter button, so it is best used with fairly static subjects.

Remote Control
3S Remote Cont. 3s delay

These two drive selections are intended for use with an optional wireless Remote Control F accessory that lets you fire the camera without touching it. When *Remote Control Unit* is selected, the camera will fire immediately; the other selection (*Remote Cont. 3s delay*) produces a three second delay. Both are intended for use with a tripod-mounted K10D.

Note: Pentax also markets an optional wired remote release accessory with a 0.5 m (19.7 inches) long cable, the Cable Switch CS-205, which can be used with any of the standard drive modes.

Exposure

In digital photography, exposure is defined as the amount of light that is required to create an image on the camera's image sensor. Ideally, the exposure will depict the scene realistically, with clean whites, rich, dark blacks, and midtones that are not excessively light or dark. Subject detail should be visible in both highlight and shadow areas.

A camera's light-metering system is calibrated to measure the exposure of average, or mid-tone, subjects such as

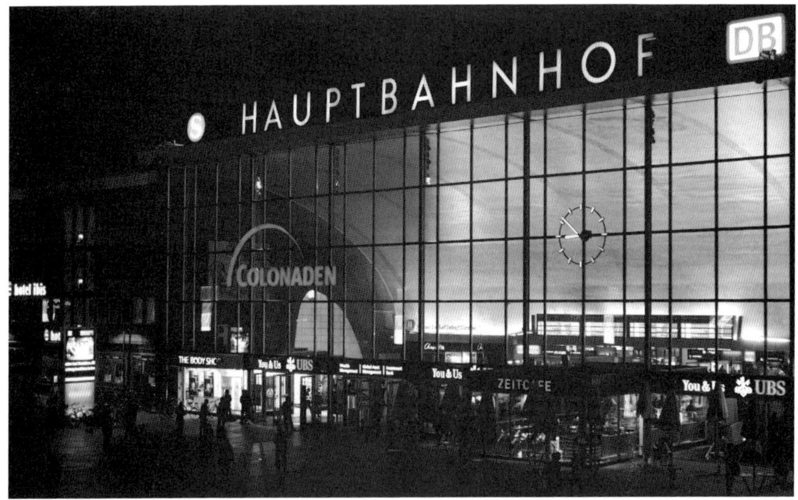

When shooting high-contrast subjects that exceed the latitude of the sensor, the photographer must decide how the exposure will render the scene. In this case, the camera recorded the bright parts of the image accurately, while sacrificing detail in the darker portions. Had the photographer wanted to show detail in the dark areas, the whites would have washed out, creating a less acceptable, less realistic image.

grass, rocks, trees, or a gray card. This type of metering works well with most common scenes and subjects. However, if the subject is very light or the scene includes a vast expanse of bright snow, sand, sky, or water, the resulting image may be too dark or underexposed. This is because the meter "assumed" the scene was a mid-tone and attempted to balance out the bright areas, effectively making them appear as gray. Conversely, a black lava field or other very dark subject may end up being too bright or overexposed. It will look gray. Again, this is because the meter "considers" all subjects to be average and tries to render them as mid-tones.

The Pentax K10D's Multi-segment metering mode uses sophisticated algorithms to compute the exposure. Hence, it is less likely to produce very poor exposures than more basic types of metering. Even so, this sophisticated system will not always produce a perfect exposure. Extremely light or dark-toned subjects may still cause exposure errors. Also, sometimes a "perfect" exposure may not be the most pleasing or most appropriate for creative expression. That's why the K10D includes options such as an EV compensation control for adjusting the exposure.

Note: Some of the exposure methods discussed in this chapter will not function fully when older lenses are mounted on the K10D. For a guide to these limitations, see page 220.

The Role of ISO

ISO is an international standard for quantifying a film's sensitivity to light. While digital cameras don't use film, ISO numbers are still used to quantify the camera's recording sensitivity, which the camera's microprocessor changes by adjusting the gain (signal amplification). A low ISO number such as 100 denotes a low sensitivity to light. A high ISO number such as 800 or 1600 denotes a high sensitivity to light. The camera's exposure system, in turn, uses the ISO information in making its calculations about the aperture and shutter speed combination that should be used to produce a good exposure.

ISO numbers are mathematically proportional, just like shutter speeds and f/stops. As you double or halve the ISO number, you double or halve the sensitivity (i.e., at ISO 800, half as much light is required than at ISO 400; and at ISO 800, twice as much light is required than at ISO 1600.

The K10D allows you to use ISOs from 100 to 1600, although you'll rarely need to use the highest option. Since digital noise (discussed on pages 16-18) increases with ISO, select ISO 100 for the best image quality, and higher ISO levels as needed.

Setting the ISO: To select an ISO, press the Fn button to display the Fn menu and then scroll right to ISO. Next, scroll up/down to select an ISO numeral. Press the OK button to confirm your selection. One of the ISO choices is *AUTO* (not to be confused with AUTO exposure mode). When it is selected, the camera will set a low ISO in bright light for the best image quality. In lower light, it will set a higher ISO to allow the camera to use a faster shutter speed, minimizing the risk of blur from camera shake. (The Shake Reduction system is useful for this purpose too, but it cannot compensate for subject movement or for camera shake at very long shutter speeds.)

Note: The K10D provides an ISO warning (see page 109) that can be activated in its Custom Setting menu. This option provides three choices: *ISO 400, ISO 800,* and *ISO 1600*. The camera will display "ISO" in the viewfinder whenever the designated level (or higher) is in use.

AUTO ISO: At its default setting the K10D will automatically select ISOs from 100 to 400 when the AUTO ISO feature is selected in the Fn menu. This works well for daytime outdoor photography when higher ISO levels are rarely required. While you could also set a desired ISO in the Fn menu at any time, AUTO ISO mode can be useful in rapidly changing light conditions when you want to shoot quickly.

Changing the AUTO ISO Range: The K10D also allows you to set different ISO ranges for use with AUTO ISO mode, letting you determine the lowest and highest ISOs from which the camera can choose. To do this, select ISO in the Fn menu and scroll to the *AUTO* item. To set the lowest ISO that the camera can use in this mode, rotate the front e-dial; note the low ISO numerals changing in the viewfinder. When you reach the setting that you want to establish as the lowest ISO the camera should use, stop rotating the dial.

Next, using the rear e-dial, set the highest ISO that the camera can use in AUTO ISO mode. As you rotate that dial, you'll see higher ISO numerals changing. Stop rotating when you reach the desired highest setting. When both steps are finished, press the OK button to confirm your selections.

Once it is set, the AUTO ISO system will choose only ISOs within the range you have specified. You can change the parameters at any time, perhaps to ISO 800-1600 in dark locations to make sure the camera will always use the faster shutter speeds.

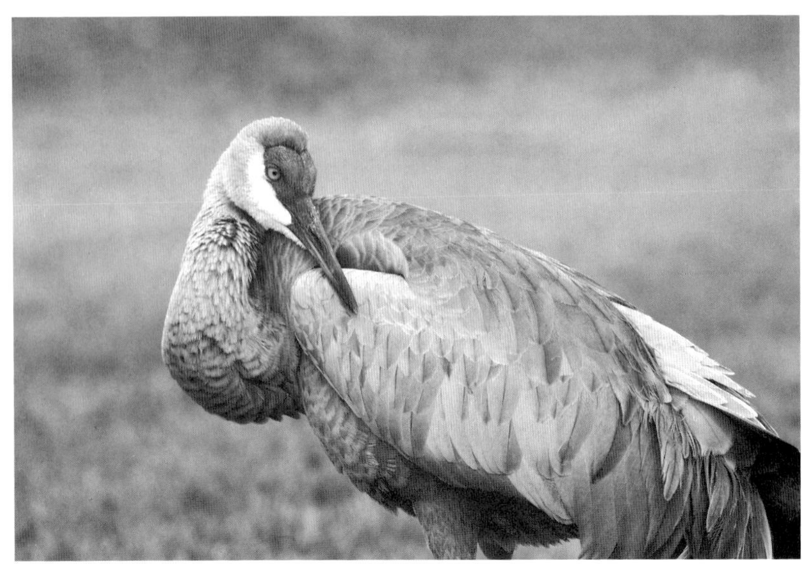

Some scenes consist mostly (or entirely) of mid-tones, allowing virtually any light metering system to provide a technically accurate exposure.

On a very bright, sunny day however, you might limit the range for AUTO ISO to ISO 100–125 for example, to make sure the camera always sets a low ISO for optimal image quality.

The Role of Shutter Speed and Aperture

At any given ISO setting, two factors control the amount of light that reaches the camera's image sensor and produces a photo: (1) the length of time the camera's shutter is open, and (2) the size of the aperture (opening) in the lens. The longer the shutter speed, the greater the amount of light that will strike the image sensor. The larger the aperture, the more light that will enter during any given exposure time.

Shutter speeds are denoted in seconds or fractions of a second. Aperture size is denoted with f/numbers, also called f/stops. The smaller the f/stop number is, the larger the aperture. A wide aperture such as f/4 will allow far more light to enter the camera than a small aperture such as f/16.

Equivalent Exposure: The camera's shutter speed settings and f/stops both increase and decrease exposure in equal amounts. Each full step increment doubles or halves the amount of light reaching the sensor. Thus, if you decrease the length of the shutter speed by one full stop and then increase the size of the aperture by one full stop, the exposure will remain the same.

Measuring Brightness (Metering)

There was a time when cameras did not contain any built-in system for measuring subject brightness. In those days you needed to use an accessory light meter, or rely on estimates and expertise to determine the correct exposure. Modern digital SLR cameras have very sophisticated built-in metering and exposure systems and the K10D is no exception. It offers three light-metering options, and it's important to understand the light measurement strategies for each of them. These are selected by rotating the metering-mode lever under the mode dial to one of the metering options.

Multi-segment Metering : This is an evaluative system, using artificial intelligence, that considers brightness in 16 sections of a scene. It's available only when DA, DA*, D FA, FA J, FA, F and A series lenses are used. The camera's CPU (central processing unit) reviews the data using algorithms designed to produce correct exposure in most types of lighting. This system may automatically ignore an ultra-bright zone in an otherwise evenly lit scene and it can automatically apply EV compensation when "necessary." This sophisticated approach often produces more accurate exposures than other types of metering.

Because this is an "intelligent" system, it is quite successful at metering subjects with unusual reflectance. For example, in strong backlighting, such as a friend posed against a setting sun, the system increases exposure automatically to compensate for the bright background, reducing the risk of a dark image. It uses the same strategy for any scene possessing high reflectance, whether a sunny, snow-covered landscape or a close-up of a bride in white. The Multi-segment metering system should also compensate for a dark-toned subject, such as a black car parked in a dark parking lot, reducing exposure to render it as a detailed study in black, not gray.

While this system often provides close to optimal exposures, no technology is foolproof. Very light-toned or dark-toned scenes may be underexposed or overexposed, requiring EV (exposure) compensation for optimal results. Slight exposure errors may or may not be a problem, depending on whether or not you can correct the errors with image processing software. But even when shooting with RAW files, which offer more capacity than JPEG for post-shooting exposure correction without degrading image quality, it is worth taking the time to get a well-exposed image in-camera, using EV compensation when necessary.

You can also choose to link the active AF point to exposure during Multi-segment metering only. Select the *Link AF Point and AE* option in the Custom Setting menu; choose *On* and press the OK button. If you do so, the meter will consider the brightness of the focused subject more heavily than usual during the exposure calculation. That option can be useful, unless the focused area is either very bright, such as a bride's white dress, or very dark-toned, such as a groom's black tux. In truth, a subject of either type would probably produce some exposure error—though perhaps less serious–even if you did not link the active AF point to Multi-segment metering.

Center-Weighted Metering : Designed to measure brightness over most of the scene and average the data, Center-weighted metering applies extra bias to a large central area. This old style system does not utilize "intelligent" evaluation and does not automatically compensate for backlighting or unusual reflectance. Hence, it's more likely that you will need to set EV compensation–and in larger increments–than with Multi-segment metering to get accurate exposures with "difficult" scenes.

Photographers who worked with film SLRs that used center-weighted metering may prefer to use this option with the K10D. When applied with expertise, this metering technique can produce excellent exposures. However, in general, you will get better results with the camera's Multi-segment metering system. You may also occasionally want to use the K10D's Spot metering function when it is advantageous to precisely meter a small area.

Spot Metering [•] : This metering pattern measures a very small (2.5%) portion of a scene in the center of the frame. To use Spot metering, point the lens so that the central circle etched on the viewing screen covers the target you intend to meter.

One of the most valuable uses of Spot metering is to measure light values in different parts of a scene for comparison or to determine the exposure gradient in the scene. Another common scenario is a spot-lit performer (small in the frame) against a dark background. Or you might be shooting a small, mid-tone subject located in very bright surroundings, such as a cabin in the snow on a sunny day. When measured with other metering patterns, these types of shots often produce an exposure that is not optimal.

In the above cases, meter your primary subject, then press the AE-L (autoexposure lock) button (on upper right corner of camera back; see also page 160). This will lock the exposure as long as the * symbol in the viewfinder is visible. This step will ensure that the locked-in exposure does not change while you recompose. When the photo is recorded, the exposure will be optimized for the primary subject.

Spot metering can be tricky because the exposure is based on the brightness of the small, selected area. If the target is a mid-tone (a tanned face, for example), the exposure may be accurate. But if you take a spot meter reading of a light-toned area, underexposure may occur unless you apply plus EV compensation before taking the photo. And if you spot meter a dark area, the image may be overexposed unless you set the correct amount of minus EV compensation before taking the photo. With experience, and a full appreciation of these concepts, Spot metering can be a useful light-metering option.

Setting the Active Metering Time: By default, the camera turns off the exposure metering circuits after ten seconds if you haven't touched the shutter release button or used certain camera controls. This length of time can be shortened to 3 seconds or extended to 30 seconds in the Custom Setting menu (see page 110).

Exposure Modes

The K10D provides a large choice of exposure modes to suit many subjects and shooting situations. These modes are selected by rotating the mode dial (on the left top of the camera) to the desired position.

Green or Full Auto ■ : This fully automatic mode is designed for easy point-and-shoot operation with little risk of user error. The camera has total control of the aperture/shutter speed combination and certain camera controls are deactivated. You cannot use AE lock (AE-L), EV compensation, Auto bracketing, Multi-exposure, or flash exposure compensation. However, some other overrides and functions remain available.

This mode is most useful when you loan the camera to a friend, for example, and want to make sure it will be easy to use for snapshots. In that case, you will first want to take advantage of the *Reset* options in both the Set-up menu and in the Custom Setting menu to return all camera settings to the defaults.

Using the Green or P exposure modes is a good strategy when you don't want to take the time to alter camera settings for each individual picture. This allows you to shoot quickly so you don't miss a scene, such as action at a child's party or an outing for ice skating.

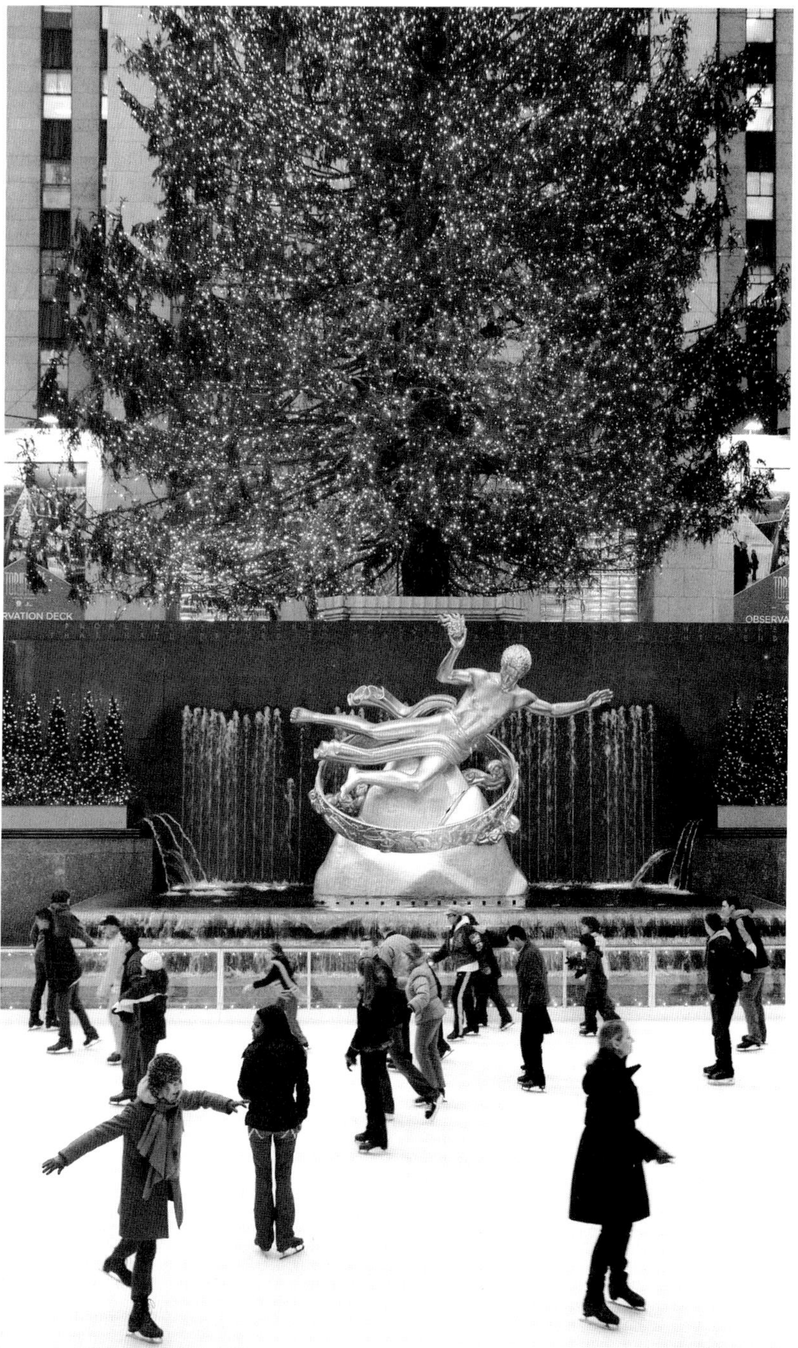

Hyper-Program (P): In this fully automatic mode, the camera sets both the shutter speed and aperture, but allows more user control than Green mode. Initially, the camera sets an aperture (f/stop) and shutter speed to provide a correct exposure based on its light meter and built-in algorithms. You can change the aperture or the shutter speed, however, using Hyper-program, a feature that is sometimes called "Program shift." Rotate the front e-dial to select a different shutter speed and the camera will automatically set the suitable aperture. (In this respect the K10D operates in the same way as it does in Tv mode, discussed later.) Rotate the rear e-dial to set a desired aperture (f/stop) and the camera will automatically set a suitable shutter speed. (In this respect the K10D operates in the same way as it does in Av mode, discussed later.)

The settings that are made automatically by the camera will be determined by the meter's analysis of the scene. In some cases, EV (exposure) compensation may be required for a perfect exposure. You can also return to fully automatic aperture/shutter speed operation at any time, by pressing the camera's Green button, beside the main (ON/OFF) switch on the right top of the camera in front of the LCD panel.

When you use the so-called "Program shift" or "Hyper" feature, you can affect a change in the shutter speed/aperture combination, but the exposure does not change. If you set a wider aperture, the camera will, in turn, set a faster shutter speed. Should you set a longer shutter speed, it will set a smaller aperture. This automated response strategy was intended to maintain the equivalent (same) exposure.

Out of Range Warning: In certain conditions when a scene may be too bright or too dark, it is possible to get an improper exposure in Hyper-program mode (or other exposure modes) with the current ISO setting. In such situations, the K10D will provide an advance warning by displaying a blinking shutter speed numeral or f/stop numeral (or both) in the viewfinder and LCD panel. If you are shooting in a very dark location and notice this blinking, you should switch to a higher ISO (or longer shutter speed and/or wider aperture). Should you get the warning in extremely bright conditions, switch to a lower ISO, or a smaller aperture and/or faster shutter speed.

Note: In some unusually bright or unusually dark locations, a suitable aperture/shutter speed/ISO combination (to provide a good exposure) will not be possible. That can occur when the scene brightness is out of the range of the camera's capabilities. A landscape at midnight, for example, might require an exposure time of several minutes even at the maximum lens aperture and an ISO level of 1600. Since the camera cannot set such a long shutter speed, it would set the longest available, 30 seconds, and that numeral would blink as a warning of incorrect exposure.

In P mode, when flash is on, the camera will set a flash sync speed as fast as 1/180 second, but never longer than 1/30 second. The brighter the conditions and the higher the ISO that you're using, the faster the sync speed that the camera will set, up to the top sync limit of 1/180 second.

Take care when selecting a very small aperture, such as f/16, because the range of flash will be fairly minimal unless you're using a very high ISO. Your flash photos may be underexposed. The camera provides no advance warning of this problem in P mode when flash is active. (If you're using an accessory flash unit with a distance scale however, you can pre-determine the flash range at any f/stop and ISO. You'll find a great deal of additional information and advice about flash photography and accessories in subsequent chapters of this book.)

Custom Programs: You can modify P mode with the field for *Program line* in the Custom Setting menu by selecting any of three options other than *Normal*. These include *Hi Speed* (the camera will favor fast shutter speeds), *Depth* (to favor small apertures), or *MTF* (denoting the Modulation Transfer Function, causing the camera to favor the apertures that will provide the best image quality with any lens.) After setting any of these three options, P mode will use that program until you change it or return the K10D to default settings with the *Reset* option in the Set-up menu.

Avoid User Error: You can minimize the need for the incorrect exposure warning in very dark or very bright conditions in exposure modes P, Av, Tv, TAv, or Sv. Set the *On* option in the *Auto EV Compensation* item in the Custom Setting menu. With this activated, the camera will automatically override your selected aperture/shutter speed/ISO settings that would not allow the camera to provide an acceptable exposure.

I recommend setting this valuable custom function to *On*. However, this feature does not guarantee ideal exposures in every situation, since no light meter is perfect. With some scenes, you may need to use EV (exposure) compensation, for reasons discussed in the metering sections of this chapter. Auto EV Compensation was designed simply to prevent exposure problems caused by user error: making a totally inappropriate f/stop, aperture, or ISO setting in certain conditions.

Aperture Priority (Av): Selected by choosing the Av (for "aperture value") on the mode dial, this is a traditional semi-automatic exposure mode that's available with many cameras and is used frequently by many photographers. Av mode was designed for depth-of-field control; you can set any aperture available using the rear e-dial (if the lens has an aperture ring it must be locked in the "A" position (see page 220). The camera automatically sets a shutter speed that should yield a "good" exposure, according to its light meter's calculations. All functions and overrides are available.

For information on flash photography in Av mode, refer to the comments provided in P mode (see page 140); they apply equally in AV mode.

Using Aperture Priority exposure mode to select a wide aperture when shooting portraits will isolate your subject against a blurred background. Shooting with a moderate telephoto focal length also enhances this effect. ⇨

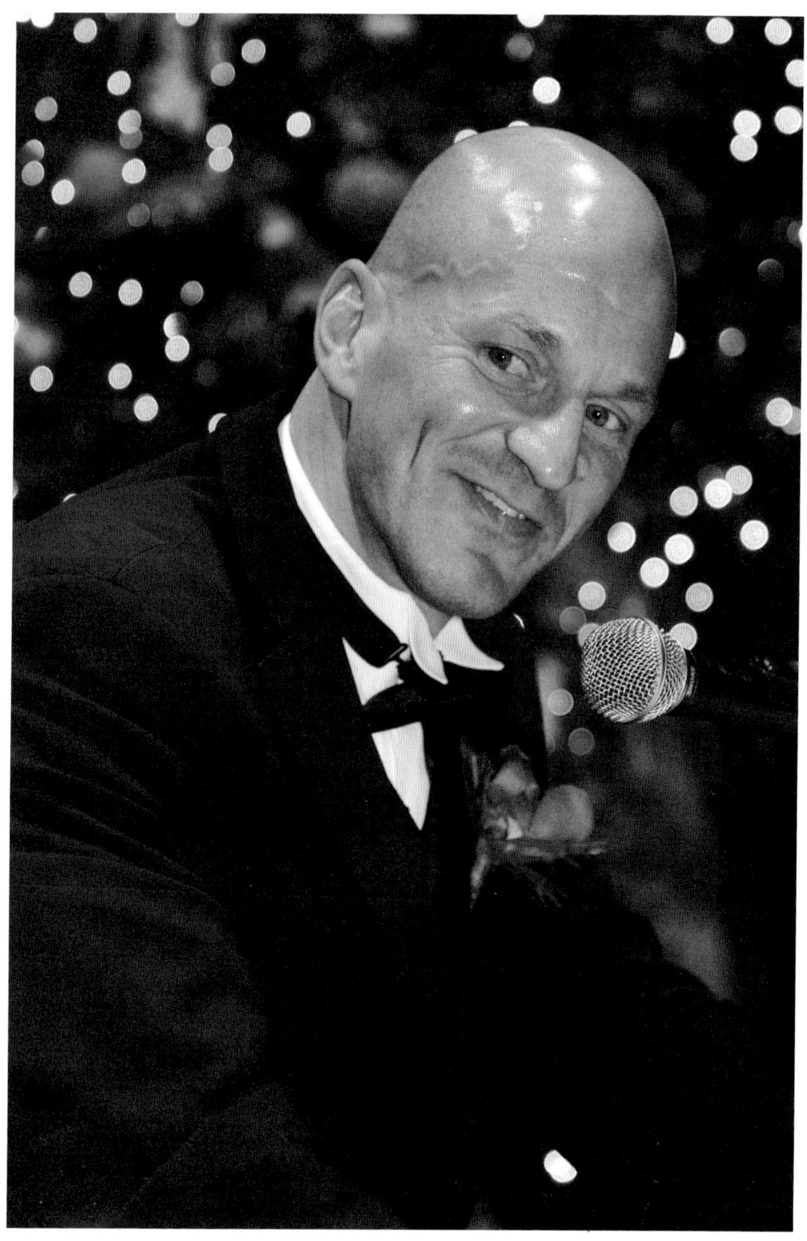

Out of Range Warning: If it is not possible for the camera to produce a proper exposure in Av mode with the current selected aperture, ISO setting, and scene conditions, the shutter speed readout in the viewfinder data panel will blink. This alerts you that you are beyond the adjustment capabilities of the camera's exposure control system at the current settings. If you are shooting in a very dark location and notice this blinking, open the aperture (lower f/stop number) or switch to a higher ISO. Should the shutter speed blink as a warning in extremely bright conditions, stop down the lens (use a higher f/stop number) or switch to a lower ISO.

Depth of Field—A Short Course

While the objects in a scene are usually three-dimensional, they are recorded on the sensor in two dimensions with a single plane of exact focus. In other words, if you focus on a subject that is about 3 yards (2.75 meters) from the camera, everything at the same distance will be sharply focused. Everything at distances other than the focused distance will appear less sharp.

However, when an image is viewed, there is an area in front of and behind the plane of sharp focus that is perceived to be in focus. This range of apparent sharpness is referred to as the depth of field. The factors that influence the amount of depth of field are: the focused distance, the focal length in use, and the shooting aperture.

If the focal length and subject distance are constant, depth of field will be shallower with large apertures (lower f/numbers) and deeper with small apertures (higher f/numbers). If the aperture and focused distance are constant, depth of field will be shallower with longer lenses (telephoto range) and deeper with shorter lenses (wide-angle range). If the focal length and aperture are constant, depth of field will be greater at longer focused distances and shallower at closer focused distances.

These factors should be considered when planning your composition and the look of the finished photograph. The K10D provides full aperture control in several modes while providing appropriate exposure at the f/stop that you select. The camera sets an appropriate shutter speed, or a suitable ISO in some cases, for a "good" exposure.

Depth-of-Field Preview: Like many D-SLR cameras, the K10D offers a feature that previews your scene's depth of field. Pentax calls this Optical Preview (a default setting). It's available by rotating the main switch (right top of camera) to the right, pointing to the icon. When you do so, the diaphragm within the lens closes down to the aperture you have selected. This allows you to view the scene at the actual taking aperture.

That is necessary because today's cameras/lenses are designed for open-aperture metering. This means that they don't close down to the shooting aperture until a split second before the shutter opens to record an image. Until then, the aperture stays wide open, allowing the viewfinder to be as bright as possible for composing and focusing. However, that means we always view a scene at a lens' widest aperture, such as f/4 or f/5.6. Hence, we cannot evaluate depth of field at the taking aperture, unless we use the technique described in the above paragraph.

If you set a small aperture such as f/11, f/16, or especially a very small f/22, the viewfinder will become dark when you activate Optical Preview. (That's because you'll be viewing the scene through a smaller aperture or lens opening.) Still, on bright days at least, you should be able to see the elements in the scene well enough to judge relative sharpness. Wait a few seconds to allow your eye to become accustomed to the darker view.

You can check the depth of field at various apertures, but must release the depth-of-field control when you want to change f/stops. That can be useful while experimenting with control of this important aspect of serious photography.

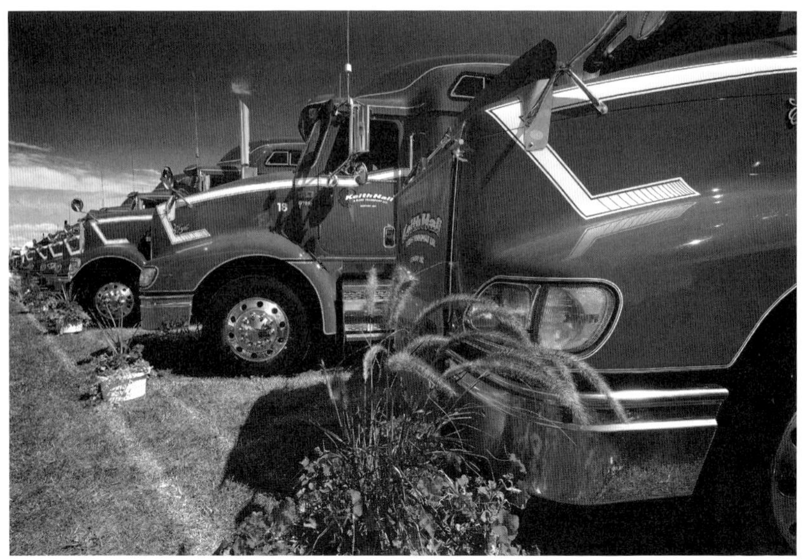

When you want extensive depth of field, use a short (wide-angle) focal length and a small aperture such as f/16. Focusing on a point about a third of the way into the scene further maximizes sharpness in the photo.

Sometimes you will want all elements of a composition, from foreground to background, to be rendered sharply–so you should use a small aperture. Other times you will want some elements, such as a cluttered background, to be softly blurred so they don't compete with the subject; that can usually be achieved with a wide aperture. Either way, Optical Preview is the easiest and most precise method of judging the degree of sharpness of various parts of a composition, at various apertures.

Note: The K10D can also be set for *Digital Preview*, with the *Preview Method* tab in the Custom Setting menu. Moving the camera's main switch to causes the camera to take a photo that you can view on the LCD monitor. This allows you to evaluate various aspects of the photo, including depth of field. (This preview photo is not recorded to the memory card.) Digital preview can be useful, although on a relatively small 2.5-inch (6.35 cm) display, it's not easy to judge the actual depth of field.

Depth-of-Field Shooting Tips: In close-up photography, depth of field is limited. So to maximize it, choose a small aperture (such as f/11). You may also wish to control the point of focus to further maximize depth of field. (Remember that focused distance is part of the formula and it is especially important at close ranges.) Take advantage of the camera's depth-of-field preview options. If depth of field is not adequate, you can use an even smaller aperture (such as f/16 or f/22), or readjust the point of focus. For example, when photographing a flower, you may find that overall sharpness will be improved by focusing on a different part of the blossom. Also, for best results in close-up photography, use a tripod or other camera support to prevent blur from camera shake.

A soft, out-of-focus background (shallow depth of field) is preferred for portrait photography because it will not draw the viewer's eye away from the subject. To accomplish this, choose a large aperture (small f/number such as f/4). Because telephoto lenses have less inherent depth of field than shorter focal lengths, they are ideal for isolating the subject against a softly blurred background. You can always check the effect using the camera's depth-of-field preview.

For landscape photography, maximizing depth of field will render more of the scene in focus. Besides using a small aperture (higher f/number such as f/16), controlling the point of focus will make the most of the depth of field. As a rule of thumb, depth of field will extend about 1/3 in front of the point of focus and 2/3 behind it. Thus, focusing roughly one-third of the way up from the bottom of the frame will yield the greatest amount of sharpness. Take advantage of the lens or focal length to create a pleasing scenic view. Not only does a wide-angle lens allow you to capture sweeping vistas, but it also maximizes the depth of field in the photograph.

Hint: Another fast and simple way to get the best possible depth of field is to take the same shot at several aperture (f/stop) settings: f/11, f/16 and f/22, perhaps. One of the images may be just right.

Shutter Priority (Tv): This is useful when you want to control how motion is rendered in a photo. To set it, turn the mode dial to Tv, or "time value" mode. After you select the shutter speed, the camera will set the appropriate f/stop for a "good" exposure. (If you are using a lens with an aperture ring, it must be in the "A" position.) In some cases, EV compensation may be required for a more accurate, or visually pleasing, image.

The chart below may be useful to show the meaning of common shutter speed abbreviations found in the camera's exposure modes. (Note for example that the ″ symbol is used as an abbreviation for seconds.) The list does not include every possible option, but once you understand the concept, you'll have no difficulty in determining the exact shutter speed.

1000:	1/1000 second
60:	1/60 second
15:	1/15 second
0.5″:	one half second
5:	1/5 seconds
1″:	1 second
1″5:	one and a half seconds
15″:	fifteen seconds

Out of Range Warning: If it is not possible for the camera to produce a proper exposure in Tv mode with the current selected shutter speed, ISO setting, and scene conditions, the aperture readout in the viewfinder data panel will blink. This alerts you that you are beyond the range of the camera's exposure control system at the current settings. If you are shooting in a very dark location, and notice this blinking, switch to a much higher ISO or lengthen the shutter speed (lower number). You may need to turn on Shake Reduction or use a tripod. Should the f/stop blink as a warning in extremely bright conditions, use a faster shutter speed or switch to a much lower ISO.

Shutter Speed Selection—A Short Course

In handheld photography, it is important to use a shutter speed that will produce a sharp photo without blur from camera shake. This minimum hand-holdable shutter speed changes with the focal length in use. A general rule of thumb is that the minimum hand-holdable shutter speed should be equivalent to the reciprocal of the focal length in use. Hence, if you are shooting with a 100mm focal length, the minimum shutter speed recommendation is 1/125 second. However, using the camera's Shake Reduction technology can extend the minimum shutter speed. For more information on using Shake Reduction, see pages 120-122.

There's another important reason for selecting a slow or fast shutter speed–the ability to control how motion is portrayed in the photo. To appreciate this concept, take several shots of moving cars at a fast shutter speed such as 1/500 second. Do the same with a slow shutter speed such as 1/15 second. Analyze the resulting images and you should find that the first set is quite sharp while the second depicts the subject with motion blur.

This is useful for creative purposes, allowing you to control the way that a moving subject will appear in your images. Think of a waterfall for example. If you shoot at 1/500 second, the droplets of water will appear to be frozen in mid-air; that may not provide the flowing effect that you want. Put the camera on a tripod and switch to a shutter speed of 1/4 second and the water will be blurred, producing a convincing portrayal of the motion of flowing water.

Note: When you select a faster shutter speed in Tv mode, such as 1/500 second, the camera will set a wider aperture to assure correct exposure, so depth of field will therefore be reduced. When you select longer shutter speeds, the camera will set a smaller aperture, so the resulting image will exhibit greater depth of field. If you want to use fast shutter speeds, plus smaller apertures for more depth of field, switch to ISO 400 in bright light and ISO 800 on overcast days.

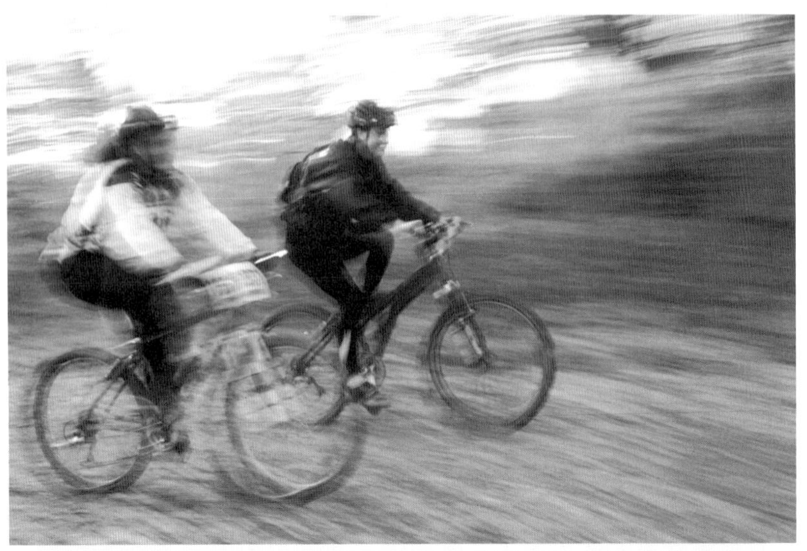

Here, a 1/8 second exposure, plus panning with the movement of the subject, produced an unconventional effect that is quite pleasing and communicates motion.

In action photography, we often use fast shutter speeds to "freeze" the subject without motion blur. But sometimes it may be preferable to convey the feeling of motion by using a relatively slow shutter speed, such as 1/30 second. In this case the subject will be blurred instead of "frozen" or static. This option works best with subjects moving through the frame from the left or right, across your line of vision. Pan by smoothly moving the camera at the same speed as your subject is moving. It helps to use a tripod with a pan head and to begin a little before tripping the shutter release. In the resulting image, the subject should be quite sharp, though with some motion blur, while the background will exhibit obvious blur, which will communicate the movement to the viewer. If the action is occurring close to the camera, try also using flash in Rear curtain sync mode during a long exposure for some of your shots, as discussed in the chapter on flash photography.

The pan/blur technique takes practice because it requires you to move the camera at exactly the right speed. You may need to shoot quite a few frames to get one that's nearly perfect technically and aesthetically. By using this technique, you'll become more skillful, so if you like the effect, practice it whenever you have the opportunity. Remember, with digital photography, you don't have to worry about running up film and processing costs!

Shutter & Aperture Priority (TAv): This new time/aperture value mode is unique to the K10D. It allows you to set the shutter speed, the aperture, or both. After you do so (with the e-dials) the camera will adjust the ISO level to provide a "good" exposure. That's the basic explanation of the TAv mode, but it's important to fully appreciate a couple of the aspects.

In TAv mode, the camera automatically switches to AUTO ISO, overriding any specific ISO that you had set. Naturally, the AUTO ISO system can use only the pre-set ISO range; at default, that's ISO 100-400. But you can set an entirely different range in AUTO ISO by making a range modification (see page 133). For great versatility in selecting a desired aperture and shutter speed in TAv mode, set a wide AUTO ISO range, such as 100-800, or ISO 400-1600 in dark locations when not using flash.

When first working with the K10D, I did not understand the value of the TAv mode, but the following comment by C.W. (Bill) Gouge of Pentax provided some insight, "The best way to think of TAv is that it is equivalent to changing film [low, medium, or high ISO] in 35mm photography. By automatically adjusting the ISO, TAv mode allows you to work with a desired shutter speed/aperture combination for a specific reason."

Sensitivity Priority (Sv): Also unique to the K10D, this "sensitivity value" mode allows you to set a desired ISO level when shooting with or without flash. The camera will then automatically vary the aperture and/or shutter speed as necessary for a correct exposure. (In flash photography it will not set a sync speed higher than 1/180 second.)

You can use exactly the same approach in P mode too, of course, but there is a notable difference in Sv mode: ISO selection is streamlined by use of the camera's rear e-dial. That's much quicker than using the Fn menu and it does not require you to remove the camera from your eye. Hence, you're less likely to miss a photo opportunity. As a bonus, the ISO number is shown in the viewfinder data panel in Sv mode as a reminder about this important factor.

The Sv mode is most useful in situations where the light is changing rapidly, from very bright to dark. For example, this might occur when moving between an outdoor and an indoor location quickly and frequently. In such situations, "sensitivity" control is certainly important. You'll probably want to use low ISO outdoors for optimal image quality and switch quickly to a high ISO when moving indoors for faster shutter speeds to minimize the risk of blur from camera or subject movement.

Hyper-manual (M): In this fully manual mode, you can set any aperture and any shutter speed at any time even if they will produce a technically incorrect exposure. (The Auto EV Compensation custom function discussed on page 110 will not operate when M mode is used.) M mode is intended to allow for intentional exposure adjustment quickly, without the need to use overrides such as the EV compensation control. It also allows full control of exposure for creative purposes.

When you set the K10D to M mode, a scale called an EV bar appears in the viewfinder and LCD panel as an exposure guide. It shows the amount of deviation from the meter-recommended exposure at the aperture and shutter speed you have set.

While experimenting with M mode, start with the "correct" or light-meter-recommended exposure for a scene. That can be achieved instantly by pressing the green button next to the camera's main switch. The K10D will then consider scene brightness and the ISO in use and it will set an aperture/shutter speed combination for a "good" exposure. The cursor on

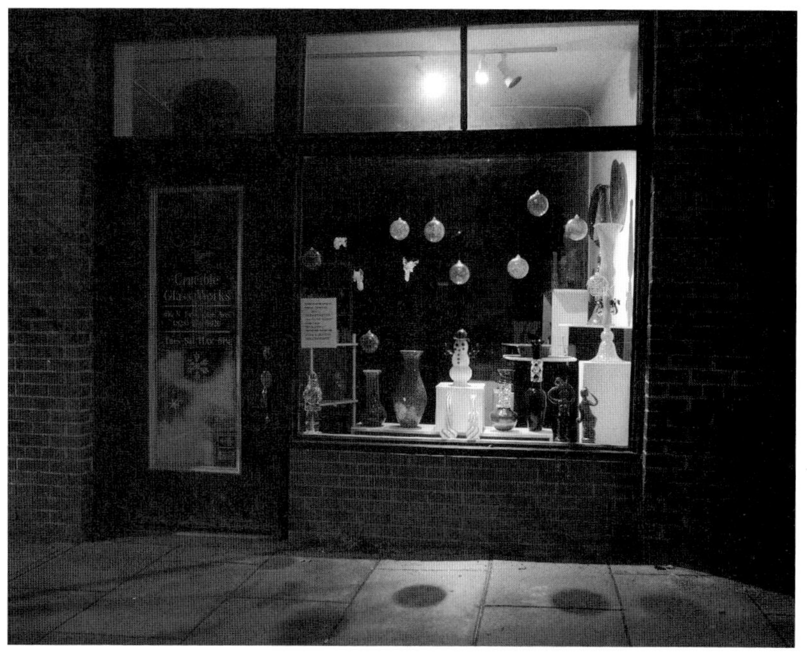

For unusual lighting, it is possible to control the exposure with automatic modes and overrides, but some experienced photographers find it more convenient to use Manual exposure mode. ©Kevin Kopp

the EV bar will settle at the central position indicating zero deviation from the meter recommended exposure.

Afterwards, you can modify this exposure by changing the shutter speed with the front e-dial and/or changing the aperture with the rear e-dial in M mode. Check the EV bar and you can see the exact deviation from the meter recommended exposure in a range of up to +3 or -3 Exposure Values (EV). A reading of +1 for example, indicates that the image will be overexposed by one EV, while -1 indicates underexposure by one EV. The scale is marked in increments of one-third (0.33) EV.

One EV is equivalent to one aperture stop or one shutter-speed step. It's quite a large increment in digital photography; over or underexposure by one EV is certainly obvious in an image. An EV factor of 0.33 is less noticeable in an image.

The manual exposure technique is not quick or easy to use. Frankly, you can generally achieve exactly the same result with less complexity by using the semi-automatic modes and EV compensation. Those modes allow you to select an aperture (f/stop) and/or shutter speed; the camera will maintain the same exposure as you change settings. When you want to make a darker or brighter image, set some minus or plus EV compensation. Unless you are already proficient in manual exposure control, you may want to experiment extensively with Hyper-manual mode before relying on it for important images.

Note: Unlike most other D-SLR cameras, the K10D allows the use of the AE-L (autoexposure lock) control in M mode; that's why Pentax refers to it as Hyper-manual. When you press the AE-L button, the exposure is locked based on the aperture/shutter speed that you have set; a * symbol appears in the viewfinder to confirm that. Whether it's "correct" exposure or not, the value will remain locked until the light metering system turns off or until you disengage AE lock by pressing the AE-L button again.

While AE-L is active (denoted by the * symbol), you can change the f/stop or the shutter speed in M mode without affecting the exposure. If you change one of these factors, the camera will change the other factor to maintain the same exposure. When using M mode, the AE-L feature is most appropriate when you are confident that your current settings will produce a desired exposure but you want to use different shutter speed or f/stop. If you are a very creative photographer or if you just enjoy shooting in fully manual mode, this feature may be appealing to you.

Bulb (B): In any of the modes discussed so far, the longest shutter speed that you (or the camera) can select is 30 seconds, but there is another option for making even longer exposures: B, an abbreviation for the term "bulb." That relates to an antique photo accessory that used a blower bulb attached to a thin hose. Squeezing the bulb tripped the camera's shutter.

Set the mode dial to B and use the rear e-dial to select an aperture (f/stop). When you then press the shutter release button, the camera's shutter mechanism will remain open as long as the button is held all the way down. (An optional remote-control accessory should be used to trip the shutter and then lock it open.) A tripod must be used for sharp images during long exposures; turn the Shake Reduction function off when using a tripod, as recommended by Pentax.

The camera's light meter is disengaged in B mode, so you will need to use a handheld meter to calculate exposure or use a published "rule of thumb" for correct exposure in night photography, for example. This option is indeed most useful at night: to record the moon and stars, a dark cityscape, or a long fireworks burst, for example. Since digital noise is always more prominent in images made during long exposures, you may want to activate *Noise Reduction* in the Custom Setting menu.

Flash X-Sync Speed (X): This mode is specifically intended for use when working with a flash unit that cannot automatically set the camera's shutter speed for flash sync. That's most common when working with older or non-dedicated flash units. When you set the mode dial to X, the shutter speed is locked at 1/180 second; you cannot set a faster or slower sync speed.

Of course, you could also use Tv or another mode that allows you to set a desired shutter speed; in that case, do not set a shutter speed (sync speed) faster than 1/180 second for flash photography. In X mode, you can control the aperture, selecting an f/stop using the rear e-dial. You can also allow the camera to automatically select an appropriate aperture by pressing the Green button. Note too that if you're using AUTO ISO when shooting in X mode, the camera will automatically select the lowest ISO available in the range that you have set for automatic ISO selection.

USER Mode: While it's not technically an exposure mode, this feature is discussed here because it's selected with the mode dial. Selecting USER automatically recalls your favorite settings, including exposure mode, ISO level or AUTO ISO range, capture format, drive mode, exposure compensation factor, and so on. (None of the custom functions are included so those cannot be recalled using the USER function.)

First, you need to determine your favorite mode and various settings and set up those preferences. Then, in the Set-up menu, select the *User* item and scroll to the right; a screen appears with confirmation of all current camera settings. Press the OK button, and these are saved. Once you have done this, at any time in the future, you can reset the K10D to your preferred settings simply by selecting the USER item on the mode dial. Neat, huh?

EV (Exposure) Compensation

This feature allows you to make adjustments to exposure. After taking a shot, check it on the LCD monitor, perhaps in Playback mode with the histogram (see page 165) and/or the Bright/Dark area warning (see page 163). Or, use the camera's Digital Preview function (see page 146) to make a preview image for evaluation purposes. If the image appears too bright or too dark, set some EV (exposure) compensation and re-shoot. (This feature is not available in Green, M, B, or X mode.) EV compensation–also called exposure compensation–can be set by depressing the button (on the back of camera) and rotating the front e-dial.

Set a + (plus) value if you want to make a brighter image, or a – (minus) value for a darker image. While the button is depressed, the exact amount that you have set is displayed in the LCD panel and in the viewfinder. Remember to check it occasionally, and make sure to reset compensation to zero when it's no longer required. You can also do this using *Reset* in the Set-up menu.

Note: In its default setting, the K10D will allow you to set EV compensation in increments of 0.5 EV. If you prefer to make changes in slightly smaller increments, you can set the camera to do so by selecting the *1/3 EV Steps* option in the *EV Steps* field of the Custom Setting menu. Making this change, however, will also affect the increment for Exposure bracket, causing it to vary exposure by 0.33 EV instead of the default of 0.5 EV. This also sets the K10D to allow aperture and shutter speeds to be selected for more precise control in approximately 1/3 EV increments, instead of the slightly larger 1/2 EV increments.

You can make EV compensation changes toward the plus side or the minus side. The term EV denotes exposure value, and one full EV change in compensation will double or half the amount of light used to make a photo. When shooting with Multi-segment metering, rarely will you need to apply more than a value of +0.7 or -0.7 for EV compensation. Take a shot without compensation and review it for exposure accuracy. If you're not satisfied, set a plus compensation factor for a brighter image or a minus factor for a darker image, and re-shoot.

Exposure Bracket

This function allows you to shoot three or more successive frames while the camera automatically applies different exposures to each. This increases your chances of getting the optimal exposure with any given subject and lighting condition. The Exposure bracket function is selected with the button on the camera back (above the MENU button).

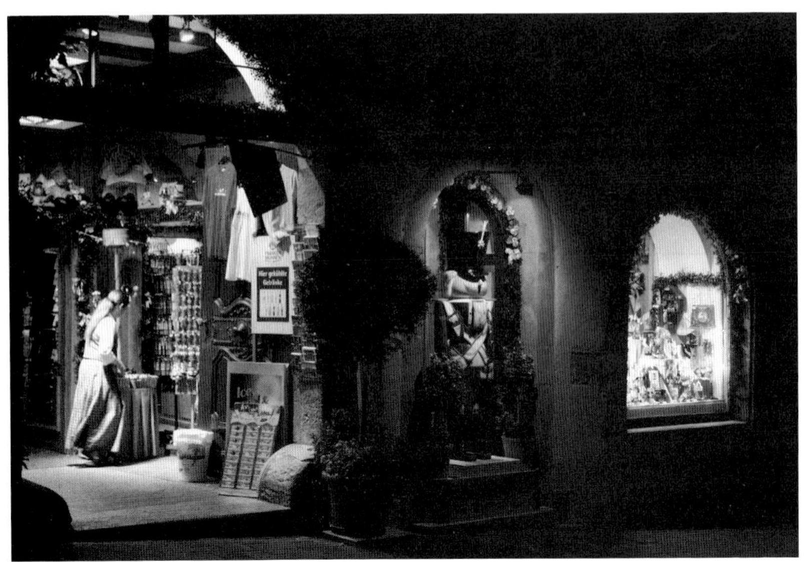

In tricky lighting, exposure bracketing can be very useful. This scene included very dark and bright areas, which made it difficult to estimate the amount of exposure compensation that would produce the best possible image. By bracketing, the photographer was able to review several exposures and select the best rendition of the scene.

Rotate the front e-dial while depressing the Exposure bracket button in order to set the number of frames that will be made during a bracketed series: 3 (the most common choice) or 5. Then, rotate the rear e-dial while depressing the Exposure bracket button to select the amount of EV compensation that will be automatically applied by the system during exposure bracketing: from +/-0.3 EV (a small amount) to a full +/-2.0 EV (a large amount.)

After you set both parameters for Exposure bracket, press the shutter release button and the camera will fire a burst of three or five frames in a sequence, in Single frame shooting mode. The first frame will receive no EV compensation, while the subsequent frames will be over or underexposed by the increment you have pre-set. Only the last image of the series will be displayed in the LCD monitor in Instant

Review. If you use Continuous shooting mode, the camera will keep firing bracketed series for as long as you wish, useful in some action photography.

Compensation Plus Bracketing

Exposure bracketing can be valuable when you are not certain how much EV compensation to set, or whether or not some plus or minus compensation would produce the most visually pleasing exposure. Before you set Bracketing, you can apply general exposure compensation. For example, you might set a +1 compensation factor in a situation where you are quite sure that underexposure would be a problem otherwise. When shooting the bracketed series of frames, the camera will consider the compensation level that you had pre-set.

Note: When the built-in flash is active, or when using an accessory flash in P-TTL mode, the exposure bracketing function will vary the flash exposure only. Remember that the flash needs time to re-cycle after taking a shot. Be sure to allow the camera to take one shot at a time, and not three in a quick sequence; otherwise, the second and third images may be underexposed. Remove your finger from the shutter button after an image has been taken; take the next shot only when the flash is ready again.

Making Multi-Exposures

This feature offered by the K10D was common with high-end 35mm SLR cameras but is rarely found on most other D-SLRs. In a nutshell, it allows you to record two to nine photos as a single digital image. Note too that the K10D can automatically adjust the exposure to prevent the overexposure that can occur when several exposures are combined to create a single image. That eliminates the need for complicated exposure compensation calculations that would otherwise be necessary.

Select *Multi-exposure* in the Rec. Mode menu and scroll to the right to specify the number of shots (from 2 to 9) that you want to combine into a single image. Then scroll down to the *Auto EV Adjust* entry, scroll to the right to put a check mark into the box, and press the OK button. This will ensure automatic exposure correction. After you make the multiple-exposure, the camera will revert to normal operation.

Let's say you have specified three frames in Multi-exposure mode. Shoot three JPEG, RAW or RAW+JPEG frames as usual, and the camera's processor will automatically combine them into a single image. If you used Multi-segment metering, the exposure should be close to correct, unless the subject was very dark-toned or very light-toned. In that case, you'll need to set some minus or plus EV compensation, set Multi-exposure again in the Rec. Mode menu, and re-shoot.

Note: If you press the MENU button or the RAW button, or if you set Exposure bracket during Multi-exposure mode, the multiple-exposure function will be de-activated (assuming that you activated it first before activating the other features mentioned above). Multi-exposure and Exposure bracket or Extended Bracket cannot be used simultaneously; the feature that is set last (bracketing or multi-exposure) will be the one that is used by the camera.

Autoexposure Lock (AE-L)

In any K10D mode except Green, B, or X, or when flash is active, the AE-L control lets you meter a portion of a scene and lock the exposure value so that you can recompose your shot. The exposure will not change while you do so, as long as AE-L (also called AE lock) is active, as confirmed by a * symbol in the viewfinder data panel. This allows you to take a meter reading from a certain subject–such as mid-toned foliage or grass–and recompose without losing the locked-in exposure value.

The AE-L control has already been discussed in the section about the Hyper-manual mode on page 152. It's worth re-reading the description again, because the basic method of operation is the same in the other exposure modes as well. However, when using any of the autoexposure modes, you cannot further modify the exposure by changing aperture or shutter speed as you can in M mode.

If you plan to use the AE-L technique, set some EV (exposure) compensation if your target is light-toned or dark-toned. This should help to assure correct exposure. For example, set perhaps +1 if you plan to take the light meter reading (using Spot metering) from a white egret. Or maybe set -2/3 if taking the meter reading from a black cat. Then press the AE-L button once, recompose for the desired framing, and take the shot.

Exposure and Focus Lock

There is a second method for locking exposure, combining AE lock (AE-L) with AF lock. That's available by selecting On for the *AE-L with AF locked* item in the Custom Setting menu. Now, slight pressure on the shutter release button will lock not only autofocus but also the exposure value.

If you want to experiment, select that option in the menu, and here's how it will work: Let's say you focus on a person in the distance and recompose with slight pressure on the shutter release button. Your focus will not change while exposure will also remain locked until you take the photo or remove your finger from the shutter button. So, whether you use the AE-L button or the shutter release button (when the pertinent custom function is set), the exposure value remains locked. The * symbol is visible in the viewfinder data panel to confirm that AE lock is active when you use either control.

Every camera owner needs to make a decision about the value of the combined AF Lock and AE lock feature. Some experienced photographers recommend against this combination, insisting that you control focus and exposure separately by using the shutter release button to lock only focus and use the AE-L button to lock exposure (this is the camera's default method). That approach allows you to focus on one part of a scene, such as a white blossom while exposing for mid-toned grass, for example.

I agree with that technique for occasions where there's plenty of time to set focus and exposure separately, as in landscape photography. In quick shooting however–as in

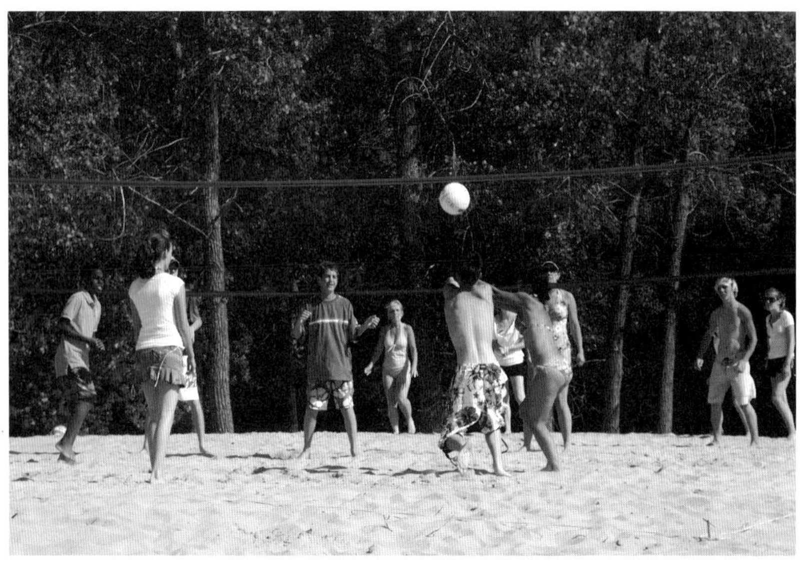

The Bright/Dark area warning can be useful when it warns about loss of detail in important highlight or shadow areas. However, this information always needs to be interpreted. Here, the camera warned about loss of shadow detail in the background, but this was not an important part of the photo.

candid picture taking–I prefer to have control of both focus lock and AE lock with a single control (the shutter release button). That makes it easy and quick to optimize focus and exposure for a subject and keep both factors locked while recomposing. It takes only a few seconds to change the AE-L with AF locked custom function from *On* to *Off*, or vice-versa. I recommend using the most appropriate option depending on the picture-taking situation as demonstrated by the examples above.

Exposure Evaluation

The K10D provides three methods for viewing an image to check for exposure accuracy: Instant Review, Playback mode, and Digital Preview (described in detail on page 146). In their most basic applications, any of these allows you to look at an image and determine whether it's correctly exposed. Such visual reviews can be useful, helping you to decide whether you need to re-shoot the photo with some EV compensation (plus or minus).

Two more objective features are offered to evaluate exposure: the histogram and the Bright/Dark area warning. Either or both of these tools are available in Instant Review, Digital Review, and in Playback mode.

Bright/Dark Area Warning

Quite common in many digital cameras, this feature is sometimes called "highlight/shadow detail warning." Regardless of terminology, it provides an alert about image areas that are so dark or so bright that they do not hold detail. Though available with all of the image review methods, this warning must be activated. In the Playback Menu, scroll down to the *Instant Review, Digital Preview* or *Playback Display* item, then scroll right when you have come to the desired item. Next scroll to *Bright/Dark area* and set that option by scrolling right again to check the box, and confirm by pressing the OK button. I strongly recommend activating this for all viewing options so the camera will always provide a highlight/shadow detail warning.

Note: Remember that Digital Preview is not always available with the K10D. If you want to use this feature, you must select it from the *Preview Method* item in the Custom Setting menu. Select that option for now; later you can always reset the Preview Method to the default, *Optical Preview,* if you prefer that feature.

Whenever you view an image using the Bright/Dark area warning, the K10D will provide a yellow colored blinking overlay on shadow areas that are too dark to hold detail (blocked up). It will also provide a red blinking overlay over

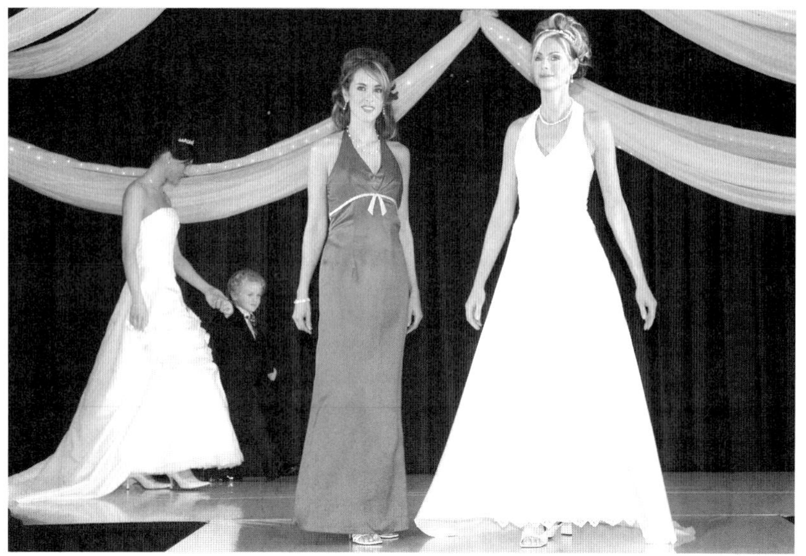

Loss of highlight detail–as in the first model's dress–is a serious problem. No amount of work in the computer can recover detail that wasn't recorded in the first place. Check your images while on location and, when necessary, set EV (exposure) compensation to correct problems such as this.

highlight areas that are too bright to hold detail (blown out). Each type of warning flashes alternately. The Bright/Dark area warning is not as detailed in its information as the histogram display, but it's logical, intuitive, and easier to interpret. It can certainly help you avoid the most serious exposure problems.

When highlight detail or texture is important, as in shots of a bride's dress or a flower petal, check the image after shooting to look for a highlight warning in the pertinent area. If it flashes, you'll probably want to modify the exposure and shoot again. Set a –0.3 EV (exposure) compensation, then re-shoot and review the new image, looking for a warning. If necessary, re-shoot a second time using a –0.7 EV compensation factor, and review that image for a highlight warning. Also keep an eye on any shadow warnings if there are also important details in shadow areas.

Hint: Although highlight detail is often your greatest concern, be careful when shooting a dark-toned subject. If the warning blinks in a dark portion of the scene, underexposure of that area will occur. You may be able to correct that later in a computer, but lightening shadow areas with computer software will often cause noise to be more noticeable: Noise is far less prominent when an image is properly exposed in the camera, especially in images made at ISO 400 and higher. When it's important to have detail in a shadow area, re-shoot several times, using a slightly different amount of EV compensation for each shot. You can always darken the image in the computer, which will not affect digital noise.

The Histogram

The histogram is a graph, in this case appearing on the LCD monitor, that indicates brightness distribution from black (on the left side of the graph) to white (on the right side) along the horizontal axis. A dark image will be weighted to the left, a bright image will be weighted to the right. Mid-tone brightness distribution is represented in the central area of the graph. The vertical axis indicates the pixel quantity existing for the different levels of brightness.

Note: The K10D offers several different histograms. The default histogram is for brightness (also called luminance), but there are also RGB histograms–red, green, and blue–that indicate brightness distribution for each color channel. Frankly, the RGB histograms are most useful to imaging experts, so my discussion centers on the conventional brightness histogram.

The K10D can always provide a histogram in Playback mode: Press the INFO button to see the screen where the histogram is displayed. If you want to see a histogram in Instant Review and in Digital Preview as well, activate in the Playback menu using the same method as that was described for viewing the Bright/Dark area warning (see page 163). You can also deactivate at any time if don't want a histogram display.

Histogram Interpretation: Experiment by taking a photo and viewing its histogram. If the graph rises in the approximate pattern of bell-shaped curve–from the bottom left corner of the histogram to a peak in the middle, then descends to the bottom right corner–all the tones of the scene are captured. If the graph starts or ends too far up on either the left or right vertical axis of the histogram, so that the "slope" looks like it is sharply cut off, then the sensor is not recording data from those areas. Some loss of detail is inevitable when the contrast range is beyond the capabilities of the camera, for example a dark-toned subject surrounded by extremely bright sky or water.

When the histogram is heavily weighted towards either the dark or bright side of the graph, detail may also be lost in the sparser of the two areas. However, some scenes are naturally dark or light in tone. In these cases, most of the graph can be on one side of the scale.

To render detail in highlight areas, control exposure so the slope on the right reaches the bottom of the graph before it hits the right vertical axis and "drops off" that side. If a scene includes detail elements in shadow areas, manage exposure so that the left side of the slope reaches the bottom of the histogram before it hits the left vertical axis, realizing that the "real" world is not perfect and you can't always produce a perfect histogram.

Check the histogram after taking a shot and, if necessary, re-shoot using a plus or minus EV (exposure) compensation setting. Then check the histogram again for the new image. Also see whether the compensation has produced any undesired blown-out highlights or blocked-up shadows by checking for the blinking warnings. Of course, when shadow detail is most important, you may need to tolerate some loss of detail in the brightest areas, and vice versa.

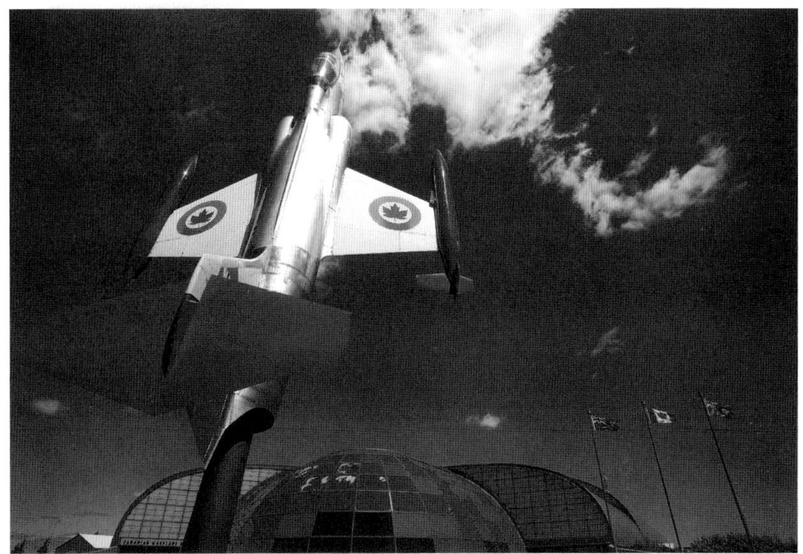

The Brightness histogram indicated the first version of this photo was overexposed in the light areas. A second shot was taken using -2/3 EV compensation.

Both the Bright/Dark area warning and the Brightness histogram provide feedback on exposure and contrast. Once you review the information they provide, you can choose to reshoot the image with a different exposure and/or contrast level. Although some people count on "fixing" exposure problems with software after downloading image files into the computer, you can't add detail that was never captured in the first place. Whether shooting JPEGs or RAW files, always get the best image possible in camera.

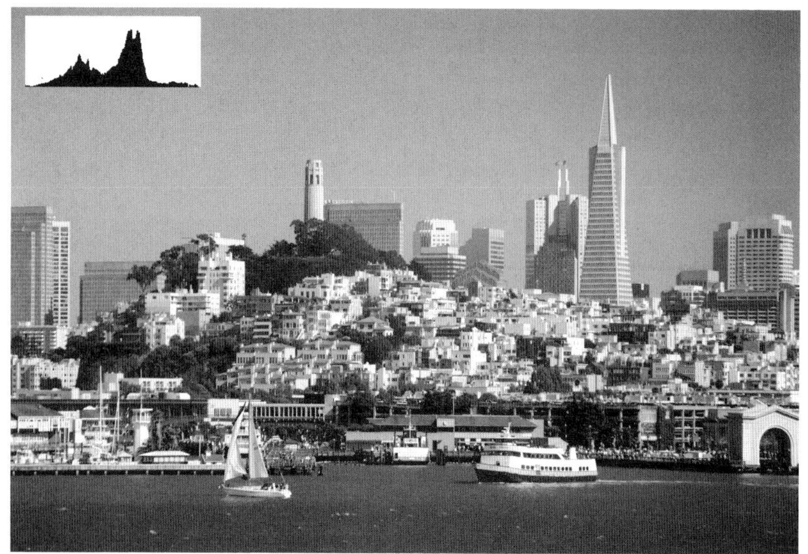

Image A

Image A: If the graph rises from the bottom left corner of the histogram, then descends towards the bottom right corner, all the tones of the scene are captured. (There may be a few peaks and valleys involved, but the graph still rises from the left and ends very close to the right axis). The image will include pure black, pure white, and a good distribution of mid-tone, for an exposure that's correct overall.

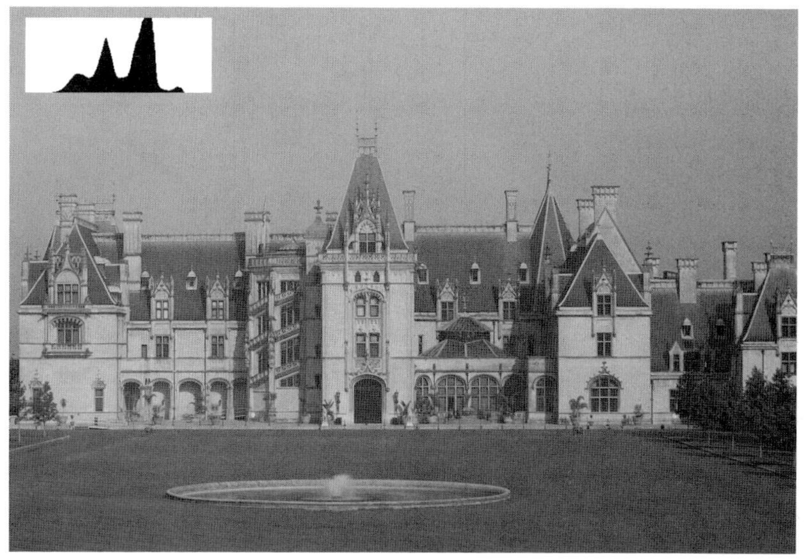

Image B *© Kevin Kopp*

Image B: With some images, the slope will drop before it reaches either the left or right side of the scale. In other words, the graph starts too far in from one or both edges. This indicates that the image does not contain rich dark blacks or bright pure white tones. (Remember, black is represented on the left of the graph and white on the right.)

The image consists primarily of mid-tones and grayish blacks and grayish whites. This does not necessarily mean poor exposure; it may represent low contrast. That's easy to correct in the computer, or by setting a slightly higher contrast level in-camera (see page 84). Of course, you may decide to set some plus or minus exposure compensation before taking the shot again. That will produce brighter whites or darker black tones.

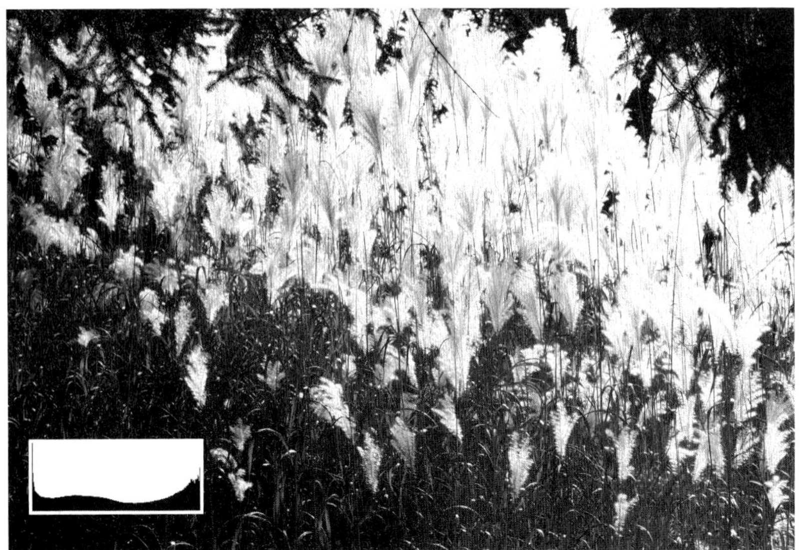

Image C

Image C: With extremely high-contrast subjects (including very dark shadow areas plus very bright highlights), the histogram may show a slope that is cut off at both ends. This indicates that detail will be lost in both highlight and shadow areas. Dark sections of your photo may be dense black, and brighter sections may appear completely washed out.

Try re-shooting an image of this type, using a low contrast setting in-camera. For nearby subjects, try using flash to even out the lighting for gentler overall contrast. If the light is changing, wait until a cloud covers the sun, moderating excessive contrast.

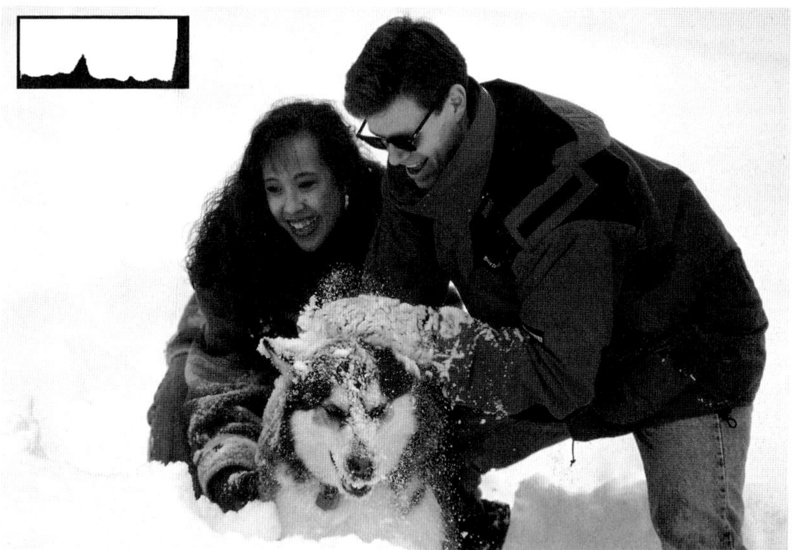

Image D

Image D: In some images, a scene in snow for example, you'll definitely want texture or detail in highlight areas. In those cases, be sure the slope on the right reaches the bottom of the graph before it hits the right side. Otherwise, the image will not hold detail in bright areas of the photo; these details will be blown out as demonstrated in the white portions of this shot of a couple with their playful dog after a new snowfall. Re-shoot using EV (exposure) compensation.

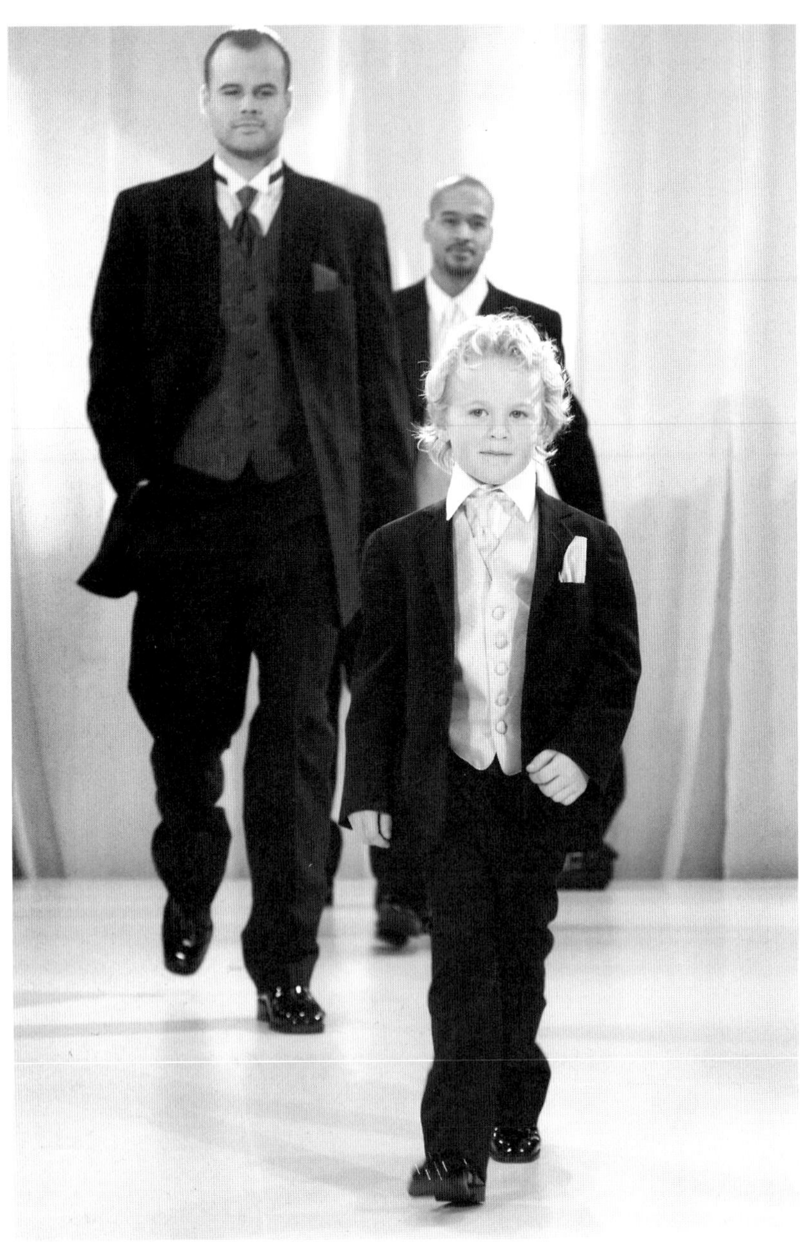

Flash Photography

Electronic flash is not just a supplement for insufficient lighting; it can also be a great tool for creative photography. Flash is highly controllable, its color is precise, and the results are repeatable. However, many photographers shy away from using on-camera flash because it can be harsh and unflattering, and taking the flash off the camera used to be a complicated procedure with less-than-sure results. The sophisticated flash options available with the Pentax K10D–especially when it is used with a compatible accessory flash unit–eliminate many of these concerns. Remember too, the LCD monitor provides instantaneous feedback, showing whether the flash exposure was right or not. You can make adjustments if you are not satisfied with the flash or ambient exposure.

Despite all the automation, it is still helpful to understand the basics of how flash photography works. The following is an overview of some of the basic principles of flash photography.

The Inverse Square Law

It's not difficult to understand one of the essential concepts at work with flash photography. This is, as light travels away from its source it also spreads outward, losing intensity. Consequently the Inverse Square Law, a fundamental principle of light, says that light intensity is reduced by a factor of four as the distance from a source, in this case your flash unit, doubles. Thus, the light level drops dramatically according to distance. In fact, if you take a picture

⇦ *Light from a flash decreases in intensity as it travels away from its source. Thus, the flash that was positioned to light the front of this image exposed the boy more than it did the man in the back.*

three feet from your subject, then move six feet away from the subject, you will need four times as much light to maintain the same level of exposure.

Guide Numbers

Guide numbers (GN) are a comparative reference used to quantify the flash output. They are expressed in feet and/or meters for a particular ISO–ISO 100 is often used in specifications. For example, Pentax states that the ISO 100 GN for the K10D's built-in flash is 36.3 in feet (11 in meters). The formula to determine guide numbers is GN = distance x aperture. So (according to the Inverse Square Law), a flash unit with a GN of 100 in feet (30.3 in meters) puts out four times the amount of light as one with a GN of 50 in feet (15.15 in meters). When using an accessory flash that's equipped with a zoom head, the GN will vary with different zoom-head settings. Fortunately, in this automatic age, people rarely need to work with guide numbers other than for the purposes of comparing the power output of flash units when shopping.

Flash Synchronization

The K10D has a focal plane shutter that consists of two shutter curtains. When you press the shutter release, the first curtain opens to uncover the camera's sensor and the second curtain covers it. The shutter speed determines the length of time between the first curtain opening and the second curtain closing. To take a photo with flash, the flash must fire when the camera's first shutter curtain is open across the entire frame and before the second curtain begins to close. The fastest speed at which the flash fires while the shutter is fully open is called the flash synchronization speed or sync speed. The highest sync speed possible with the K10D is 1/180 second. Whether you're using the built-in flash or a dedicated accessory flash, the camera will not let you set a shutter speed faster than the

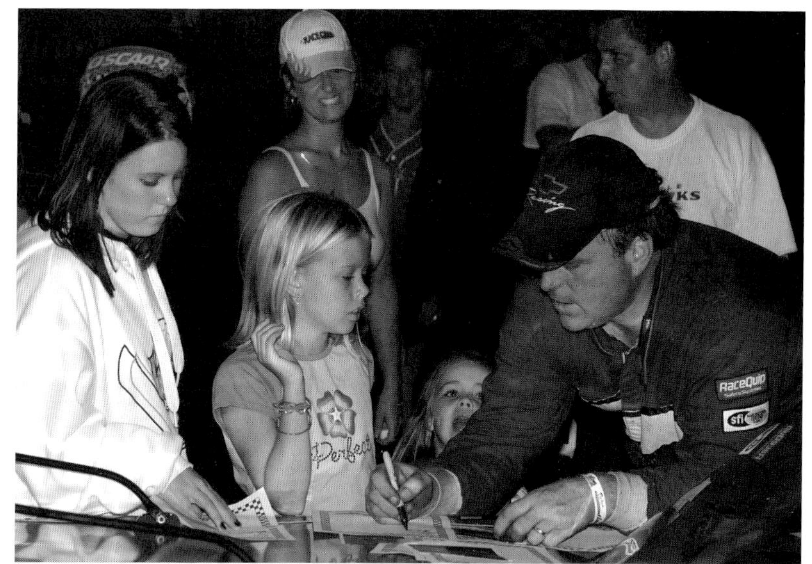

The built-in flash uses sophisticated P-TTL metering to compute exposure. As long as the subject is within range of the flash, your photos should be properly exposed.

sync speed. (Some accessory flash units have a high-speed sync function, which allows the use of flash with faster shutter speeds, but this involves rapid pulsing of the flash, not just a single burst. See pages 203-205.)

Flash with Camera Exposure Modes

Flash modes are selected by pressing the Fn button to access the Fn menu. You can select a mode using the camera's four-way controller: *Flash On* (or Auto Discharge mode), *Flash On + Red-eye, Slow-speed sync, Slow-speed sync + Red-eye,* or *Trailing curtain sync*.

Note: Not every flash mode is available in every camera exposure mode (see the list on the next page).

Flash Modes with Camera Exposure Modes

Green Mode: Auto Discharge, Auto flash+Redeye reduct

P Mode: Flash On, Flash on+Red-eye, Slow-speed sync, Slow-speed sync+Red-eye, Trailing curtain sync

Sv mode: Same options as in P mode

Tv mode: Flash On, Flash on+Red-eye, Trailing curtain sync

Av Mode: Same options as in P mode

TAv mode: Flash On, Flash on+Red-eye, Trailing curtain sync

M mode: Flash On, Flash on+Red-eye, Trailing curtain sync

B mode: Flash On, Flash on+Red-eye, Trailing curtain sync

X mode: Flash On, Flash on+Red-eye

Using the Built-in Flash

To use the built-in flash, you must activate it by pressing the flash up button. Next, press the Fn button to access the Flash mode Fn menu and select a mode (see list above) using the four-way controller.

Thanks to P-TTL flash metering, you can get good results with the built-in flash. P-TTL is a digital version of TTL (through-the-lens) flash metering; the P designates pre-flash. Before a photo is actually taken, the flash unit generates a short burst of light to determine subject distance and reflectivity (brightness). The flash metering system uses the 16

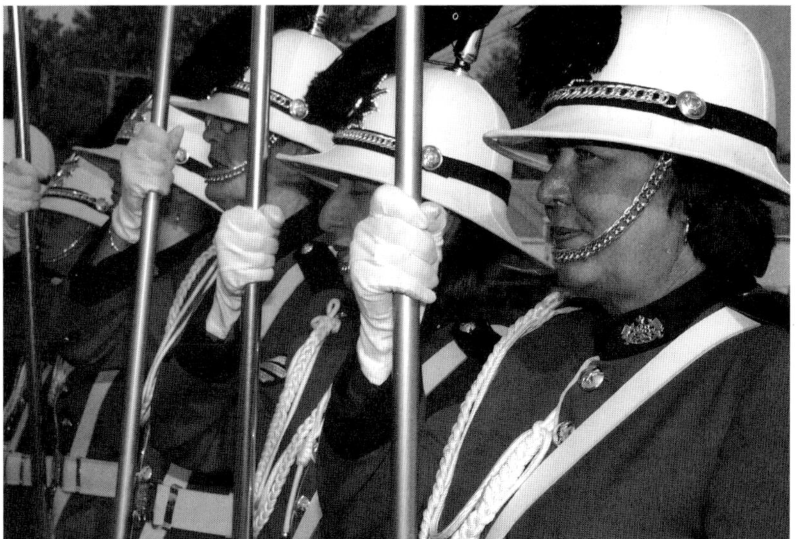

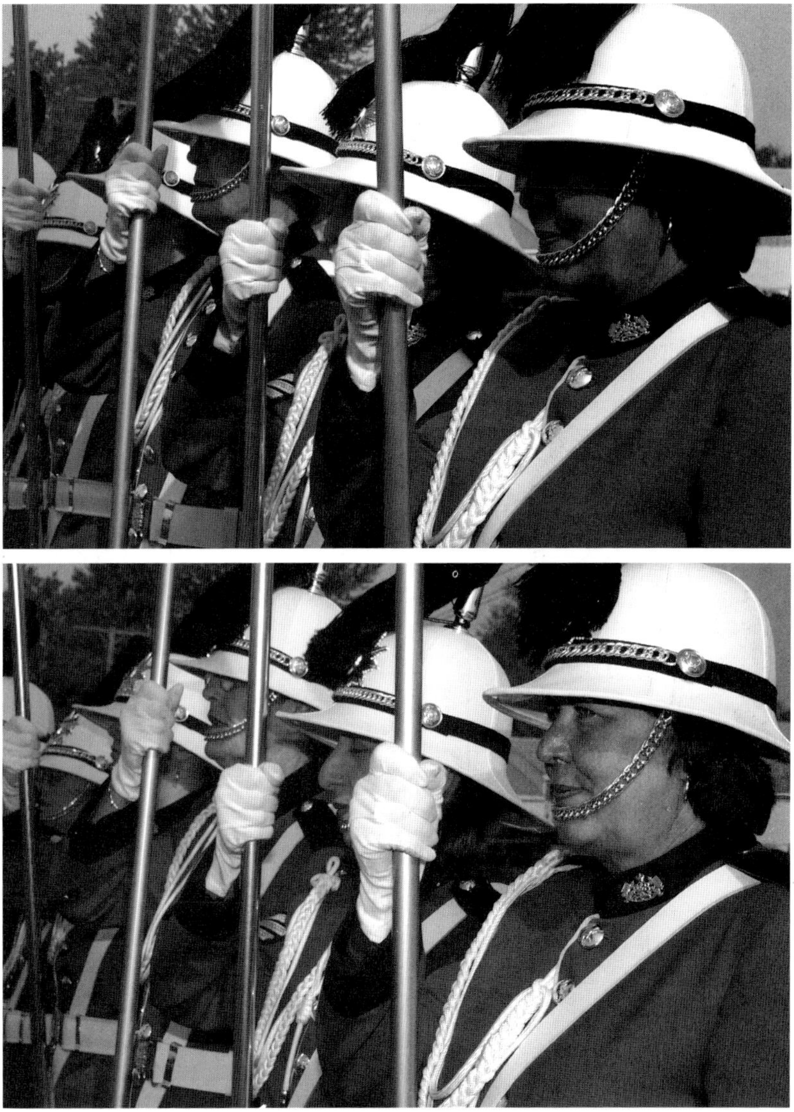

Flash is often useful outdoors for filling in shadow areas and lowering the overall contrast gradient of a scene. As you can see from the strong shadows and high contrast in the top photo, it was taken with existing light only. In the bottom photo, flash was used with -1 flash exposure compensation, so that the light from the flash would remain secondary to the existing light in the photo. Fill flash with flash exposure compensation usually gives the most natural looking results.

zone Multi-segment light meter. A microcomputer analyzes the scene based on the pre-flash to determine the appropriate light output for exposure. Most of your flash exposures will be fine, unless the subject is unusually light or dark, or is located against a very bright or dark-toned background.

Hint: Light, highly reflective subjects may produce underexposed flash photos, while very dark, deep subjects and can cause overexposure. Check your images on the LCD monitor. If an image would benefit by adjusting the flash intensity, set plus or minus flash exposure compensation (see pages 184-186).

Flash photography is particularly easy in the fully automatic Green mode. When the flash is charged and ready to fire, as confirmed by a lightning bolt symbol in the viewfinder data panel, the camera automatically sets the aperture and sync speed. The flash power output, or intensity, is automatically adjusted. The image should be well exposed as long as your subject is fairly standard and within the flash range (see chart page 181).

You cannot take additional shots while the flash is recycling or charging and the lighting bolt is blinking (unless you have set the *On* option in the *Release When Chrging* Custom function item (see page 116). When the blinking stops, the flash is ready. Remember, that the built-in flash draws power from the camera's battery. Frequent flash use will reduce battery life. Thus, it's always a good idea to carry a charged spare battery if you plan to shoot flash pictures.

Note: When in Green mode, you cannot select the *On* option in the *Release when Chrging* item of the Custom Setting menu.

Lens Compatibility with Flash

The K10D will accept many types of lenses (see pages 218-222), but not all camera functions work with older lens types. This is also true with flash. If you use a lens that does not allow you to lock the aperture ring to A, the built-in flash will always fire at maximum output. Exposure can be adjusted by changing the aperture for the flash-to-subject distance using the GN formula (see page 174) or the chart on page 181. Since this is cumbersome, we recommend using only DA, DA*, D FA, FA J, FA and F series lenses if using the built-in flash.

Also note the additional compatibility issues when using the built-in flash:

- It is incompatible with the DA Fisheye 10-17mm zoom.

- It is compatible with the 17-28mm fisheye zoom, but you'll get dark corners (vignetting) at focal lengths of less than 20mm.

- When using the FA*28-70mm f/2.8 AL or the DA16-45mm f/4 ED AL zoom, vignetting will occur when using focal lengths shorter than 28mm if the subject is less than 1 yard (1 meter) from the camera.

- Pentax warns that the built-in flash should not be used with the following lenses: FA* 250-600mm zoom, DA 14mm f/2.8 lens, FA* 300mm f/2.8, and FA* 600mm f/4lens.

- The soft focus lenses, FA Soft 28mm and FA Soft 85mm will cause the built-in flash to fire only at maximum output. Exposure can be adjusted by calculating the correct aperture for the distance using the guide number formula.

Note too that a lens hood may block some of the light from the built-in flash; this can be a problem especially when the subject is less than about 6 feet (2 meters) from the camera. Check your photos if using a lens with a hood attached; if the problem has occurred, remove the lens hood and re-shoot.

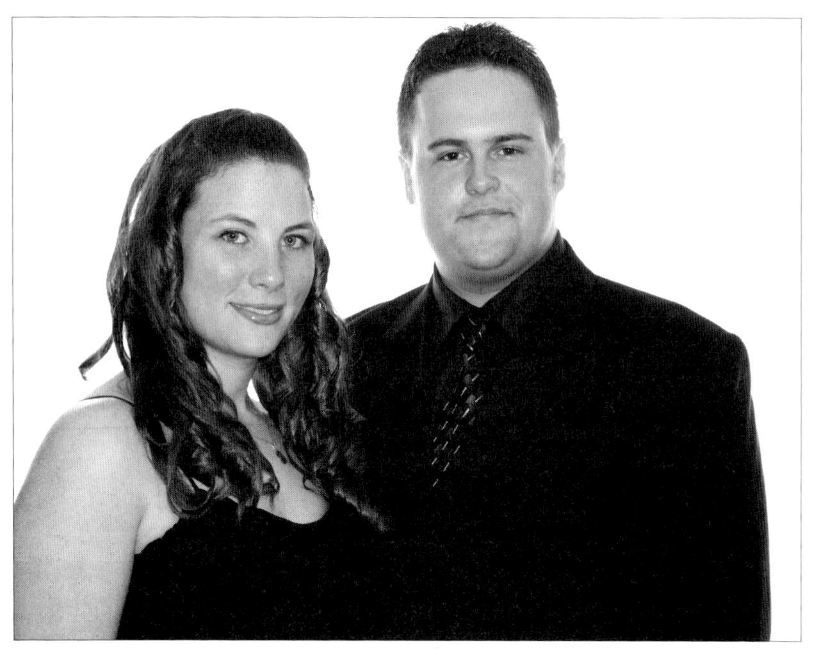

Particularly at ISO 400, the built-in flash has plenty of range for most indoor photography because subjects are usually not too far from the camera. A well-exposed ISO 400 image made by the K10D will exhibit little or no evidence of digital noise.

Flash Range

The built-in flash is not particularly powerful, but it has adequate range for most typical snapshots and people pictures. For optimal results at ISO 100, Pentax recommends it for subjects that are about 2-1/4 feet (0.7 meters) to 13 feet (4 meters) from the camera. The flash will adjust the exposure automatically as the subject is within this range. As with any flash unit, the effective range varies with the aperture that's used: it's greater at larger apertures (f/4 for example) than at smaller ones (f/11). Effective range also varies depending on the ISO–at higher ISO settings, the flash range will be greater.

Built-in Flash Shooting Range

ISO	f/stop	Max. Distance (ft)	Max. Distance (m)
100	2.8	12.9	3.9
	4	9.0	2.7
	5.6	6.4	1.9
	8	4.5	1.4
	11	3.3	1.0
	16	2.2	0.7
200	2.8	18.4	5.5
	4	12.8	3.9
	5.6	9.2	2.8
	8	6.4	1.9
	11	4.6	1.4
	16	3.2	1.0
400	2.8	26.0	7.9
	4	18.2	5.5
	5.6	13.0	3.9
	8	9.1	2.7
	11	6.6	2.0
	16	4.5	1.3

Hint: Photocopy this chart and carry it in your camera bag along with the wallet card found in the back of this book. And don't ignore the minimum range. Moving very close for a frame-filling close-up–especially when using a high ISO setting–can produce excessively bright flash photos.

While the flash range is much greater at higher ISOs, remember that image quality will be lower due to increased digital noise at ISO 800 and, particularly, at ISO 1600. Consequently, you might consider buying the more powerful Pentax AF540FGZ or AF360FGZ accessory flash units. These have a substantially higher GN so they provide much greater effective range than the built-in flash. This will allow you to shoot at lower ISO settings for superior image quality.

Accessory Flash Units

The K10D supports full-featured flash photography with the compatible accessory flash units such as the AF540FGZ or AF360FGZ. With these you can take advantage of all of the many options discussed in this chapter, including P-TTL flash metering, wireless off-camera P-TTL flash, high-speed sync speed flash, bounce flash, and advanced off-camera setups for sophisticated flash effects.

Older Flash Units

Older Pentax flash units designed for the 35mm cameras will only work with the K10D in a limited capacity. The camera will trigger the flash but will not necessarily provide a correct flash exposure. More recent Pentax flash units designed for 35mm cameras will provide basic (non-TTL) autoflash operation if they include an Auto mode. Auto flash uses a sensor on the flash unit to measure the flash exposure. It is not a TLL system, however. It will work with older lenses if you use the maximum distance/ISO/aperture recommendations provided with the flash unit.

Older flash units also work in a fully Manual mode. However you will have to use information provided with the flash unit on distances and settings at a given ISO. You can also calculate the exposure with the GN formula (see page 174), or use a separate flash meter.

Pentax changed its TTL flash system to P-TTL system when it first began the preliminary design work on digital SLR bodies several years ago. The older TTL flash units were ideal with film based cameras, but due to the difference in reflective properties between film and the filter in front of a CCD, the new flash metering system involving the use of a preflash was required. Now, Pentax manufactures only the FG and FGZ-series flash units. These can also be used on certain Pentax 35mm SLRs; when one of these units is mounted on a camera that does not support P-TTL metering, it reverts to standard TTL flash.)

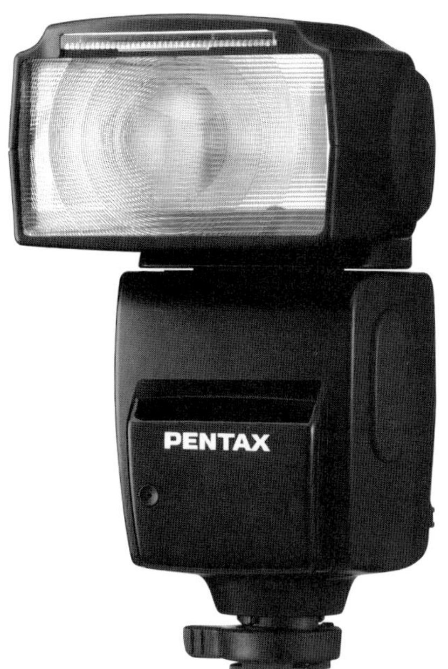

Pentax AF540FGZ

Pentax Flash Units

Pentax AF540FGZ: This is a large P-TTL model with high power output. Its ISO 100 guide number (GN) is 177 (feet)/54 (meters) at the longest zoom-head setting. This model features an illuminated LCD data panel, wide-angle diffusion panel (for use with very short lenses), focus-assist illuminator, plus several creative-flash functions. In addition to conventional upward tilt/bounce capability, this unit also tilts 10° downward for close-up photography, and can be rotated to the side for bouncing flash from a wall or diffuser.

When it's mounted on a digital SLR camera, the AF540FGZ's power zoom head will match focal lengths from 13mm to just under 57mm (it automatically adjusts for the reduced format of the digital sensor). Do note that the built-in wide-angle diffuser must be used for coverage of 13mm, 14mm, and 15mm focal lengths.

Pentax AF360FGZ

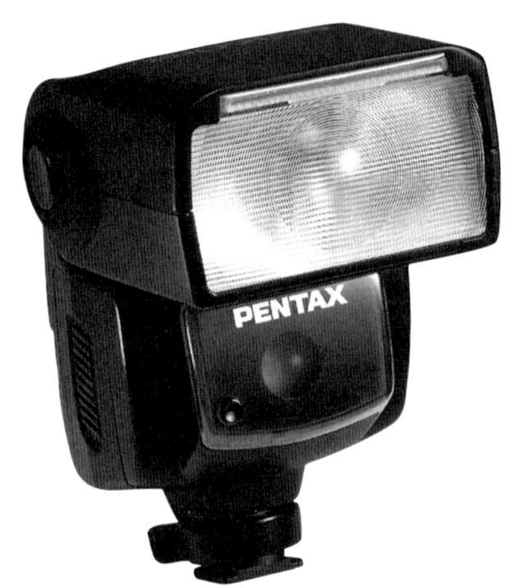

Pentax AF360FGZ: This is a more compact P-TTL unit with lower power output. The ISO 100 GN is 118 (feet)/36 (meters) at the longest zoom-head setting. It cannot swivel to the right or left and is equipped with slightly different controls than the AF540FGZ.

Controlling Flash Exposures

Before discussing the specifics of flash photography, let's consider the essential override, flash exposure compensation. This feature is similar in concept to conventional exposure compensation (for ambient light) except that it only increases or decreases the flash intensity. Press the Fn button to access the Fn menu, and select the icon for Flash modes ϟ . While that screen is visible in the LCD monitor, rotate the camera's rear e-dial to set the amount of flash exposure compensation from a range of -2 to +1. Press the OK button to confirm your selection.

While a dedicated flash unit will often provide good to excellent results without the use of overrides, flash exposure compensation can often be useful. In this case, a +1 level was employed to prevent underexposure and to make a "high key" image, one that consists primarily of whites and light tones. ➪

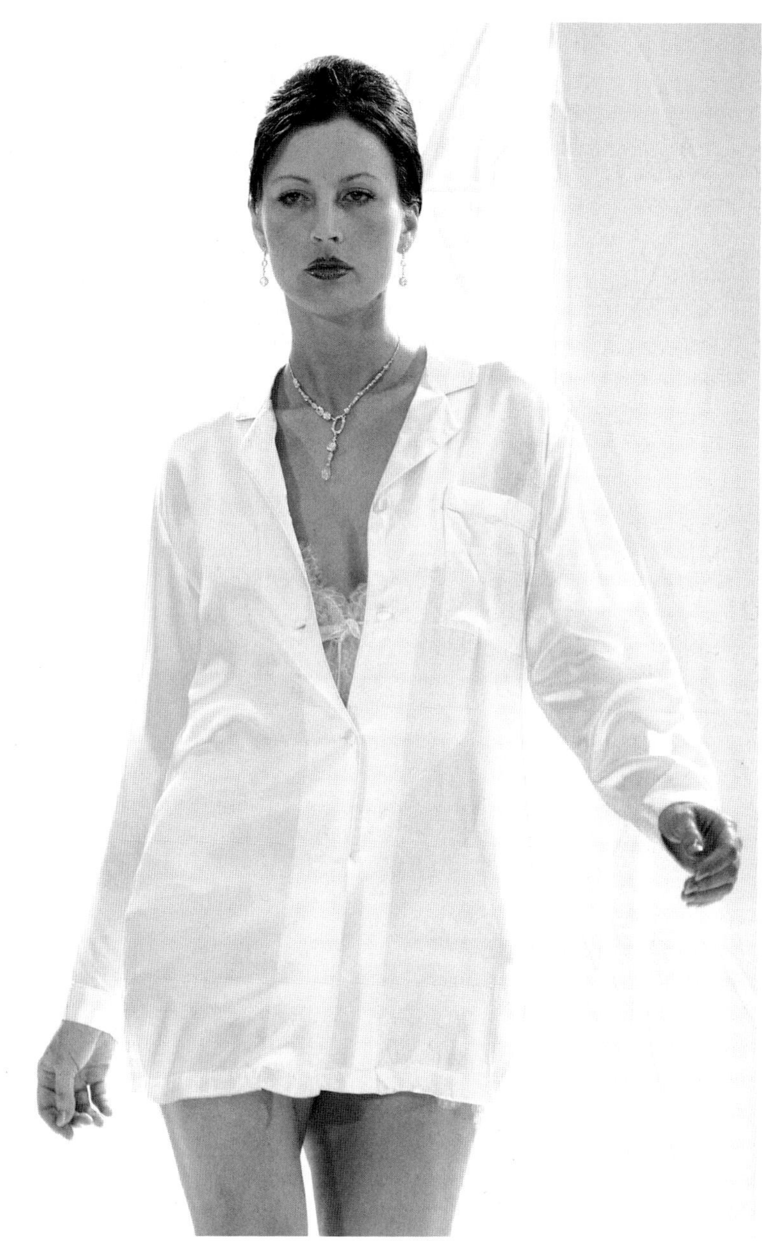

Any flash exposure compensation setting will affect the output of the built-in flash or any (fully compatible) accessory flash that you use. (If you set flash exposure compensation on both the camera and an attached accessory flash unit, the setting made on the accessory flash will take priority.)

If the flash exposure of a nearby subject is too dark, set a + flash exposure compensation factor. If the flash exposure of a distant subject is too dark, the subject is probably beyond the range of the flash unit. If setting a +1 level does not solve the problem, move closer or set a higher ISO level, increasing the effective flash range. (Digital noise is increased in images made at very high ISO.)

Flash exposure compensation is useful for fine-tuning flash exposures at any time. You'll probably use it most often to produce a very subtle flash effect in outdoor photography, with a -1 level setting for example. In extreme close-up photography, you may need to set a -2 level so the light from flash will not be excessive; if that does not solve the problem, then you are too close to the subject. Move further back or use off-camera flash–set further from the subject–as discussed later in this chapter.

Note: Flash exposure compensation is not available when the camera is set to the Green mode. If you had set compensation in another mode, it will revert to zero if you switch the camera to Green mode.

Note: You can also set Exposure bracket while flash is active to make three images, each with a different exposure, as discussed on pages 157-158. When the flash is on, this exposure bracketing only affects the light from the flash, not the ambient light exposure.

Camera Exposure Modes

Whether you're using the built-in flash or a fully compatible accessory Pentax unit, you can shoot with any of the camera's available exposure modes. For a list of flash modes that are available with the various camera exposure modes, see page 176.

Flash in Green Mode

As described earlier, operation is fully automatic in this mode. The camera makes all settings and it disables any flash overrides that you had set. Once activated, the flash will fire only when the metering system determines it is necessary. The use of flash in Green mode is most suitable for snap shots or when a less experienced person is using the camera.

Flash in P Mode

In the Hyper-program mode, the camera will automatically set an appropriate shutter speed and aperture as a starting point, but you can change either or both settings if desired. You can choose any available aperture and any shutter speed from 30 seconds to 1/180 second. The camera will not allow you to select aperture/shutter speed combinations that are certain to produce badly over or underexposed images. For example, when ISO 1600 is set on a sunny day, you will not be able to set 30 seconds and f/4 because that would definitely produce an excessively bright image.

In very dark or very bright conditions, watch for a warning signal in the viewfinder: a blinking line of numerals in the data panel. If that appears, the camera is indicating that it cannot produce a good flash exposure. Select a higher ISO in low light or move closer to the subject, or both. In extremely bright light, set a lower ISO and/or select a smaller aperture (larger f/ number) until the blinking stops.

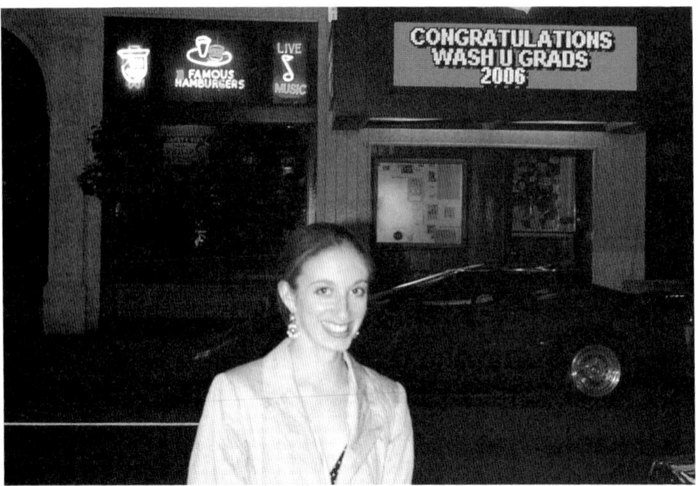

Flash works wonders for night pictures of people in front of city lights or sunsets. Just select a shutter speed and ISO for the background exposure, make sure the aperture will provide adequate depth of field, and let the P-TTL system take care of the flash. If you need to use a long shutter speed, you should use a tripod or other camera support. The flash will freeze the person in the foreground. © Martha Morgan

Flash in Av Mode

In the Aperture Priority mode, you can select any available aperture and the camera automatically sets an appropriate shutter speed. However, the slowest shutter speed selected by the camera will depend on the lens focal length in use; this is intended to minimize the risk of blurring from camera shake. During my tests, the camera never set a shutter speed longer than 1/30 second at a 16mm focal length, even in extremely dark locations when I set f/22. At 50 to 100mm focal lengths, the camera set a shutter speed of 1/60 second with flash. When longer telephoto lenses are used, the shutter speed will be faster, up to 1/180 second, helping to reduce the risk of blurring from camera shake.

Note: If you do want to use long shutter speeds in Av mode, simply select the Slow-speed sync as the Flash mode in the Fn menu (see pages 195-196). Then the camera can set shutter speeds as long as 30 seconds.

In the standard flash mode, the safety feature reduces the risk of blurring from camera shake that may occur at long shutter speeds. The problem is, your images may be underexposed (too dark) if shooting in dark locations at low ISO and small apertures. *No advance warning of underexposure is provided by the camera in Av mode.* If using an accessory flash with an LCD data panel, check the flash range in the distance scale in advance. If using the built-in flash, check your photos in the LCD monitor.

The best solution is to switch to the Slow-speed sync mode and mount the camera on a tripod if you really must shoot at low ISO and if you must use very small apertures in dark locations. Otherwise, set a higher ISO level and/or a wider aperture, such as f/4 instead of f/22. That should help to produce well exposed flash photos at the longest shutter speed that the camera will set in Av mode using standard flash modes.

Flash in Tv Mode

When using flash in the Shutter Priority mode, you can select any shutter speed and the camera will set the appropriate aperture. You can set shutter speeds as short as 1/180 second or as long as 30 seconds. (There is no need for Slow-speed flash in Tv mode.) The shutter speed cannot exceed the maximum flash sync speed, so the K10D will simply not allow you to set a shutter speed faster than 1/180 second. (Later, on pages 203-205, we will discuss high speed sync, available with the FGZ series flash units for flash at faster shutter speeds.)

The camera does not provide any advance warning in Tv mode if the exposure will be incorrect at the shutter speed that you have selected. Let's say that you select a 30 second shutter speed on an extremely bright day when using ISO 1600 in flash photography. Overexposure will definitely occur. Conversely, if you select a 1/180 second shutter speed in night photography with a distant subject when using ISO 100, underexposure may occur. In either case, no advance warning will be provided.

Refer to the hints in the Av mode section (see page 188) about checking the flash range or reviewing flash photos on the LCD monitor. If the effective range is not suitable for the subject, set a different shutter speed and/or ISO; in low light also move closer to the subject.

Try Long Exposures with Flash: Unless you select a shutter speed that is much too long or much too short for the lighting and the ISO in use, changing the shutter speed will not affect the flash exposure. However, it allows you to control how ambient light will be rendered. This is especially useful when you have a flash lit subject in front of a somewhat dark background that you want to be rendered naturally. An example would be your subject in front of a city scene at dusk or a beautiful sunset. If you don't intentionally use a long shutter speed, the picture will probably have a flash-lit subject against a very dark or black background.

Make sure you use a tripod when shooting at long shutter speeds to prevent blur due to camera shake. Tv mode, or Slow-speed flash in another operating mode, is also useful when you want to render ambient light motion-blurs and a sharp flash-exposed subject. You should set the camera for Trailing curtain sync mode (see page 196) and use a long shutter speed to capture the ambient exposure of the moving subject. The camera will produce an image with light trails that follow a sharp subject (illuminated by the brief burst of light).

Flash in Sv and TAv mode

The Sensitivity Priority (Sv) mode is not a very useful choice for general flash photography since its primary purpose is for quick selection of ISO levels using the K10D's rear e-dial. The camera sets both the shutter speed and aperture providing no control over either of those aspects. As well, the aperture/shutter speed combination does not change very much regardless of the ISO you select in Sv mode.

When you select the Shutter and Aperture Priority (TAv) mode, the camera automatically switches to Auto ISO (automatic ISO level selection). It allows you to select any aperture/shutter speed combination, even if those settings will produce serious over or underexposure. *No advance warning is provided in the viewfinder.* This mode is most useful when using an accessory flash unit with an LCD data panel that allows you to check flash range in advance, after you set an aperture/shutter speed combination.

Note: Because a high-power flash unit has a great range even in dark locations, the risk of underexposure is not great in TAv mode, based on my extensive testing. Even in almost total darkness indoors, with a subject 15 feet from the camera, I got good flash exposures at f/22 at 1/180 second, when using the AF540FGZ. The camera set an ISO 400 level and that was adequate. The same finding applies when using other exposure modes and setting small apertures and/or fast shutter speeds in low light. When the camera was set for ISO 400, none of my images was underexposed in the conditions used for informal testing with the most powerful Pentax flash unit.

The risk of *over*exposure is greater; that can certainly occur in extremely bright light–in other operating modes too–especially if shooting at a very wide aperture, particularly at a high ISO setting, with a nearby subject. If you wish to use that technique, plan to use the high-speed sync mode available with the AF540FGZ and the AF360FGZ (see pages 203-205).

Flash in M Mode

When using flash in the camera's Manual mode, you set the desired aperture as well as shutter speed up to the top sync speed of 1/180 second. Using Manual mode for flash photography provides more creative control. The photographer can adjust the relationship between the flash and ambient light. In Manual mode, the exposure scale in the K10D's viewfinder operates, but it only provides a reading for the ambient light in the scene.

If you want the lighting on the subject and the background to be balanced, set the shutter speed and aperture for correct ambient light exposure. If you wish to make an

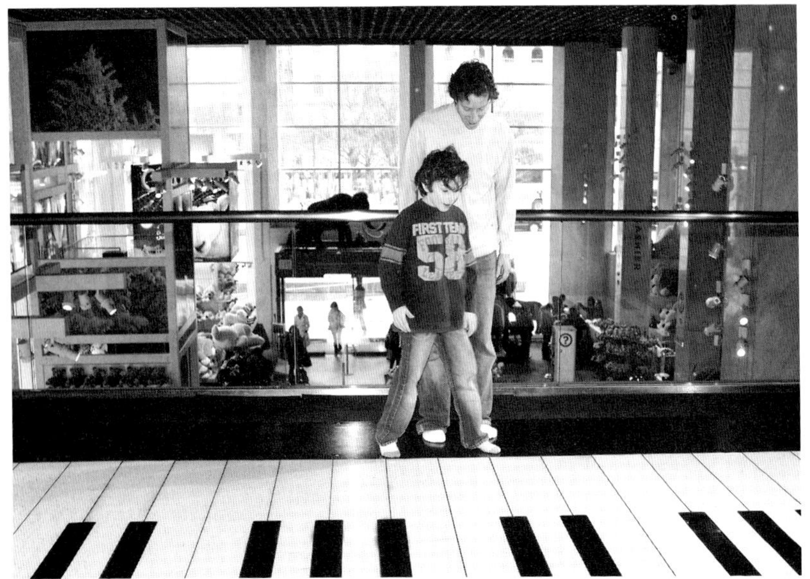

The camera's M mode can be useful in flash photography when you want great control over the "look" of your image, particularly background brightness. For this photo, a bright background was important for a natural effect and that was easy to achieve by selecting a shutter speed, 1/60 second in this case.

image with a brighter or darker background, you can adjust the shutter speed or aperture. A longer shutter speed provides a brighter background. To set off your subject against a darkened background, use a faster shutter speed or a smaller aperture. (If you close down the aperture, make sure the subject distance is still within the flash range. Since flash range is affected significantly by the aperture, be cautious in adjusting the aperture. It is better to adjust the shutter speed as much as possible.) Watch the scale in the viewfinder and stop making adjustments when the marker indicates a desired level of difference between subject brightness and background brightness. If the marker on the scale indicates -2 for example, the background will be about 2 stops darker than the subject illuminated by the flash.

The scale provides data in a +2 to -2 EV range. In many typical conditions, the brightness of the background is not substantially higher or lower than the subject brightness, so the +2 to -2 scale should be adequate. If the background brightness is substantially different than subject brightness–common in very dark locations or with extremely bright backlighting–the plus or the minus symbol at an end of the scale will blink as a warning.

Think about the flash range especially after setting small apertures when using low ISO levels; the camera provides no advance warning that the settings will underexpose the shot. Also check your photo on the LCD monitor. If it's dark, set a wider aperture or a higher ISO. When using one of the compatible accessory flash units with a data panel, check the effective flash range before taking a photo. As in other exposure modes, the range varies depending on the ISO, the aperture, and the position of the flash unit's zoom head.

Other Flash Options

In addition to selections already discussed in detail, let's consider the other options for flash photography, selectable in the Fn menu: Red-eye reduction, Slow-speed sync, and Trailing curtain sync. These are available with both the built-in flash and the fully compatible accessory flash units.

Red-Eye Reduction

This feature is recommended for use when photographing people or animals in dark locations. When selected, the flash unit fires a burst of light intended to reduce the size of the subject's pupils and minimize the red-eye syndrome. (With pets this is often a blue or green effect, but the cause is the same.) After the pre-flash, the actual flash burst is fired in order to take the actual photo. This feature is occasionally successful in reducing red-eye when used with the built-in flash, but people tend to be annoyed by the bright pre-flashes.

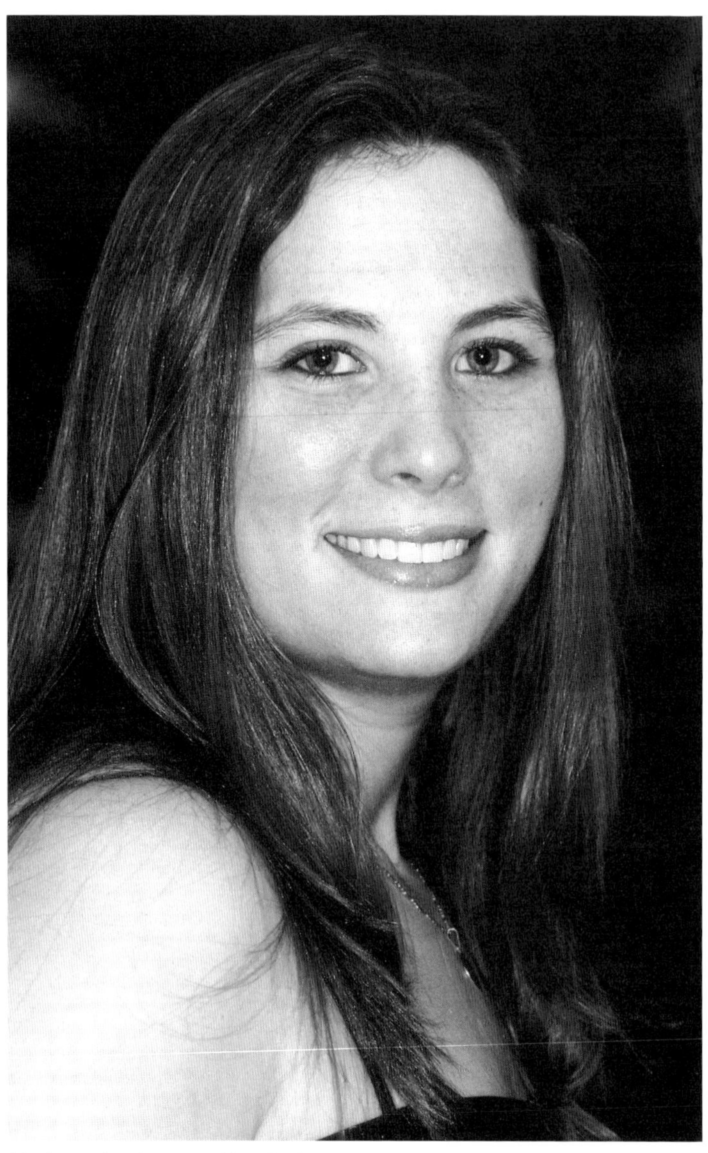

Red-eye is always a big challenge in portrait photography with flash. While there are methods for minimizing the effect, it's easy to correct a photo if your image editing software offers an automated red-eye correction feature; Elements 5.0 was used for this photo.

Note: Do not set the Red-eye reduction flash mode in wireless off-camera flash photography. If you do so, the preliminary burst of light (intended for red-eye reduction) will trigger the remote flash unit.

I do not recommend using Red-eye reduction mode unless you find that the camera/flash produces terrible red-eye in certain circumstances. There are two drawbacks. The bright pre-flash may cause your subjects to blink or appear unnatural. And there is a short delay from the instant that you press the shutter release until the actual exposure is made; during that time, your subjects' expression may change.

Effective Ways to Reduce Red-eye:

- Ask the subject not to look directly at the lens.
- Turn up the room lights to cause the iris in the eye to close down reducing the risk of red-eye.
- Use an accessory flash unit that sits higher above the camera, and hence, further from the lens; a greater flash to lens axis distance minimizes red-eye.
- Using an accessory flash unit, bounce the light from a ceiling or wall if your flash unit includes a tilt or swivel head feature.
- Use wireless off-camera flash (see pages 201-203); hold the remote flash unit above and to one side of your subject.
- Use the red-eye correction tool if that is available in your image-editing software program.

Slow-Speed Sync

As discussed earlier in this chapter, you can set a long shutter speed for flash photography in several of the camera's exposure modes without the need to set the Slow-speed sync feature. However, you may want the camera to automatically set long shutter (sync) speeds in some circumstances for greater simplicity. When you activate this feature in P, Sv, or Av mode, the camera will set a long shutter speed whenever flash is active. A second flash mode, Slow-speed sync + Red-eye, works in the same manner, but simply activates the red-eye reducing pre-flash. The actual shutter speed will depend on the scene brightness and the ISO that has been set.

On a bright sunny day for example, especially at ISO 400 or higher level, the camera will not set a very long shutter speed. In a dark location however, especially at low ISO levels, the shutter speed will be quite long. That can be several seconds long in a dark room, for example.

Do note however that Slow-speed sync is not available when the camera is set for any other exposure mode: this feature does not appear as a flash mode option in the Fn menu. When you're using the Tv, TAv, or M exposure modes, you would need to specifically set a slow shutter (sync) speed if you want to use flash while making a photo using a long exposure. In the fully automatic Green mode, the camera does not allow for slow-speed sync at all.

This function can be useful when taking photos of a nearby subject lit by flash against a distant, not excessively dark, background. For example, use this setting to photograph a person with a nighttime cityscape in the background. The long exposure time will record the ambient light in the scene without affecting the flash exposure. Use a tripod to avoid blur from camera shake and have your subject remain still during the entire exposure.

Trailing Curtain Sync

A feature that's generally called rear curtain sync, this function causes the camera to fire at the end of an exposure, and not at the start of an exposure as it does in conventional flash photography. This feature can be selected in any camera exposure mode except Green. When it's set, the camera will automatically activate slow-speed sync as well in P, Av, or Sv modes. When you're using the Tv, TAv, or M exposure modes, you would need to specifically set a slow shutter (sync) to take advantage of Trailing curtain sync. (At normal "fast" shutter speeds in flash photography, the flash effect would be the same with or without trailing curtain sync.)

When used for shooting moving subjects at long shutter speeds (preferably 1/15 second and longer), this feature produces the effect of motion streaks that follow the subject instead of preceding it. Some photographers also use Trailing (or rear) curtain sync for long exposures of static objects or people, moving the camera to produce interesting flash blur effects.

Motion Blur–How It Works: In order to create motion trails that follow an object instead of preceding it, the flash must be fired at the end of the exposure with Trailing curtain sync. If the flash is fired using the standard flash mode (usually called front curtain sync), the moving object is "frozen" at the beginning of its travel and then the motion trail is recorded. This captures the action but the motion trail appears to be in front of the moving object. However, if the flash fires just before the shutter closes, the camera will record the ambient light motion blur and then freeze the object. Thus, the photo will appear natural, with the motion trail following the object. This technique can produce dramatic action shots, so take the time to experiment with your camera and flash until the effects you want become second nature.

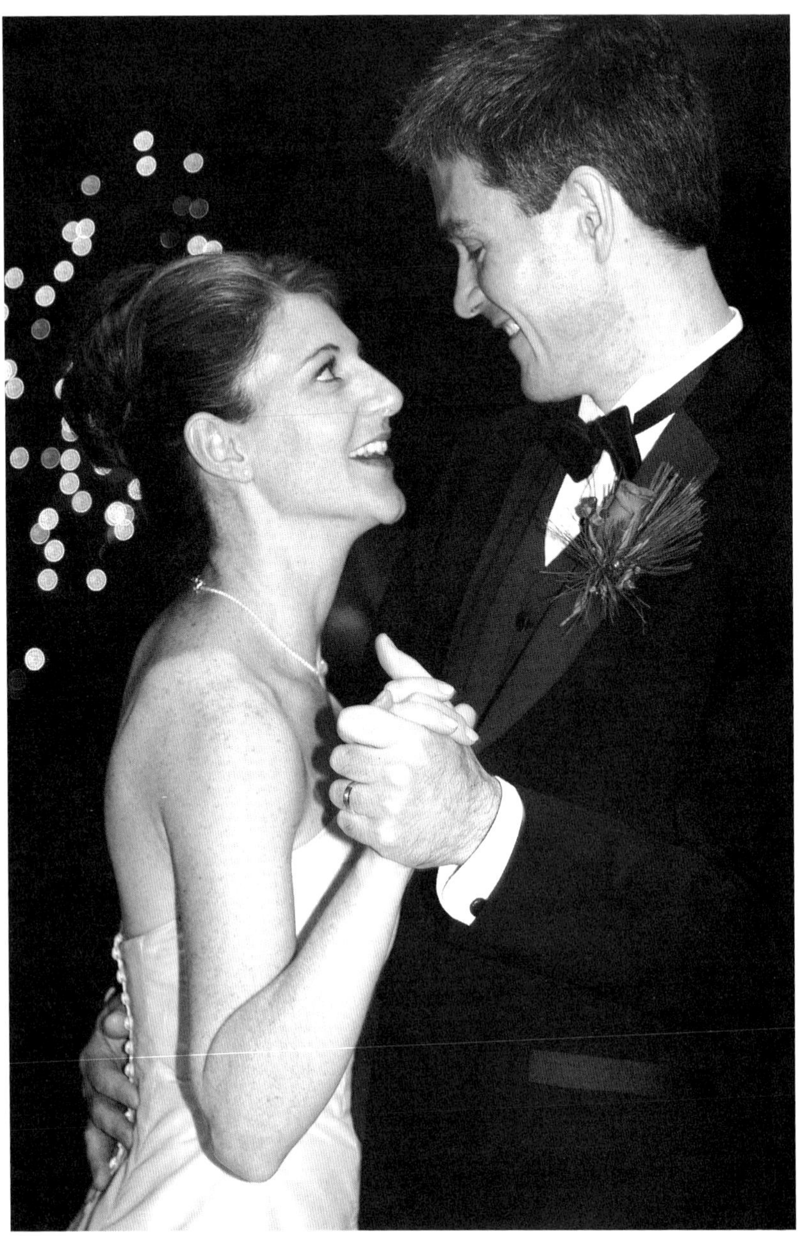

Off-Camera Flash

While on-camera flash is certainly convenient, serious photographers often prefer to use off-camera flash for more sophisticated flash lighting effects. The K10D can be used with one or more off-camera flash units using connecting cables or with Wireless P-TTL Flash when using the Pentax AF540FGZ or AF360FGZ flash unit. Let's consider each of these distinct options individually.

Wired Off-Camera Flash

This technique requires three optional accessories, the Hot Shoe Adapter F, the Off Camera Shoe Adapter F and a long or short Extension Cord F5P. Attach the Hot Shoe Adapter F to the camera's hot shoe and attach the Off Camera Shoe Adapter F to the bottom of a flash unit. Then, connect the two accessories with the Short (3 foot) or Long (9.5) foot Extension Cord F5P. When the hookup is finished, you can hold the "remote" FGZ-series flash unit wherever you wish. You can also mount it on an accessory flash bracket (made by aftermarket accessory manufacturers) or on a tripod; the Off Camera Shoe Adapter F accessory includes a built-in tripod mount.

Off-camera flash, mounted on a bracket on the right side of the camera, was used for this image. While a higher flash position would have caused the shadows to drop down more and been even less obvious, it would have required the use of an assistant.

All of this is simpler than it sounds and the setup extends power and full automation–including P-TTL flash control–from the K10D to the remote flash unit. When you turn the camera on, flash photography works in exactly the same manner as if you had mounted the FGZ-series flash unit in the camera's hot shoe. There is one additional benefit however: the built-in flash unit can be popped up and it will also fire when the remote unit fires. (That is not possible when a flash unit is in the camera's hot shoe; only the accessory flash can be used in that case.)

You can also use two or more off-camera AF540FGZ and/or AF360FGZ flash units. For each additional remote flash that you want to connect, you'll need an extra Hot Shoe Adapter F, Off Camera Shoe Adapter F and a long or short Extension Cord F5P. Connect the remote units as described in the instruction manual that accompanies the accessories and you can fire two or more remote flash units; the built-in flash will also fire if it's in the up position. This is no more complicated than using one wired off-camera flash, but can lead to a tangle of connecting cords.

Contrast Control Sync Flash

Pentax provides an additional flash feature that is available when at least two flash units (including the built-in flash if that is being used) are active in wired off-camera flash photography. When you connect one external flash unit and also activate the built-in flash, or when you connect two or more external flash units to the K10D, a contrast control option becomes available. This allows you to control the intensity of each flash unit.

In its most basic form, this feature can be used when you connect one AF540FGZ or AF360FGZ to the K10D using the accessories described in the previous section. (Contrast control flash is not available in wireless off-camera flash photography.) On the remote flash unit, set the sync mode to Contrast-Control-Sync option. Set the K10D for the P, Tv, Av, or M exposure mode using the mode dial. Activate the remote flash and pop up the built-in flash. Now, the flash output ratio will be automatically set to 2:1. In other words, the remote flash unit will provide two thirds of the light while the built-in flash will provide one-third of the total amount of light.

Wireless/Remote Flash

The K10D also allows for remote flash without the need for the adapters and extension cord using wireless communication that maintains P-TTL flash control. In its simplest configuration, this allows you to position an AF540FGZ or AF360FGZ off camera and it will be triggered automatically by a burst of light from the built-in flash or a hot shoe mounted flash unit. That concept is often referred to as "slave" flash.

Flash Firmware Update: Originally, the K10D did not allow for triggering a remote flash unit using the built-in flash. An on-camera accessory flash unit was required for that purpose. Subsequently, Pentax developed new firmware that would allow the camera to do so. The new firmware, Version 1.10, available for download and installation by any K10D owner who does not already possess that version or higher (cameras made since about mid January 2007 are already equipped with Version 1.10. Check the Pentax website from time to time to see if even higher versions of the firmware, that may include this plus additional features, have been.)

To activate that feature, scroll to the Flash mode item in the Fn menu and select Wireless mode as the option. Now, the built-in flash can trigger a remote flash. (When the built-in flash–instead of an on-camera FGZ unit–is used as "the trigger", High speed sync flash will not operate.) If you cannot find Wireless mode as an option, your K10D is still equipped with the older version of the firmware; make enquiries through a Pentax Service center in your country (or check their website) for information on where to find new firmware and how to download and install it to your K10D.

You also get two options when using the on-camera flash to trigger the remote unit. Access the Custom Setting menu and scroll down to the *Flash in Wireless mode* item. Two options are available under "Built in flash works as master discharge". If you select *ON*, the built-in flash will trigger a wireless remote flash unit and it will also provide some of the total light. If you select OFF, the built-in flash will fire only a brief (barely visible) burst that will trigger the remote flash but will not add to the total amount of flash lighting.

Wireless Remote Flash Techniques

Whether you use the built-in flash or an on-camera FGZ flash unit to trigger off-camera flash, the procedure is similar. However, there is some additional complexity when using an accessory flash as "the trigger"; the procedure is discussed at length in the flash owner's manual and is beyond the scope of this book about the K10D. Initially, we recommend using the built-in flash and one off-camera FGZ flash unit. In that case, follow this procedure:

1. Hold or place to remote flash unit in the desired location. Turn the power switch to Wireless instead of the standard ON.

2. Set the wireless mode of the remote flash to S, denoting Slave and the channel to 1 so the LCD screen shows Slave 1. Also set the FGZ flash unit's zoom head to a wide angle or telephoto setting as desired. (While experimenting, try using the 34mm zoom head setting.)

3. Turn the camera on and set it to any desired exposure mode.

4. Scroll to the Flash mode item in the camera's Fn menu and select the option for *Wireless*; also set the desired option under the "Built in flash works as master discharge" custom function. Both steps were discussed in the previous section.

Metering control is P-TTL, making it quite easy to get good flash exposures without any calculations. The flash exposure compensation control (discussed in the next section) of the built-in flash and the remote flash unit remains functional. You can use that feature if you want more output (plus level) for greater brightness or less output (minus level) for a more subtle flash effect.

Initially, practice with a single remote flash unit. If you own two of the compatible FGZ flash units, try more advanced setups with one illuminating the subject and the other illuminating the background. (Follow the procedure for making the appropriate settings on both of the remote units as detailed in the flash owner's manual.) Make sure that both remote units maintain line of sight with the on-camera flash and are no further than 13 feet (4 meters) from the K10D. To be certain that your setup will work well, take a test shot.

Wireless Flash Range

Wireless flash photography works best indoors, in a location that is not excessively bright. It's important to position the remote flash unit so it's not too close to, or too far from, the subject. As well, the remote flash should not be too far from the camera; otherwise, it may not be triggered.

The remote flash-to-subject distance should be no less than 2.6 feet (.8 meters). The maximum distance between flash and subject will vary depending on the power of your flash unit. It will also vary depending on the aperture you have set on the camera and the ISO level in use.

Note: When you return to conventional flash photography, do not use the camera's wireless flash mode. Set the accessory flash unit to ON instead of Wireless. Select one of the camera's other flash modes, using the Fn button.

High-Speed Sync

When using an AF540FGZ or AF360FGZ accessory flash, the K10D allows for high-speed sync, the opposite of slow-speed sync; it's available only when the camera is set to the Tv or M exposure modes. This allows for flash at shutter (sync) speeds faster than 1/180 second, which is otherwise

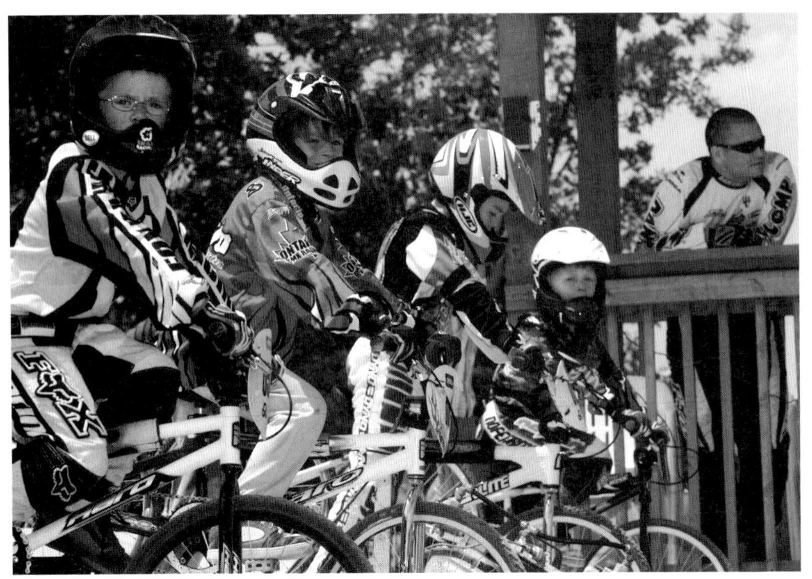

Since the camera's top sync speed is a high 1/180 second, you won't often need to use high-speed sync. Still, it could be useful for fill flash on extremely bright days.

the fastest shutter speed available for flash photography. When high-speed sync is active, the flash unit does not fire a single burst of light when the shutter is open; instead, it fires short, lower intensity bursts as the curtain travels across the image plane.

To activate high-speed sync, simply set the accessory flash unit to the HS mode. Set a fast shutter speed, such a 1/250 second. To prevent underexposure, use this technique only in bright lighting conditions. In darker locations, conventional flash should be used.

Fast shutter speeds are associated with stopping subject motion, consequently people may mistakenly think high-speed sync is for photographing moving objects with flash. It is not. This setting is useful when you want to use flash for a subject in bright sunlight, especially with a large aperture (such as f/2.8). Typical situations are when you want to use flash to fill shadows or balance the overall exposure latitude of a scene. When using flash at the conventional 1/180 second sync speed, it is likely the image would be overexposed. Using a fast shutter speed controls only the bright ambient light exposure and prevents it from overpowering the flash exposure. By making the photo with a faster sync speed, such as 1/500 second, you can correctly expose for the ambient light and flash.

When experimenting with HS, use the camera's Shutter Priority (Tv) mode and set a desired shutter speed, such as 1/500 second on a very bright day. Check the information on the flash unit's data panel as to flash range. (At high shutter speeds, flash range is very short unless a high ISO level has been set.) If the range is not suitable for the camera-to-subject distance, select a different shutter speed and check the data panel again. Setting a higher ISO level in the camera can increase the effective flash range at any shutter speed.

Although you can select shutter speeds (sync speeds) as fast as 1/4000 second, you'll rarely need to use anything faster than about 1/500 second. The flash unit's guide number is dramatically reduced when you use high-speed sync as you select faster shutter speeds. This limits the flash range. Unless you're using a very high ISO setting for extreme close-ups in very bright sunshine, a sync speed of 1/250 second to 1/500 second will often be perfect when shooting at wide apertures.

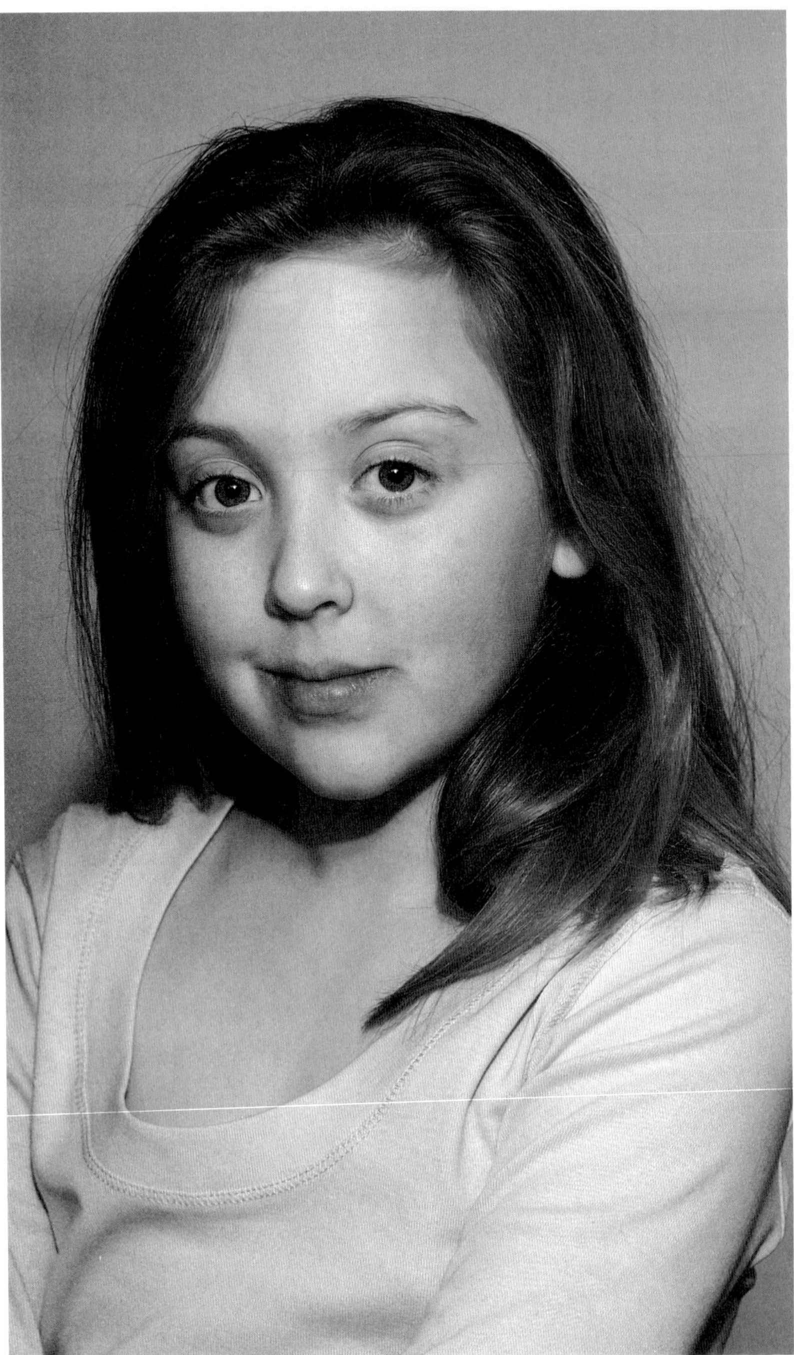

Bounce Flash

Direct flash can often be harsh and unflattering, causing heavy shadows or a "deer in the headlights" appearance in your subject. Bouncing the flash diffuses the light to soften it and create a more natural-looking effect.

The Pentax AF540FGZ and AF360FGZ feature heads that are designed to tilt for bouncing flash from a ceiling, for example. The AF540FGZ can also swivel, for bouncing flash from a wall beside the subject. Either technique can be useful for allowing a shoe-mounted flash to be adjusted so it is not aimed directly at the subject. Experiment by pointing the flash toward the ceiling at a point about halfway between the flash and the subject. If the head also swivels, try bouncing the flash light from a wall as well. Either technique can produce softer lighting. However, the ceiling and walls must be white or light neutral gray or they may cause an undesirable color cast.

Note: When you bounce flash, the LCD data panel will not show the effective flash range. Nor is such data published in owner's manuals because it depends on the distance from the camera to the bounce surface plus the distance to the subject. It also is affected by the condition of the bounce surface and how much light it absorbs. As a rough estimate, assume that flash range is about half of what it would be with direct flash photography. It can be greater than that if the bounce surface and subject are quite close, or less if the subject and/or the surface is very far from the camera or each other. After taking a photo, check the LCD monitor. If it's too dark, use a larger aperture or select a higher ISO setting to increase the effective flash range.

Bouncing the flash off a ceiling not only softens the quality of the light, but also directs it to fall on the subject from above, making it appear more natural. Always make sure that the bounce surface is neutral to prevent unwanted color casts. © Simon Stafford

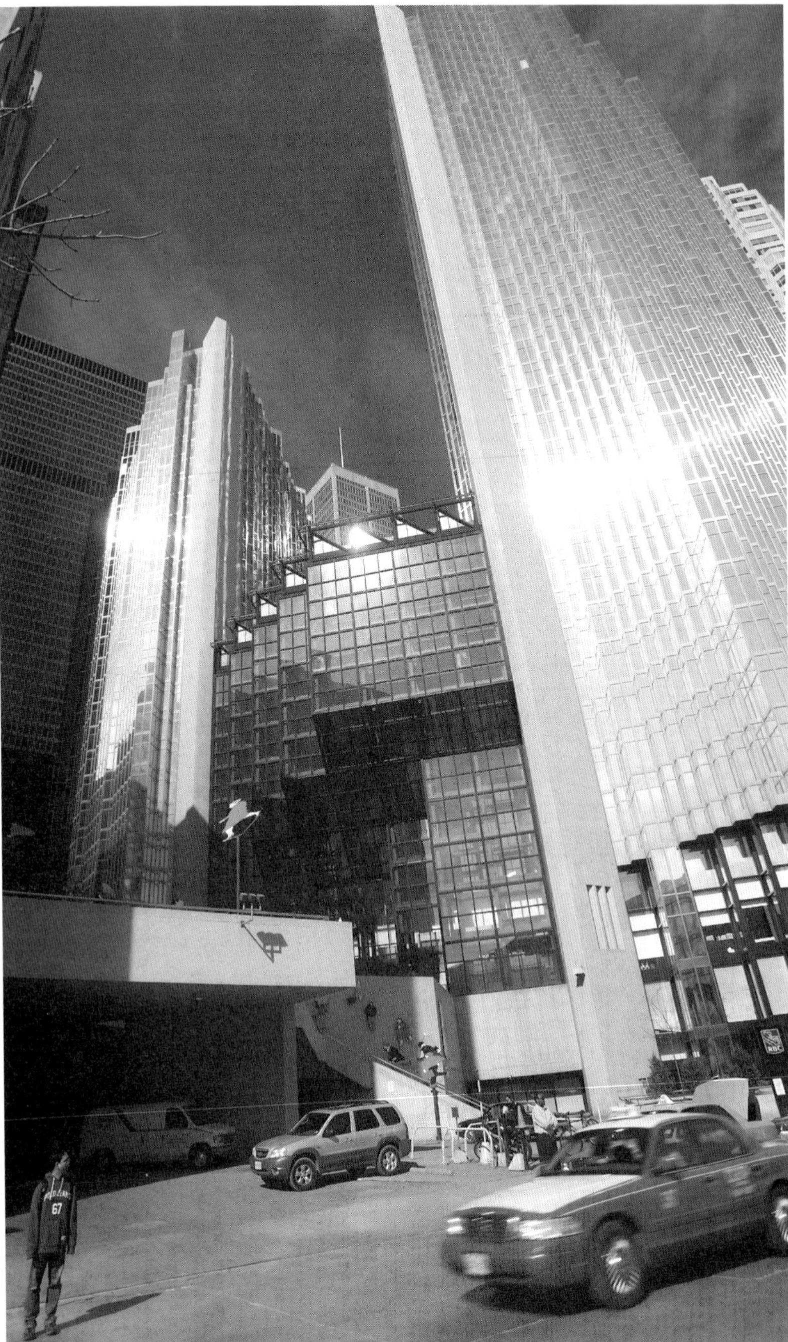
RBC
67

Lenses and Accessories

Composed of various types of multiple elements, modern lenses focus light rays on a plane (the sensor in the K10D). But lenses have several other essential functions. They control the amount of light that will make an exposure, the range of acceptable sharpness within a scene (depth of field), the focus, the subject magnification, and the angle of view (the amount of any scene which will be included in the image). You should think hard about your specific photographic needs before adding a lens to your system. The focal length and design of a lens will have a huge affect on how you photograph. The right lens will make photography a joy; the wrong one will make you leave the camera at home.

One approach is to determine if you are frustrated with your current lenses. Do you constantly want to see more of the scene than the lens will allow; do you love to shoot interior scenes? Then consider an ultra wide-angle lens such as the 12-24mm model. Or maybe the subject is often too small in your photos because it is far from the camera. Then look into acquiring a telephoto lens such as the DA 50-200mm f/4-5.6 ED, or the longer 100-300mm zoom. Many people like wide-angles for landscapes, but telephotos can come in handy for isolating the most appealing elements of a distant scene. And if portrait photography is your main interest, think about lenses with focal lengths between 60 and 90mm, although some photographers appreciate the effects produced by a 135mm lens.

It's certainly possible to make ultra wide-angle images with a digital SLR such as the K10D, although you'll need to purchase an extremely short focal length, such as 12mm.

Note: This book assumes you are using a fully compatible lens, so it does not usually provide information on non-compatibility issues in discussions of the various camera features and functions. If you are using another lens type, be sure to note the information about functionality limitations with the K10D (see pages 218-222).

Effective Focal Lengths

If the sensor in a digital camera is smaller than a 35mm film frame (36 x 24 mm), the field of view (or angle of coverage) with any lens will be narrower than if that same lens were place on a 35mm camera. The smaller sensor is responsible for this field of view crop. In practice, this crop gives the lens a view that has more "telephoto effect" than it would on a 35mm camera. The result is sometimes referred to as "focal length magnification" and calls for a conversion factor to calculate the "effective focal length" on a full frame (35mm) camera.

That may sound complicated but is quite straightforward. At 23.5 x 15.7 mm, the K10D's sensor is smaller than a 35mm film frame. If you are used to using certain focal lengths on a 35mm camera, the focal length of a lens used on the K10D must be increased by 1.5x in order to visualize the field of view that you will get. For example, images made with a 20mm lens on the K10D will look like images made with a 30mm focal length on a 35mm film camera. A 300mm telephoto used on a K10D produces the field of view that we would expect from a 450mm lens on a 35mm camera.

That's great news if you practice sports and wildlife photography, where the K10D used with even a moderate telephoto lens can now produce frame-filling images of distant subjects. But it's less than ideal if you prefer wide-angle landscape or travel photography, with images that include scenic vistas. Fortunately, you can find short focal-length lenses such as the Pentax DA 12-24mm f/4 ED AL (IF) that produces the field of view that 35mm film photographers would expect from an 18-36mm zoom.

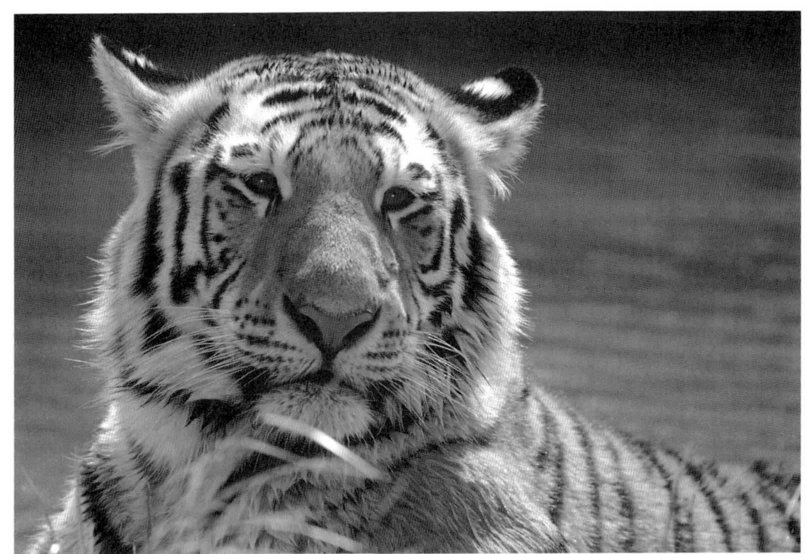

On the K10D, a 300mm focal length provides a super telephoto effect, useful when you don't want to get too close to your subject.

In fact zoom lenses, which you can adjust to cover a wide range of focal lengths, offer the advantage of versatility. A single zoom can replace several other lenses, making for greater convenience and portability, though zooms do have some limitations (see pages 217-218).

Note: Unless otherwise indicated, lenses will be referenced by their actual focal length, not their effective focal length.

High Tech Glass

Technology has brought welcome advances to modern lenses. Some of the current Pentax lenses bear an ED designation indicating that they include elements of extra-low dispersion glass. These modify the way that light rays are

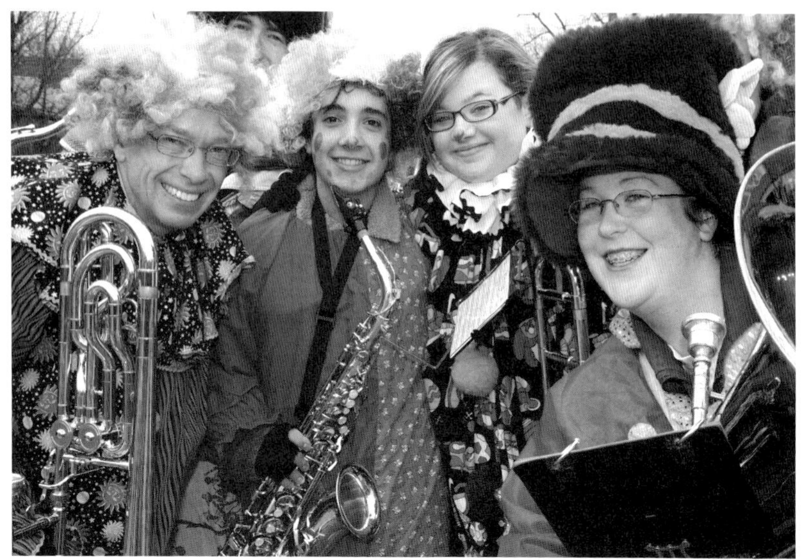

Designed and optimized for use with digital SLRs, the DA (and new DA series) lenses are not suitable for use with 35mm cameras. However, the K10D accepts nearly all lenses originally designed for 35mm film photography.*

bent, producing superior color rendition as well as higher sharpness across the entire image frame. The benefits are most obvious in images made at large apertures and long focal lengths.

An increasing number of wide-angle lenses, including some of the Pentax zooms and the single focal length Limited lenses, are designated as AL, indicating the use of element(s) with a non-spherical surface. Such "aspherical" lenses boast reduced flare, more consistent sharpness across the frame at large apertures, and less bending of straight lines near the edges of the image. A single aspherical element can take the place of two conventional elements, reducing size and weight of the lens.

Lenses for Pentax Digital SLRs

The digital-only DA and DA* lenses are optimized for use with a digital SLR camera, as is the D FA series. There are models available in wide-angle, standard (normal), telephoto, macro, and zoom focal lengths. Digital optimization minimizes vignetting (darkening at the corners), maximizes sharpness near the edges of the frame, and prevents internal reflections that can cause flare. The latter is achieved through the use of new chemicals applied in multiple layers to an increased number of optical elements. The digital optimization features are especially advantageous when using wide-angle lenses with digital cameras at apertures larger than f/8. Use of these lenses on 35mm film cameras will result in vignetting because these smaller lenses do not project an image circle that covers the larger 36 x 24 mm film frame.

Note: The FA J, FA (KAF or KAF2), and the F (KAF) series are multi-platform Pentax lenses, meaning they are suitable for both digital and 35mm SLR cameras.

Ultrasonic Focusing Motor

DA* lenses utilize entirely new Supersonic (ultrasonic) motors for faster, virtually silent autofocus operation and excellent starting/stopping response. Do note however, that the new technology is not compatible with all Pentax cameras. Only the K10D (and future Pentax D-SLRs) will provide autofocus when using one of the D* Supersonic lenses. With other cameras, only manual focus is available. The first three DA* lenses are wide aperture high-grade models with ED and/or AL optical elements: the 16-50mm f/2.8 ED AL (IF), 50-135mm f/2.8 ED (IF) and the 60-250mm f/4 ED (IF).

Types of Lenses

Normal Lenses

The focal length of a normal lens roughly corresponds to the diagonal of the format. With 35mm film, this measurement would be exactly 43.3 mm; but for design reasons, most normal lenses for 35mm SLRs are about 50mm. Because of the K10D's sensor size, a focal length of about 35mm becomes equivalent to the field of view you would get when using a normal 50mm lens on a 35mm film camera. Pentax does not currently make a 35mm focal length lens, but the digital-only DA 40mm f/2.8 Limited model is pretty close, just a bit longer than normal (a "short" telephoto).

If you use a zoom lens set for the 35mm focal length, subjects in the K10D's viewfinder appear about the same size as they look to the naked eye. However, if you want to achieve a closer view without moving physically closer to your subject, you will need longer focal lengths. Conversely, if you want to photograph a sweeping vista or a group of people inside a room, a shorter focal length will give a wider field of view.

Telephoto Lenses

Lenses with focal lengths that are greater than a normal lens are telephotos. In the case of the K10D, this would be any lens with a focal length greater than 35mm.

Telephoto lenses not only bring distant subjects "closer," they also compress perspective, reducing the apparent distance between objects in a scene. This is useful for creating interesting effects such as stacking near and distant hills or making a traffic-filled city street look especially congested. In addition, a telephoto's narrow angle of view often limits the number of components included in the image, eliminating clutter. In high magnification photography, depth of field is very shallow, so only the focused plane is sharp; that's useful for blurring away a distracting background, particularly at a wide aperture (small f/number). This makes a telephoto lens an excellent tool for isolating a subject and making it "pop."

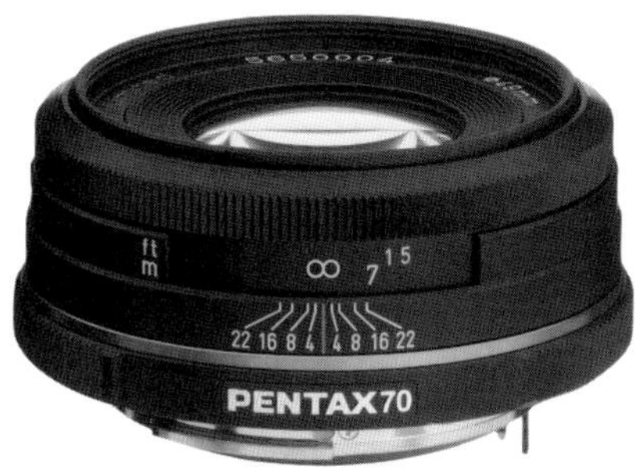

The Pentax DA 70mm f2.4 Limited lens is lightweight and designed exclusively for use with Pentax digital SLRs.

Moderate Telephoto Lenses: These are lenses from about 50mm through 135mm on the K10D. They often feature larger maximum apertures than longer lenses. In the current Pentax line, that includes several single focal length lenses: the very compact (digital only) DA 70mm f/2.4 Limited and multi-format FA lenses such as the 77mm f/1.8, 85mm f/1.4 (IF) and 135mm f/2.8 (IF). The longer two lenses are somewhat large because their wide maximum apertures require the use of large diameter optical elements. Lenses in the lower half of the moderate telephoto range are regarded as excellent portrait lenses.

Long Telephoto Lenses: With the K10D's smaller sensor, even moderately long telephotos from 135-300mm will give you quite a bit of reach. Such Pentax lenses, like the FA J 75-300mm f/4.5-5.8 zoom, are relatively compact, lightweight and affordable. Pentax also offers larger, pro caliber telephotos such as the FA 80-200mm f/2.8 ED (IF) and the FA 300mm f/2.8 ED (IF). Large maximum apertures make these useful in low light because they allow the camera to set fast shutter speeds with less need for high ISO levels.

Lenses with focal lengths greater than 300mm magnify the subject more than eight times and greatly compress perspective. The increased subject magnification and size of these lenses often exaggerate camera shake, but the K10D's Shake Reduction system is helpful in reducing this. Still, it is good advice to use a tripod or other form of support with these lenses.

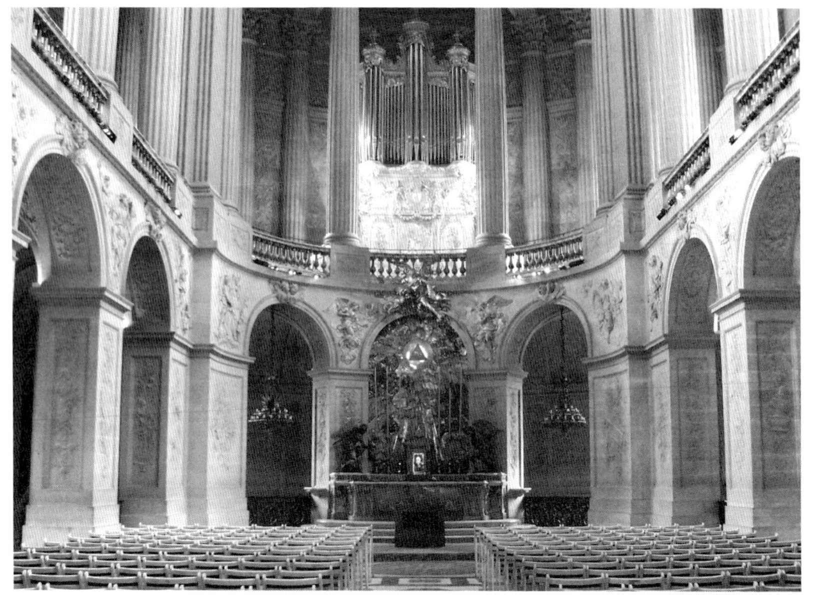

Wide-angle focal lengths are ideal for photographing interiors. Be careful to keep the back of the camera perpendicular to the floor to prevent convergence distortion or "keystoning."

Wide-Angle Lenses

Wide-angle lenses produce a broad field of view and expanded spatial perspective. Foreground elements become prominent while more distant objects are "pushed back," rendered smaller than the eye perceives. You can exploit this trait with a variety of subjects, including cramped interiors, yachts at a marina, or land and cityscapes. Depth of field is also extensive, so an entire vista can be rendered in reasonably sharp focus at moderately sized apertures.

A focal length of 16mm provides a wide, though not ultra wide, field of view that is often ideal for point-and-shoot photography. When trying to fit as much of a scene into your picture as possible, or while working in limited space, an even wider angle may be a better choice, such as the DA

12-24mm zoom. The DA Fish-Eye 10-17mm lens has even shorter focal lengths and can make images with a 180-degree angle of view. Because lines outside the center of the frame at not straight, this zoom is intended for creative purposes and is not an all-purpose wide-angle lens.

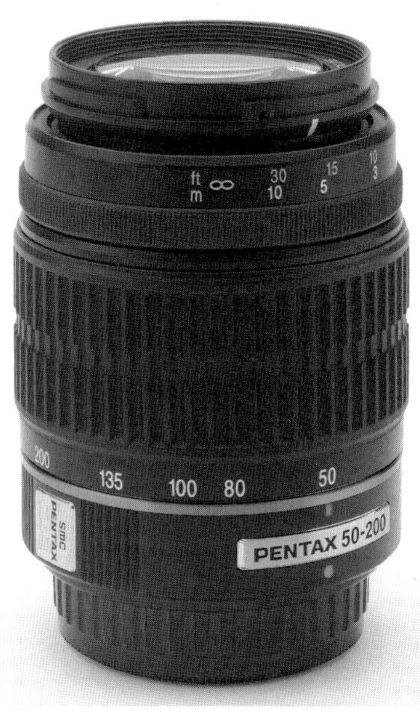

The Pentax DA 50-200mm f/4–5.6 ED zoom lens allows you to switch from auto to manual focus with a twist of the focus ring.

Zoom Lenses

Many single focal length (prime) lenses feature an aperture as wide as f/2.8, f/2.0, or even wider (though very long telephotos are often smaller). Zoom lenses, however, often have variable apertures with the maximum being relatively small. The Pentax DA 50-200mm f/4-5.6 ED zoom has a maximum aperture of f/4 at its short end that diminishes gradually as you zoom to longer focal lengths. At the 200mm setting, the maximum aperture is f/5.6. Except for a few fast professional models, such as the FA 80-200mm f/2.8 ED (IF) with a constant maximum aperture of f/2.8 though its entire zoom range, most zooms are slower than primes, meaning they feature smaller maximum apertures.

Consequently, you'll need to use a higher ISO setting for a fast shutter speed, and the images may exhibit more visible digital noise.

Note: Small maximum aperture is less relevant when shooting with the K10D, at least in terms of the shutter speeds required to prevent blur from camera shake. When using the Shake Reduction system, there is less need for fast shutter speeds. Still, in dark locations–and when a subject is moving–the shorter shutter speeds available when using a fast lens are certainly beneficial.

A wide aperture lens–whether f/1.4 or f/2.8–can be useful, but the trade-off is significant. There are many fewer choices, for one thing. The FA 80-200mm f/2.8 is much larger and heavier than the FA J 75-300mm f/4.5-5.8 zoom for example, and it's also a lot more expensive. That's why most lenses (in all brands of camera systems) feature moderate to small maximum apertures; these types outsell wide aperture lenses by a large margin.

If you need a lens with a maximum aperture of 2.8 and a focal length that's longer than 200mm, you probably need to buy a fixed focal length. Pentax makes several, such as the FA 300mm f/2.8 ED (IF) and an A 400mm f/2.8 ED (IF). For most photo enthusiasts, lenses that combine such wide maximum apertures and long focal lengths are prohibitively expensive and excessively large and heavy.

Lens Compatibility

The K10D can be used with a wide variety of lens types, including Pentax bayonet mount or thread mount lenses from 35mm camera systems. However, there are some camera functionality limitations that should be noted when using older lenses. Full compatibility with the K10D's advanced features requires a DA, DA*, or FA J series lens or a D FA, FA, KAF2, F, or A series lens with an "A" setting on its aperture ring. In that case, all the camera's features should function as described in this book.

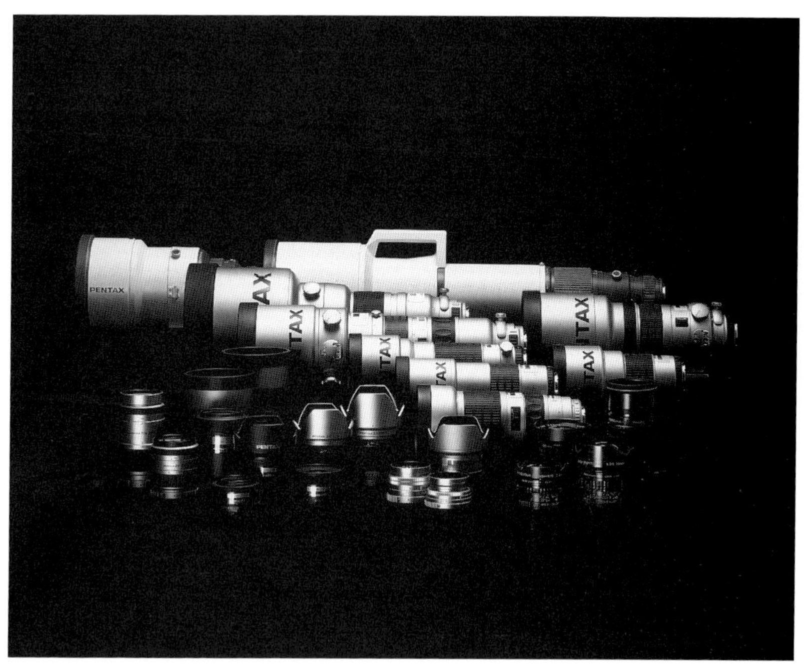

You can use many older Pentax lenses as well as the current models with your K10D. While autofocus lenses are required for all camera functions to operate, the level of compatibility is still remarkable.

Manual Focus KA Series Lenses

These offer full compatibility with three exceptions: (1) autofocus is not available, unless using the optional AF Adapter 1.7x; (2) only the single, central AF point will be active for AF or for manual focus confirmation; and (3) you'll need to provide focal length information when using the SR system (as discussed in the Shake Reduction section on page 101).

Older K Mount Lenses

When using any of the K mount lenses, or any screw (thread) mount lenses with Mount Adapter B, additional restrictions apply. Several other camera features will not be available, including Multi-segment metering, autofocus, and several of the K10D exposure modes. The built-in flash will always fire at full power and will rarely provide correct flash exposure, and the FGZ series flash units will not provide the high-tech P-TTL flash control. (Also see the comments below about the use of aperture rings.)

Some, but not all, A series lenses will communicate focal-length information to the K10D. When that data is not communicated, the Shake Reduction focal length menu will automatically appear on the LCD monitor if the proper custom functions are set when the camera is turned on or a lens is changed.

Pentax cannot guarantee compatibility with other brands of lenses, but the K10D should work with recent third-party lenses, especially if they are equipped with a mount that has been confirmed as DA, D FA, FA J or FA (KAF or KAF2) compatible. If you decide to buy such lenses, stick with well-known brands purchased from a retailer who will allow you to return the lens if it is not 100% compatible with your K10D.

Setting the Camera Aperture Ring Functionality

Many types of Pentax lenses have an aperture ring; with older cameras this was the device used to adjust the lens' diaphragm to set f/stops. If you are using a lens of this type on the K10D, Pentax recommends locking the ring to the A (automatic) position and using the K10D's e-dial for selecting an f/stop (though some photographers may prefer to select f/stops using the aperture ring instead). Note that some older Pentax lenses' aperture rings do not have an A position, so electronic f/stop selection is not possible. In either case, for proper lens functioning, you must select the *Permitted* option in the item for *Using aperture ring* in the Custom Setting menu.

While this custom function will allow the use of a lens without locking the aperture ring to A, the camera features will be restricted if you cannot or do not lock the aperture ring. For example, the K10D will switch to Av (Aperture Priority) mode even if you set Green, P, Sv, Tv or TAv mode. If you are using a D FA, FA, F, A, or M series lens with Av

Lens Functions and Compatibility Chart

Function / Lens Mount	DA, DFA, FAJ, FA KAF, KAF2 [3]	F KAF [3]	A KA
Autofocus (lens only) (with AF Adapter 1.7x) [1]	Y –	Y –	– Y [5]
Manual focus 1. With focus indicator [2] 2. Using ground glass	 Y Y	 Y Y	 Y Y
Eleven AF points	Y	Y	N [5]
Power zoom	Y [6]	–	–
Aperture Priority (Av) exposure mode	Y	Y	Y
Shutter Priority (Tv) exposure mode	Y	Y	Y
Manual (M) exposure mode	Y	Y	Y
P-TTL Auto Flash [4]	Y	Y	Y
Multi-segment metering	Y	Y	Y
Automatically obtain focal length info for use with Shake Reduction	Y	Y	N

Only DA and FAJ lenses, and DFA, FA, F, and A lenses with A on aperture ring can be used with K10D

Y = Function is available when aperture ring set to A
N = Function not available

[1] Lenses with maximum aperture of f/2.8 or brighter. Only available at A position
[2] Lenses with maximum aperture of 5.6 or brighter.
[3] For FA or F series 85mm or 28mm Soft (soft focus) lenses, you must select the Permitted option in the item for Using aperture ring in the Custom Setting menu. Photos can be shot with aperture you set, but only within manual aperture range.
[4] When built-in flash or Pentax AF540FGZ or AF360FGZ flash units in use.
[5] Center AF point only
[6] Only available with KAF2 mount FA lenses

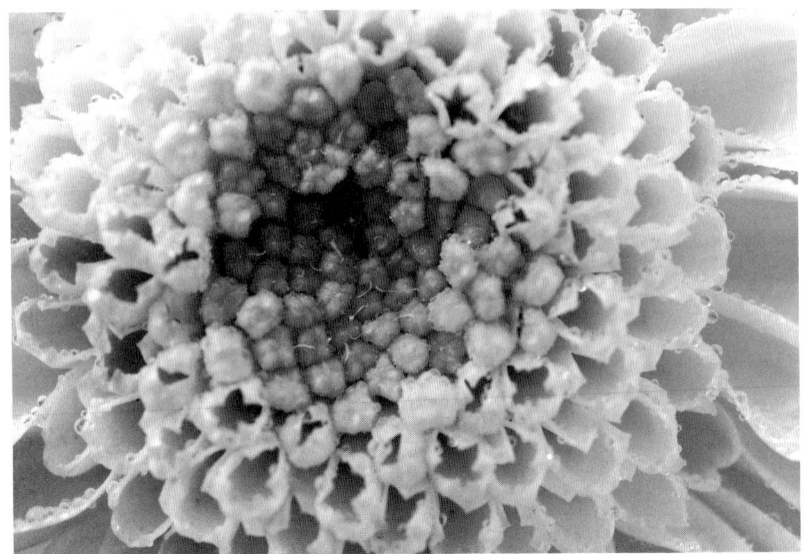

True macro lenses produce the very best image quality in close-up photography, but they are expensive. Other lenses can be used with accessories such as extension tubes or supplementary close-up lenses.

mode, the aperture will always remain at the widest setting–the f/stop will not change regardless of the position of the aperture ring. While the camera will often set an appropriate shutter speed in Av mode, exposure errors can occur in some cases. With any lens series, switching the camera to the M exposure mode allows the selection of any f/stop with the aperture ring; to activate the camera's light meter however, you must use the Optical Preview. Note too that information about the f/stop in use will disappear from the data panel whenever a lens' aperture ring is not locked to A; instead [F --] will appear.

Finally, be aware that when using the FA or F series 85mm or 28mm Soft (soft focus) lenses, the camera will revert to Av mode but exposure metering will be active only when you use Optical Preview.

Close-Up Photography

Some Pentax telephoto zoom lenses allow for close focusing in order to render a small subject about 1/4 life-size on the image sensor (also called 0.25x magnification, or a 1:4 reproduction ratio). However, Pentax also makes true macro lenses that produce a life-size rendition (1:1 reproduction ratio) at the closest focusing distance. Thus, a honeybee will be exactly bee-sized on the digital sensor, without the need for magnification. These are the Pentax FA 50mm and 100mm f/2.8 1:1 Macros as well as the FA 200mm f/4 ED 1:1 Macro. The longer macro lenses are most useful in nature photography because they provide high magnification at greater focusing distances. This eliminates the need to be extremely close to a skittish subject, such as a butterfly, and also reduces the possibility of casting a shadow in the subject.

If you don't own a lens that allows for extremely close focusing and you cannot justify the cost of a true macro lens, you have several options. Definitely check out the two types of devices described below that are effective and readily available.

Magnifying Filters

Resembling a magnifying glass in a filter mount, a supplementary close-up lens (often called a "plus diopter") is ideal for use with telephoto zoom lenses. Simply screw it into the front threads of the lens as you would with any type of filter. This type of accessory is not available from Pentax but is sold by various filter manufacturers. For the best image quality, look for models that are "achromatic" (featuring highly-corrected, multi-element lenses).

Extension Tubes

Extension tubes are hollow tubes without any optical elements. They fit between the lens and the camera, and move the optical center of the lens farther from the sensor. This allows the lens to focus much closer than it could normally. Pentax makes only the older K-mount extension tubes, which are not fully compatible with the K10D; the camera will not provide autofocus, some operating modes, and certain high-tech features. Automatic extension tubes in Pentax AF mount are available from a few third-party accessory manufacturers. These should be fully compatible with the K10D. They are designed to work with all compatible lenses, but are most suitable for fixed focal length lenses of 100mm or longer focal length.

Any extension tube causes a loss of light; in other words, less light reaches the camera's autofocus sensor. Consequently, autofocus performance may not be reliable, especially in low light. When used with lenses with small maximum apertures (such as f/5.6) autofocus may not work at all. Consequently, it is often better to use manual focus with extension tubes.

The camera's light meter reads the light actually reaching the sensor, so exposure should be accurate. Do note however, that the loss of light requires the use of longer shutter speeds. So when using extension tubes, it's wise to set a high ISO for faster shutter speeds. If you use a tripod however, then the longer shutter speed should not cause a problem with blurring from camera shake, though a moving subject such as a flower swaying in the breeze will not be sharp.

Hint: Though relatively expensive, true macro lenses are a good investment for anyone who often needs extremely close focusing capability. Such lenses are designed for superb sharpness at all focus distances from mere inches to infinity. In addition, they are typically optimized for flat-field photography. If you do not often need that capability, buy a quality supplementary close-up lens (resembling a filter), or a set of extension tubes.

Whether using a macro lens or accessories, depth of field is extremely shallow at close distances. The range of acceptable sharpness may be only a centimeter or two. Anything outside the depth of field will be unsharp to some extent. Do not confuse this effect with poor optical quality. For greater depth of field, use a small aperture such as f/16. Focus manually, with extreme care, on the most important subject element: the eyes of an insect, for example. After taking a shot, review it on the LCD monitor, using the magnify feature; if the focus or depth of field is not correct, re-shoot after modifying focus or selecting a smaller aperture.

Due to the higher magnification at extremely close focus, even the slightest camera movement or subject movement will produce an unsharp image. Use a tripod, and if the subject is moving slightly, set an ISO level that will allow you to use a shutter speed of at least 1/250 second.

Accessories

Lens Adapters

In order to use screw mount Pentax lenses (now discontinued) on the K10D's bayonet mount, a Pentax Mount Adapter B accessory is required. When this adapter is attached, the lens becomes a K-mount manual focus lens that is compatible, with certain restrictions, with your camera. Note that screw mount lenses' aperture rings do not have an A position; see page 220 for a discussion about the use of such lenses.

The AF Adapter 1.7x mentioned on page 219 allows the camera to provide autofocus operation with A (KA) series manual focus lenses that have a maximum aperture of f/2.8 or wider. (Pentax discontinued this accessory some time ago, but you should be able to find used models with an Internet search.) The aperture ring must be locked to the A position for the adapter to work properly. Note that this accessory is also a teleconverter, increasing the focal length by a factor of 1.7x. Like all converters, it causes some loss of light (about one stop or EV) to the camera's sensor, so shutter speeds will be longer. In addition, less light reaches the AF sensor so that autofocus performance can be sluggish.

Teleconverters

A teleconverter is an optical attachment consisting of a group of elements in a tubular mount. It is placed between the camera body and the lens, and it effectively increases the focal length of the lens in use. Teleconverters currently manufactured by Pentax will only fit specific wide aperture, pro-caliber telephoto lenses in the A series that are not fully compatible with the K10D. These limitations are discussed on page 225.

Several teleconverters are also available from third party manufacturers that may be suitable for use with other lenses as well. They are an alternative to the steeper investment often required to purchase top-quality telephoto lenses. For maximum compatibility with the K10D, buy only AF designated teleconverters. A Pentax retailer can help you find the best match for your equipment.

A 1.4x teleconverter extends a lens' focal length by a factor of 1.4x, and a 2x converter does the same by a factor of 2x. While increasing the effective "reach" of your telephoto or zoom lens, be aware that teleconverters reduce the amount of light that reaches the image sensor. A 1.4x converter will cause a 1-stop loss of light, while a 2x leads to a 2-stop loss; hence, either accessory is most suitable for use with a wide aperture (such as f/2.8) lens. Teleconverters without superior optical elements will also degrade image quality and even the best teleconverter should only be used with high-grade lenses for the best results.

Filters

Filters thread onto the front of the lens. They affect the light reaching the sensor by blocking certain wavelengths or angles of light in the scene.

Protective Filters: Some photographers buy haze or skylight filters to protect the front lens element from scratches. After all, a filter is less expensive to replace than a damaged lens element. A protective filter can also be useful in such conditions as strong wind, rain, blowing sand, or when going through brush. If you do use a filter for lens protection, a high-quality filter is best, preferably one that is multi-coated to reduce flare. An inexpensive filter can degrade image quality. Remove any filter when shooting toward the sun to minimize the risk of flare.

Graduated Filters: Because the color balance of an image can be controlled by white balance settings, digital photographers rarely need color balancing filters. However, one filter that is useful in digital photography is a graduated neutral density filter, or ND grad. Half of the filter is clear while the other half is dark (gray.) It is often used in landscape or cityscape photography to reduce bright areas (such as sky), while not affecting darker areas (such as the ground).

Square or rectangular ND grad filters are the most versatile. When used with a filer holder designed for them, these filters can be moved up and down until the center lines up with the horizon in the scene.

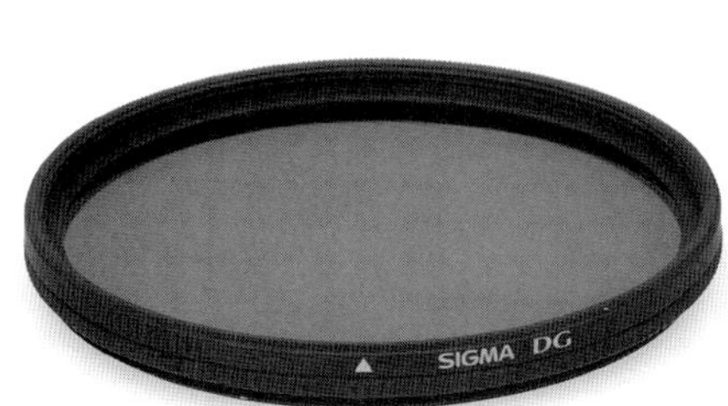

A circular polarizer comes in different diameters to fit lenses of different sizes.

Polarizing Filters: I strongly recommend the circular polarizer, preferably a multi-coated model of high optical quality. A polarizer reduces glare from non-metallic subject surfaces for richer, more saturated colors. By blocking polarized light reflected from water droplets and particles in the air, this accessory can deepen the tone of a blue sky.

Note: There are two types of polarizers, "circular" and "linear." They look identical and produce the same result, but use different technology. The K10D requires a circular polarizer for correct exposure and accurate autofocus.

As you rotate the polarizer, watch the effect–richer sky colors for example–through the camera's viewfinder. A polarizer works best when the sun is at a 90° degree angle to your position. If the sun is directly behind you, or if you are shooting directly into the light, a polarizer won't have any effect. The filter is most useful when the sun is to the side, although it can also be effective when the sun is directly overhead.

Lens Hood

Sometimes called a lens shade, this short tube attaches to the front of the lens and reduces glare by blocking undesirable light from reaching the lens. Using one will almost always improve your photos. Lens hoods are designed to match the field of view of the lens. If you are shooting with a wide-angle focal length, make sure that the lens hood is not blocking the edges of the frame (called vignetting). It also offers protection to the front of the lens.

Camera Support Accessories

If you want to get the most from your Pentax camera and lenses, be aware that camera movement affects sharpness significantly, causing image blurring. While the Shake Reduction system allows us to use longer shutter speeds in hand-held shooting, it cannot perform miracles. A sturdy tripod is an essential accessory when you cannot use fast shutter speeds, when shooting with longer telephoto lenses, and for close-up work. By holding the camera/lens rock steady, it can assure sharp images.

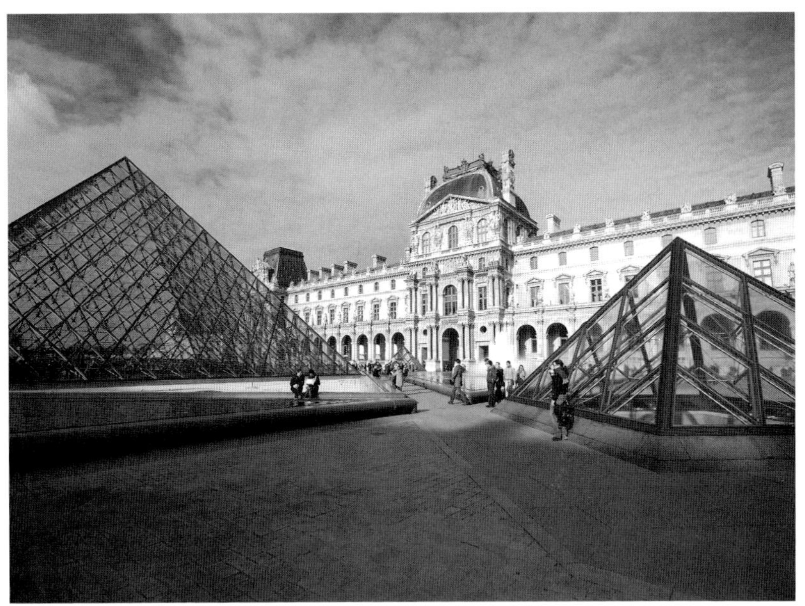

A circular polarizer is a valuable accessory that can enrich a blue sky, minimize the effect of atmospheric haze for greater contrast, and decrease glare from (non-metallic) surfaces for richer colors. When shooting with an ultra wide-angle lens, you may need to use a thin-ring polarizer to prevent vignetting: darkening at the corners of the frame.

Hint: When the K10D is mounted on a tripod, consider using an accessory to trigger the camera. Two models are available: the Cable Switch CS-205 with a 0.5 meter (19.75 inches) cord and the wireless Remote Control F that works if it's within 5 meters (16.5 feet) of the front or the back of the camera.

Consider using the camera's 2-second self-timer drive selection (use Fn button) when shooting static subjects with a tripod-mounted K10D. While that mode will produce a two-second delay, it will also provide reflex mirror pre-lock. In other words, the camera will flip the internal mirror to the up position at the start of the two-second delay; it will be locked in the up position until after the photo is taken. This feature minimizes internal vibration caused by mirror action, a benefit in high-magnification photography when using a true macro lens or a 300mm or longer telephoto.

A good tripod is an excellent investment. A cheap tripod can actually be wobbly and cause more problems than it solves. When buying a tripod, extend it all the way to see how easy it is to open, then lean on it to see how stiff it is. Both aluminum and carbon fiber tripods offer great rigidity. Carbon fiber is much lighter, but also more expensive.

The tripod head is an important consideration and may be sold separately. There are two basic types for still photography: the ball head (my favorite) and the pan-and-tilt head. Both designs are capable of solid support. The biggest difference between them is how you adjust the camera. Try both and see which works better for you. Ball heads are considered easier to operate for fine adjustments, while pan heads are better for action photography. Be sure to do this with a camera mounted because that added weight changes how the head works.

Tripods are the most commonly used camera-stabilizing device, but beanbags, monopods, mini-tripods, shoulder stocks, and clamps can be useful too. Many photographers carry a small beanbag or a clamp pod for those situations where a tripod isn't practical.

While the Shake Reduction system is useful for minimizing blur in handheld photography, it is not recommended when using a tripod. If you want to capture the essence of flowing water, a tripod-mounted camera and a long shutter speed, such as 1/4 second are required. ➪

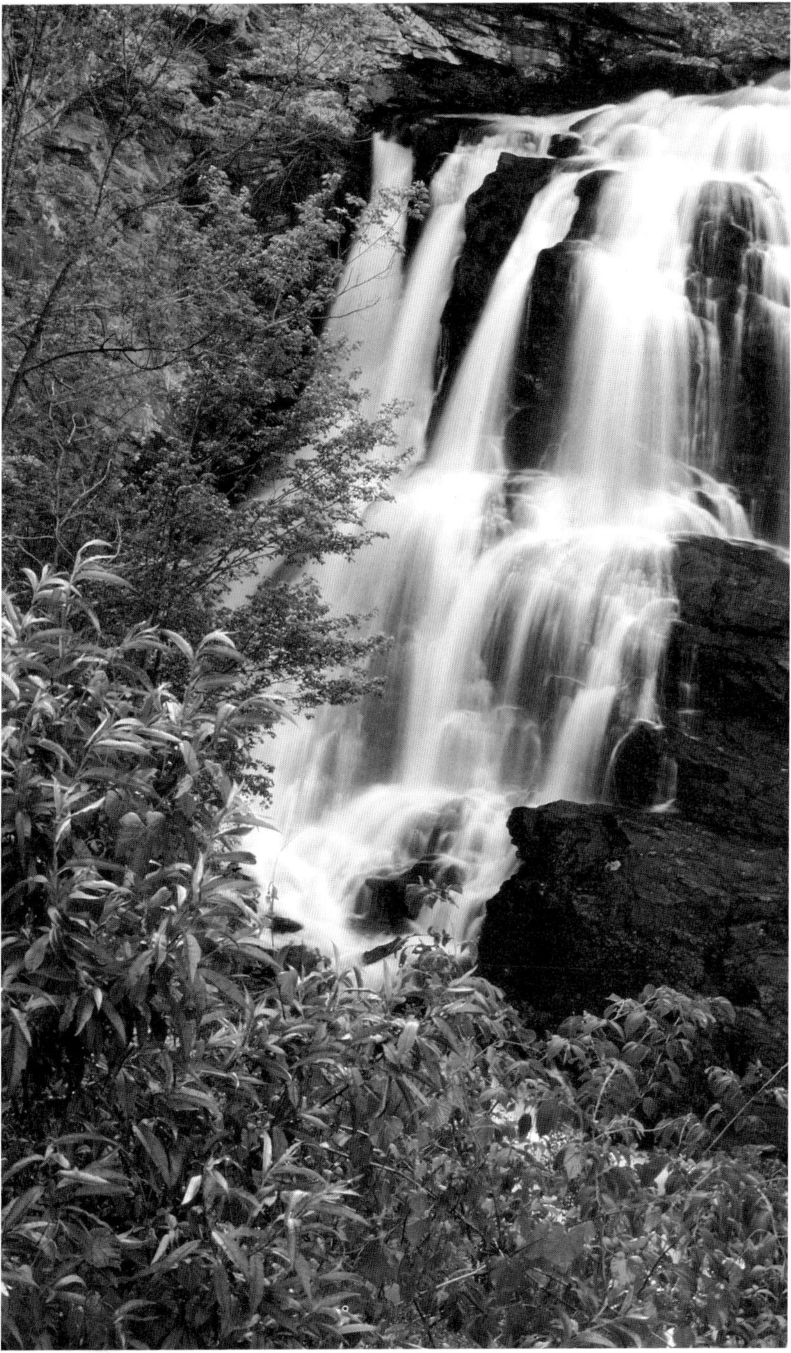

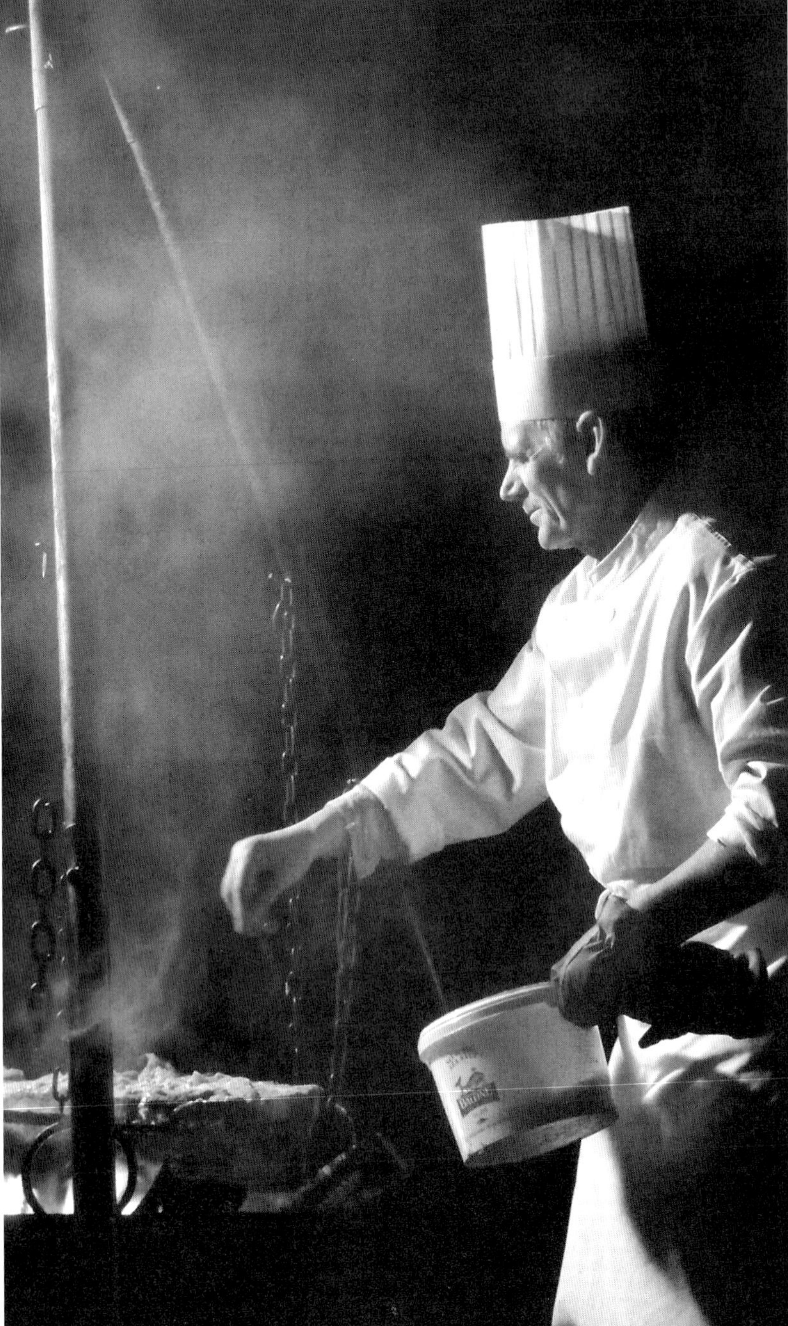

Working with Images

Taking great pictures with your K10D, and perhaps doing some quick in-camera enhancement, is only part of the digital photography experience. You may also want to download images to a computer, convert RAW files, file and store your photos for easy access and viewing, enhance them using versatile image-processing programs, and make prints.

Image Data

A wealth of information is recorded when you shoot a digital picture with the K10D. This data is stored in the Exchangeable Image File Format (EXIF–often called by the generic term of Metadata).

This EXIF data embedded with the image file includes: date and time of recording, aperture, shutter speed, ISO, exposure mode, metering mode, lens focal length, white balance setting, color mode, exposure or flash compensation, and settings for color saturation, contrast, or sharpness. Some of this information will be used by the printer in direct printing, as discussed on page 246.

You can examine some of the EXIF data on the camera's LCD monitor by pressing the INFO button three times while in Playback mode. You can also review all of it using the Pentax Photo Browser or other imaging software. It's worth looking at this data from time to time to compare pictures and camera settings to learn more about exposure, depth of field, the depiction of motion, flash exposure, and so on.

One of the best parts of digital photography is the ability to refine images in the computer using image-processing software. This harkens back to the days of the darkroom, only now you can have fun creating memorable pictures in the comfort of your home, without the stop-bath and fixer fumes!

Enhance Images In-Camera

The K10D provides features for enhancing images in-camera and for converting RAW files to JPEG in Playback mode. These are discussed in detail on pages 88-93. While they are not intended to replace more versatile image-processing computer programs, these features can be useful. Perhaps you want to make prints directly from the K10D (or from your SD memory card) using an available PictBridge compatible inkjet printer while at a birthday party or some other special occasion. The in-camera features would be more convenient and less time consuming than downloading images to a computer and using the full range of enhancement tools.

Downloading Images

There are two main ways of transferring digital files from your memory card to your computer. One is to use an accessory card reader that downloads the files from your card. Another is to download images directly from the memory card in the camera using the USB cable included with your K10D. Direct downloading eliminates the need to buy a card reader, but it means you have to connect (then disconnect) the camera to the computer each time you want to download, while a card reader simply remains connected and ready to use at all times. Also, downloading directly from the camera consumes a great deal of battery power, which is one argument for using the optional AC Adapter D-AC50.

Card Reader

A memory card reader is a simple desktop device that plugs into your computer using either a FireWire or USB connection. Card readers can be designed to read one particular type of memory card or to accept several different kinds of cards. The latter can be useful if you own more than one camera and use two or more types of card formats.

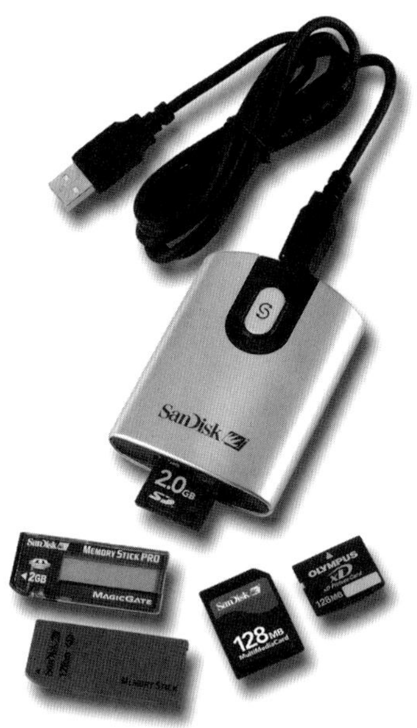

Card readers can remain connected to your desktop computer at all times. Some models are made to accept only one type of memory card, but many have multiple slots and are able to accept different types of memory cards. Courtesy of San Disk Inc.

Note: The K10D is fully compatible with the new SDHC (HC means high capacity, up to 16 gigabytes) memory cards, but many card readers were designed for use only with SD and do not do not accept SDHC cards. If you buy SDHC cards, you will also need a card reader that is compatible with them.

After you have connected the card reader to your computer, put the memory card into the appropriate slot. The card should appear as an additional drive on Windows and Mac operating systems (for other operating systems you will probably have to install the drivers that come with the card reader). Select your files from the card reader and drag them to a preferred computer drive and folder.

PC Card Adapter

If you use a laptop, you may prefer an alternative to the card reader known as a card adapter. (Some computers, especially laptops, include a built-in SD-to-PC card reader and therefore do not require an adapter.) The accessory adapter is compatible with any laptop's PC card slot. Insert the memory card into the SD PC card adapter. Then, insert the adapter into your laptop's PC card slot. The computer will recognize this as a new drive, and then you can drag and drop images from the card to the desired folder in your computer's hard drive.

Hint: Most PC card adapters use the 16-bit standard, but several companies make 32-bit PC card adapters, sometimes called Cardbus 32 Adapters. These can take advantage of internal bus speeds that can be four-to-six times faster than 16-bit. The 32-bit accessory for SD cards costs three or four times more, but it's great when you have large image files to download to a laptop computer.

Direct from the Camera

Check to see that the *Transfer Mode* option in the Setup Menu is set for *PC*. Now, be sure to turn the camera off before taking the next steps.

Make sure to use a fully charged battery or the optional AC Adapter D-AC50 to power the camera. You must use a computer with a USB port and USB interface support. USB connectivity must be installed if your computer does not include it. As well, a PC must use Windows 2000 or later; a Mac OS X 10 or later. (If your computer uses an older operating system, such as Windows ME, you'll need to use a memory card reader that's compatible with that system.)

With the K10D powered off, plug the supplied USB cable into the terminal on the left side of the camera. Plug the other end into your computer's USB port (to prevent possible problems, do not attach to a USB hub.) Turn the camera on and look at the LCD monitor to confirm connection. Data transfer will then begin.

A window should appear on your computer monitor designed to help you download images–follow the instructions it provides. An icon should also appear designating the camera as a drive, for example, "Removable Disk (D:)." If the latter does not appear, disconnect the camera and start the process over.

With Windows-based computers, some software should launch automatically; you can then designate the folder in your computer where the images should be sent. With Mac computers, you will need to drag and drop images from the DCIM folder to the desired folder in your computer. You can do the same with Windows-based computers if you do not use the automated feature.

Double click on the DCIM folder to reveal the specific files in the folder, such as 100PNTX. (The "Misc" folder contains data that may be required for DPOF printing, discussed later in this chapter.) Do not change the names of any folder or file. To copy images, simply drag and drop the file icons to a location in your computer, such as "C: My Pictures." Be sure to specify Copy instead of Move.

Note: A .jpg suffix indicates a JPEG image, which is recognized by nearly all imaging programs. The .PEF or .DNG suffix indicates a RAW file. You can download the RAW files, but you'll need to convert them to a universal image format such as JPEG or (preferably) TIFF. You can use Pentax PHOTO Laboratory for this or other RAW-compatible programs, such as Adobe Photoshop CS2 or Adobe Elements 3.0 (or later versions of each). If you were shooting in PEF format, you will need to download from Adobe's website the version of Adobe Camera Raw plug-in that supports PEF files from the K10D; be sure to install the plug-in exactly as specified by Adobe.

Caution: Never disconnect the camera, or insert or remove memory card while the camera's orange access lamp is lit. If you do, data may be lost and the memory card may be permanently damaged.

Downloading is complete when the orange access lamp on back of the K10D is no longer lit. If you want to download files from another memory card, do not disconnect the camera, just turn it off. Then change memory cards and turn the camera on to reestablish the USB connection. If you are finished, switch the camera off and disconnect the USB cable.

If your Windows system requires that you first "Stop Mass Storage Device," be sure to follow the "Unplug" or "Eject" hardware routine before unplugging the camera or switching to a new memory card. Start by clicking the Unplug or Eject icon located in the task bar. Follow the procedure required to unplug or eject the pertinent device (camera) before unplugging it or removing the memory card and inserting a new card. If using a Mac computer, drag the Mass Storage Device icon for the camera into the trash.

Imaging Software

Pentax PHOTO Browser

Compatible with Windows 2000 or later, as well as Mac OS X 10.2 or later, PHOTO Browser is a basic program for viewing and organizing images. It comes with your K10D package.

If you double click on an image in PHOTO Browser, it will appear in a new screen that provides a few features, such as cropping, rotating, and auto fix. These features support JPEG, DNG, and PEF format files. Full (EXIF) shooting data can be displayed by clicking on *View* at the top of the screen and checking the *Image Data* item; in fact, I recommend checking all of the options in that drop down menu

Pentax PHOTO Laboratory

The K10D is packaged with Pentax PHOTO Laboratory software, compatible with Windows and Mac operating systems. It was designed to read and enhance your DNG or PEF format files and convert them to JPEGs or TIFFs. This program includes tools for adjusting brightness, saturation, sharpness, contrast, hue, white balance, and so on. It's compatible only with the PEF and DNG files and cannot be used to modify

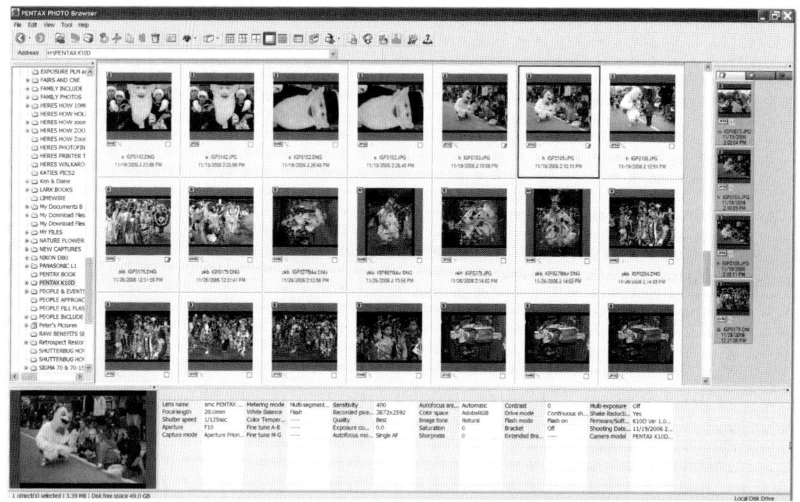

The Pentax PHOTO Browser is not designed for enhancement but it is a useful program for browsing and cataloging your image files.

JPEG or TIFF files in your computer. (Close the Pentax PHOTO Browser before launching PHOTO Laboratory; if you forget to do so, some of PHOTO Laboratory's important features will not work).

Experiment with the various tools until you get the color and exposure adjusted to your liking before converting the PEF or DNG file. But don't "over do" the adjustments when you apply contrast, color saturation, and sharpness in your RAW workflow. It's much easier to increase these attributes after exporting the files into a conventional image-processing program than it is to moderate or tone them down at that time.

After the processing is finished, save your image as a JPEG or TIFF in an appropriate file folder in your computer. Before you save the image file as a TIFF, select the option for 8-bits per channel (usually a selection within the *Mode* option), unless you own Photoshop CS2 or CS3, the programs with

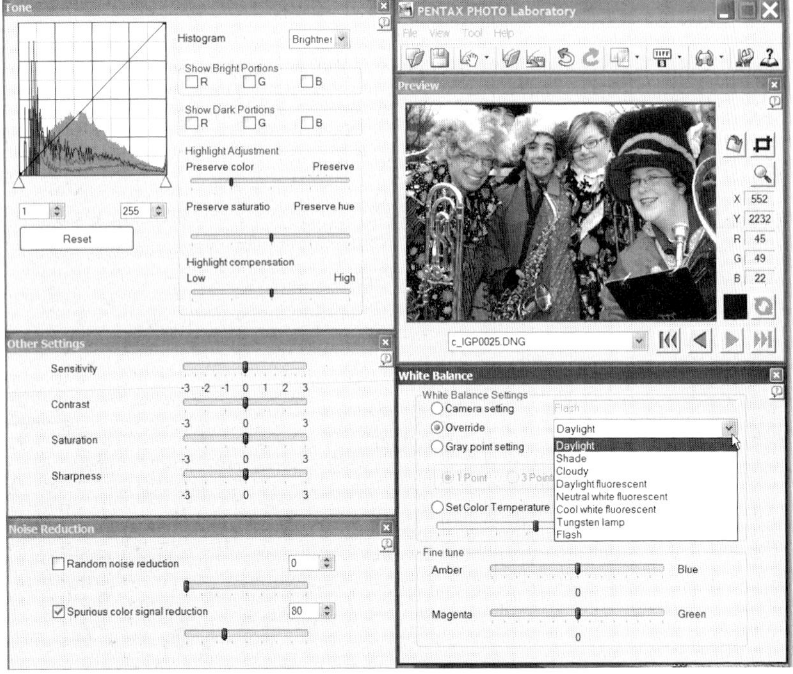

The PHOTO Laboratory software has tools for enhancing RAW images before conversion to TIFFs or JPEGs.

the most extensive 16-bit support. You can also select various JPEG compression options. It's a good idea to give each image a unique name instead of using the more meaningless file name assigned by the camera. Afterwards, you can further fine-tune or manipulate the converted image using your image-processing software.

Some of the popular image-processing programs also include RAW converter functions. These may be faster than the Pentax PHOTO Laboratory program and may include more features or provide a larger preview image. That's fine, as long as they are compatible with the PEF or DNG format files generated by the K10D.

Other Programs for Working with Images

A number of companies have developed different programs for browsing, RAW workflow, and/or image processing. Browsers are designed for viewing and organizing photos on your computer. They often include additional functions to help you manage your stored JPEG or TIFF image files, such as the ability to search, rename photos (either one at a time or in a batch), move image files to different storage locations, make basic image enhancements, resize photos for e-mailing, create simple slideshows, and more.

An important function of a superior browser program is its ability to print customized index prints. You can then give a title to each of these index prints, and also list additional information such as your name and address, as well as the photo's file location. The index print serves as a hardcopy that can be used for easy reference (and visual searches). You might want to include index prints with every backup CD or DVD you burn so you can quickly reference what is on the backup and easily find the file you need. A combination of uniquely labeled file folders on your hard drive, a browser program, and index prints will help you to maintain the quickest and most efficient way of finding and sorting images.

When the K10D was first released, DNG format was supported more widely than PEF by third-party manufacturers of RAW viewing, conversion, and enhancement software. Some browsers may allow you to view the PEF format photos, but they cannot convert the files into another file format. Do not attempt to open or to modify a PEF or DNG format file with any software that was not specifically designed for that purpose.

This lack of initial compatibility is one reason why some K10D owners use DNG as their RAW capture format. Developed by Adobe Systems, DNG is an open format that is widely available for use by camera and software manufacturers. Not all imaging programs support DNG, but a growing number do. Some browsers allow only for viewing DNG format photos while others, as well as full-featured image-processing programs, allow you to modify and convert them to JPEG or TIFF.

However, over time, more and more programs will support PEF as the software companies update their products. After viewing and processing your PEF or DNG format files in a compatible program, you can use any brand of image-processing software to further enhance them as JPEG or TIFF files. These programs usually have tools to perform a number of additional functions like cloning and layers, so it may be a good idea to consider owning such a full-featured program. Examples include the latest versions of Adobe Photoshop, Photoshop Elements, Adobe Photoshop Lightroom, Apple Aperture, Paint Shop Pro, Microsoft Digital Image Suite, or Ulead PhotoImpact, to name a few.

Note: Check the software distributor's website frequently for updates to see if your imaging software supports PEF format. Once you see it is supported, download and install the update to view, open, adjust, and convert PEF files.

Image Cataloging

If you prefer not to use a browser program that organizes your image files, how can you edit and file your digital images so that they are accessible and easy to use? One way is to create specific folders for groups of images in your computer's hard drive. For example, in "C:MyPictures," you might create a variety of folders with titles like Vacation 200X, Robin's Graduation, Alexis' Birthday, and so on. Create new folders frequently for new events or new subject matter such as Trip to Hawaii or Rob's Florida Birds. You can organize your photo folders alphabetically or by date inside a "parent" folder.

Before downloading any images to your computer, take a few minutes to review them on the camera's LCD monitor. Delete any that are obviously unacceptable, keeping those you want to look at more closely. After downloading these remaining photos, review them again on your computer monitor. Erase any additional images that you don't want in order to avoid squandering precious hard drive space.

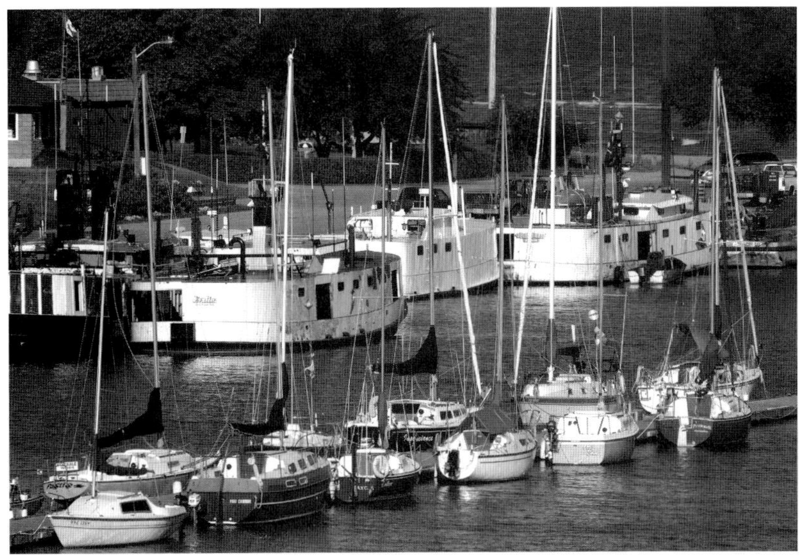

You would have difficulty finding this image in your computer if the file name was IGO9981.tif, for example. Rename your images and use Pentax PHOTO or another browser software for cataloging in order to make it easy to find any image later.

Rename the images with descriptive file names. You'll probably agree that "Lara_BDay_Candles.jpg" makes more sense as a file name than "IGO0761.jpg" for example. Later, be sure to convert any JPEG files to TIFF before enhancing with image-processing software. Processing and resaving JPEG files in a computer can cause image degradation; that's also the reason for converting your DNG or PEF format RAW files to TIFF instead of to JPEG.

Hint: After shooting an event, you may want to set up one folder for the images: Ron and Mary's Wedding, for example. After you adjust a photo using image-processing software, save it using a different file name. If the file name was "Bridesmaids_4.tif," for example, you might save the enhanced file as "Bridesmaids_4B.tif." This step will prevent overwriting of the original image so you can later return to it and try entirely different enhancing effects, or use more sophisticated image-processing software.

Image Storage

Although your images are stored as digital files, they can still be lost or destroyed without proper care. You will need a good back-up system. Many photographers use two hard drives, either adding a second one to the inside of the computer or using an external USB or FireWire drive. This allows them to easily back up photos on the second drive. It is very rare for two drives to fail at once.

However, it is recommended that you also burn your images to CDs or DVDs. Hard drives, zip discs, and memory cards are certainly useful devices, but they are not ideal for long-term storage. The life of a hard drive is unknown, but hard drive failures can occur after a couple of years, not to mention accidental erasure. And a number of malicious computer viruses can wipe out image files from a hard drive (especially JPEGs).

The answer to these storage problems is optical media. A CD and/or DVD-writer (or "burner") is a necessity for the digital photographer. DVDs can store about eight times the data that can be saved on a CD. Either option allows you to back up photo files and store images safely.

Hint: For long-term storage of images, only use R discs. The storage medium used for CD-R and DVD-R discs is more stable than rewriteable media such as RWs. If disc permanence is important, look for CD-R discs that are rated as archival such as the Delkin e-Film Archival Gold product.

Video Output

The K10D can also be connected to a television set, allowing you to show JPEG images to friends and family. If you decide to try this feature, start by making sure that the *Video Out* item in the Set-up menu is set for the correct TV standard, *NTSC* (North America) or *PAL* (Europe and most other regions of the world).

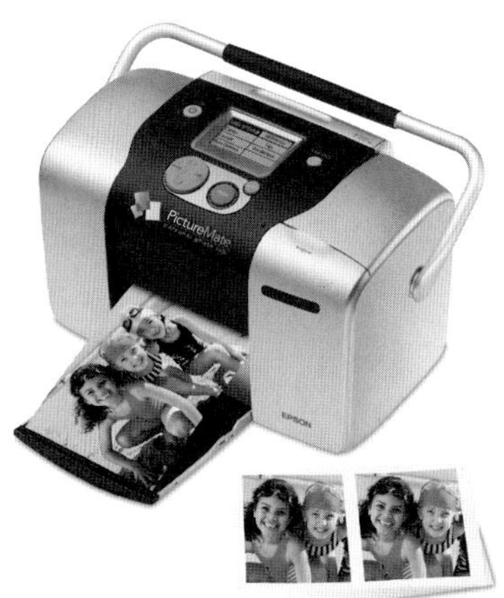

Some printers allow you to insert the SD card from your K10D directly, without need to download files into your hard drive. This can be convenient. Courtesy of Epson America Inc.

To view, start by turning off the television or the DVR as well as the camera. Insert one end of the video cable (provided with the camera) to the Video Out terminal under the terminal cover on the left side of the camera. (It's the same port that's used for USB.) Plug the other end into the video input terminal of the TV or DVR. Turn the video device(s) on and select the video channel. Turn the camera on and press the playback button.

Images will be displayed on the TV instead of the LCD, as they would in conventional camera Playback mode.

Direct Printing

You can also use the K10D for direct printing without using a computer. This feature is available when you connect the camera to a PictBridge compatible photo printer using the USB cable provided with the camera. With the vast majority of printers, this will work only with JPEG images that you made using the camera's sRGB color space.

Note: PictBridge is a technology that allows for direct printing between compliant digital cameras and printers. The K10D is PictBridge compatible, as are most Epson, Canon, Kodak, and HP photo printers released since 2004. Look for the PictBridge logo on the printer's box. Some photo printers also include slots for memory cards, allowing you to print JPEG's directly from the camera's memory card; this method does not require a PictBridge compliant printer.

Start with a fully charged camera battery or use the optional AC Adapter D-AC50. Make sure that the *Transfer Mode* option in Setup Menu is set to *PictBridge*. Turn the camera off and connect the USB cable from the camera to the printer. Then turn the camera on. The PictBridge menu appears on the LCD monitor. Select the *Print One* option if you want to select images one by one for printing; or select the *Print All* option if you want to print all JPEG's (in sRGB color space) on the memory card.

For the *Print One* option, use the four-way controller to scroll and identify the image to be printed and to choose the number of copies. Use the Fn button to specify whether the date should be imprinted or not. Press the OK button. A print settings screen will appear. If that looks fine, press the OK button twice to start printing.

Many other options are appear in the PictBridge menu that displays when the camera is plugged into a compatible printer. These allow you to control the entire printing process: to select paper size, quality, borders, and so on.

However, the amount of control you have over the photo is limited entirely by the printer. Some printers do allow minimal image enhancement during direct printing, while others offer none at all. If the image requires enhancement or retouching, you will get better results using software in the computer.

Digital Print Order Format (DPOF)

Another printing feature of the K10D is DPOF: Digital Print Order Format. This allows you to designate certain JPEG images you want to print. (The DPOF settings cannot be applied to RAW image files.) Then use a DPOF compliant printer to print those selected images after you make the USB connection. The DPOF options are available in Playback mode. Scroll to select an image to print, then press the Fn button and scroll up to the DPOF item. You can print single images or all images on your memory card.

The DPOF feature is also useful for selecting images on a memory card for printing at a photo lab that uses DPOF compliant equipment. (Ask about that before leaving your memory card at the store.)

Other Printing Options

Kiosks

Many stores offer self-service photo kiosks. Plug your memory card into the slot. Use the kiosk's controls to crop and enhance JPEG images from your memory card; specify the desired size and quantity.

Photofinishers and Mini-Labs

Most photo labs now have the capability to take your memory card and make prints or CDs from the image files.

On-Line Services

There are many photofinishers that offer their services through websites. Prices are reasonable and your prints are delivered by mail. Once you start an online album on a company's website, you can invite friends and relatives to view images and order prints. Images must usually be converted to JPEGs before uploading because most photofinishers won't accept other file types.

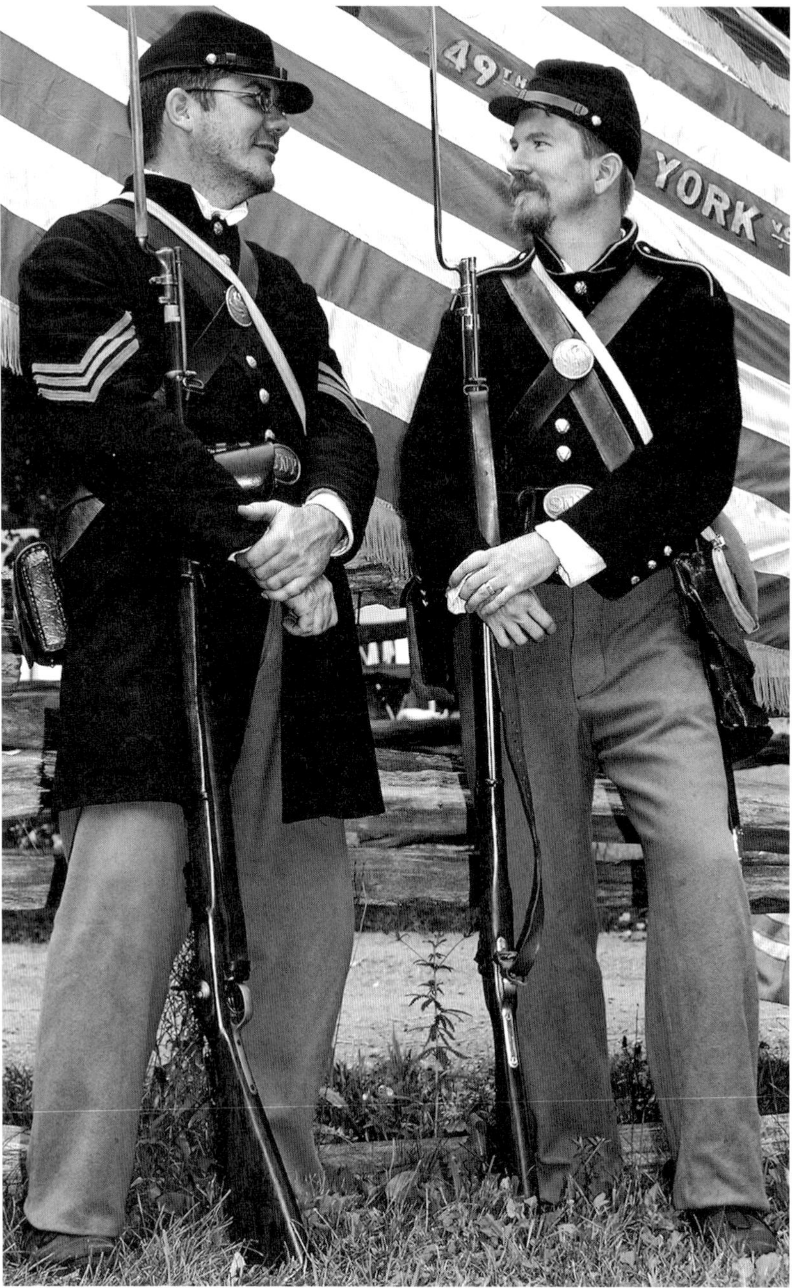
49TH
YORK

Troubleshooting Guide

The Pentax K10D is a sophisticated camera that provides reliable service. Although rare, a malfunction can occur as with any electronic device. The camera may occasionally generate an error message that is straightforward and understandable. Common examples include *Memory card full, No image* (no images on the SD card), *No card in the camera, Card locked* (SD card needs to be unlocked using the small lever on the card), Cannot use this card (format the card to delete all data or try a new card), and so on. Sometimes, a minor problem will produce frustration; the chart on pages 250-251 provides steps you can take in such cases.

Note: Unlike some cameras, the K10D does not include a reset button for use in case of electronic malfunction. (The Reset item in the menu is strictly for resetting features to the factory-recommended defaults.) However, removing the battery for 30 seconds achieves the same purpose. If you remove the battery (or disconnect the AC adapter) when the orange recording lamp on the camera back is lit, images may become corrupted or the memory card may be damaged.

Web Support

Check the Customer Care and Support section of the Pentax website (www.pentaximaging.com) occasionally for updates to firmware (in-camera software), new accessories, tips on problem solving, or information on company authorized service centers in your area. The following recommendations should solve most problems; however, if you experience camera malfunction–especially one that cannot be solved by removing the battery for 30 seconds–contact an authorized service center.

The K10D is a sturdy and weather resistant camera, so be sure to take it on your travels. Contact Pentax customer care by phone or internet for any support needs that may arise.

Problem	Solution
Cannot install battery	Make sure to insert it in the proper orientation.
Camera does not turn on	Make sure battery is charged and properly installed.
Battery life is very short	Ensure that battery is fully charged every time you remove from charger. In low temperatures, warm battery (under your coat or indoors) and try again. In other conditions, gently clean terminals with a soft cloth. If the problem persists, battery may need to be replaced.
Camera shuts down unexpectedly	See above re: battery. Also remember that the K10D goes into sleep mode after a period of non-use. Touch shutter release button to re-activate it.
Nothing is displayed in the LCD monitor	Press the Info, Fn or MENU button. For data on current settings, see the LCD panel on the camera's right shoulder. To view images on the memory card, press the playback button.
The viewfinder image is not sharp	Adjust the diopter correction control (on top of the viewfinder) until it suits your vision.
The camera will not take photos	Ensure it is ON and that the lens is mounted properly and memory card is not full. If card is full, delete unwanted images or insert another card. If using a lens with an aperture ring, lock it to A. If using flash, wait until it has fully charged. In AF.S autofocus, the camera cannot fire if focus has not been confirmed.
Autofocus does not work.	Make sure camera is set to AF and that an autofocus lens is in use. If extremely close to subject, try moving farther. If AF has difficulty in dark conditions, try manual focus. For moving subjects, select AF.C mode.
Images are too dark	Light-toned subject or shooting toward bright area may require plus (+) EV.
Images are too bright	Ensure plus EV is not set; dark-toned subjects may need minus (-) EV to prevent overexposure.

Problem	Solution
The flash does not work	Make sure built-in unit is up or that an accessory unit is ON and fully charged. Flash will not fire in bright conditions in Green Mode; switch to another mode such as P.
Flash photos are too dark	You may be beyond range of flash unit in use. Move closer and/or set a higher ISO level or switch to a more powerful flash unit. Try setting a plus (+) flash exposure compensation level, available in Flash mode section of Fn menu.
The bottom of flash photo is dark	In close-focusing, lens hood or lens barrel can block some light from the built-in flash; move farther from the subject. Remove lens hood.
Flash takes a long time to recycle	This is common after shooting several flash photos in sequence; may improve after battery is fully charged.
The corners of images are dark	Remove any filter being used on a wide angle lens; replace with a slim-ring filter. Never use more than one filter at a time. (Mild darkening of the corners is common with many zoom lenses but should not be visible if shooting at f/8 or a smaller aperture.)
The images are not sharp	Often caused by camera shake or subject movement. Enable Shake Reduction or use tripod. Set higher ISO level for a faster shutter speed, particularly if subject is moving.
Images exhibit color cast such as yellow or blue	May be an incorrect white balance setting; try using a white balance preset (such as Tungsten or Shade) that suits lighting conditions. Under artificial light (without flash) Manual White Balance may be necessary,
The camera won't play back images	Make sure to press playback button. If a file folder name (on the SD card) was changed in your computer, images can no longer be displayed on the camera. Also, images made with another camera cannot be displayed.

Index

D

E

F